Poverty, Community and Health

Poverty, Community and Health

Co-operation and the Good Society

Vicky Cattell
Queen Mary, University of London, UK

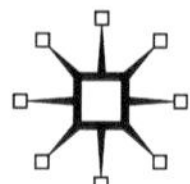

First published 2012 by
PALGRAVE MACMILLAN

Palgrave Macmillan in the UK is an imprint of Macmillan Publishers Limited, registered in England, company number 785998, of Houndmills, Basingstoke, Hampshire RG21 6XS.

Palgrave Macmillan in the US is a division of St Martin's Press LLC, 175 Fifth Avenue, New York, NY 10010.

Palgrave Macmillan is the global academic imprint of the above companies and has companies and representatives throughout the world.

Palgrave® and Macmillan® are registered trademarks in the United States, the United Kingdom, Europe and other countries

ISBN 978-0-230-01997-3

This book is printed on paper suitable for recycling and made from fully managed and sustained forest sources. Logging, pulping and manufacturing processes are expected to conform to the environmental regulations of the country of origin.

A catalogue record for this book is available from the British Library.

A catalogue record for this book is available from the Library of Congress.

10 9 8 7 6 5 4 3 2 1
21 20 19 18 17 16 15 14 13 12

Printed and bound in Great Britain by
CPI Antony Rowe, Chippenham and Eastbourne

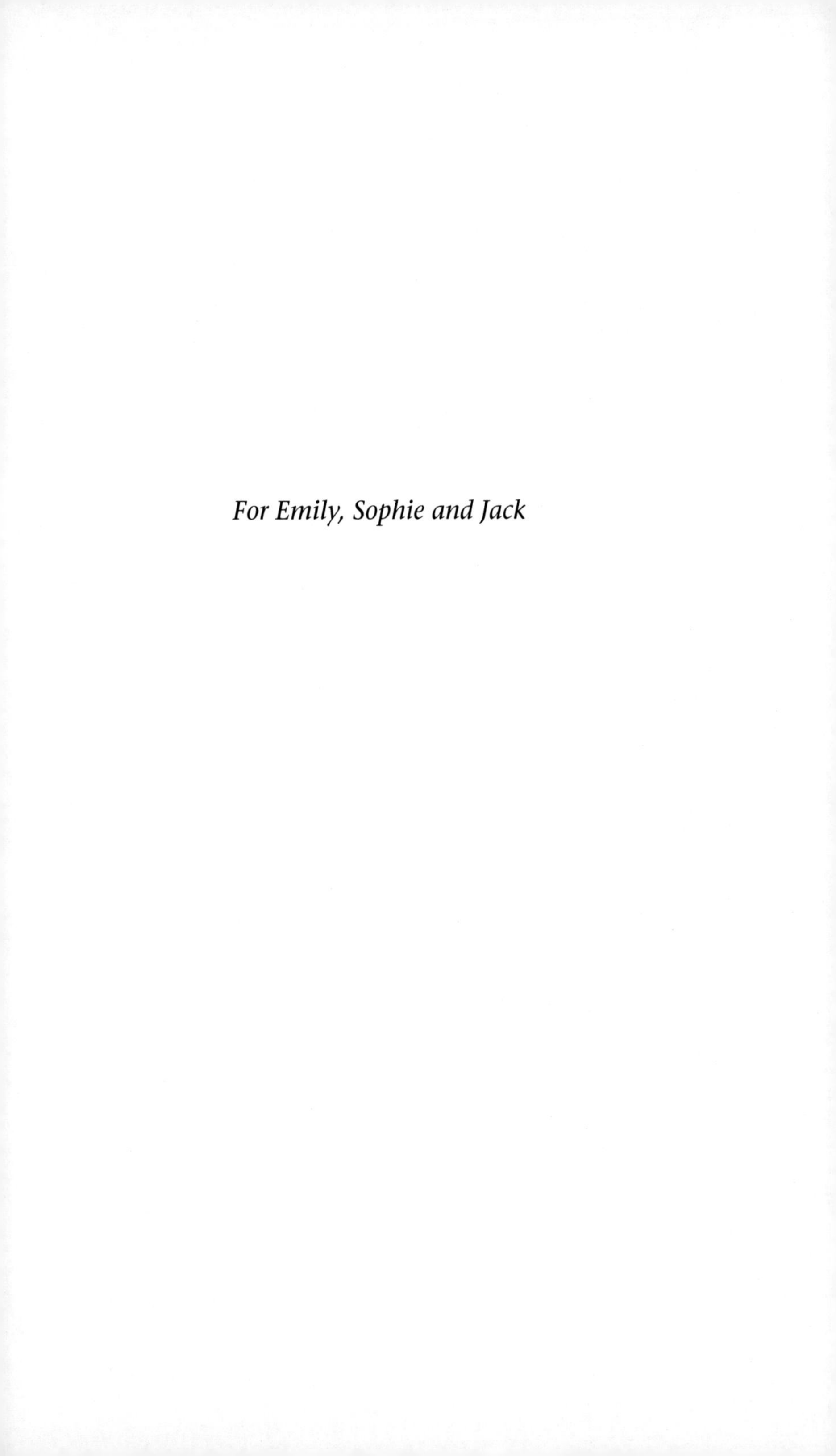

For Emily, Sophie and Jack

Contents

List of Abbreviations

BNP	British National Party
CSDH	Commission on Social Determinants of Health
DCLG	Department of Communities and Local Government
DWP	Department of Work and Pensions
IEA	Institute of Economic Affairs
IFS	Institute for Fiscal Studies
NCVO	National Council for Voluntary Organizations
ODPM	Office of the Deputy Prime Minister
OECD	Organization for Economic Co-operation and Development
ONS	Office for National Statistics
SEU	Social Exclusion Unit
SIGOMA	Special Interest Group of Local Authorities
TMC	Tenant Management Co-operative
VAT	value added tax
WHO	World Health Organization

Acknowledgements

The publishers and I would like to thank the Joseph Rowntree Foundation and NICE for permission to reproduce copyright material from:

Vicky Cattell and Mel Evans (1999) *Neighbourhood Images in East London: Social Capital and Social Networks on Two East London estates*, York: Joseph Rowntree Foundation, and Health Development Agency (2003) *Social Capital and Health: Insights From Qualitative Research,* London: HDA/NICE. Available from www.nice.org.uk

1
Introduction: Social Murder

A social transformation identified as a defining feature of the new millennium concerns the notion that people are less connected to one another and their communities than they were a generation ago. Yet the theme is familiar, social science has produced a number of different variations on this topic over a period spanning at least 150 years. Community decline or its endurance was a persistent issue explored by community studies throughout the 20th century for example (Lee and Newby, 1983; Wellman, 1979), whilst earlier, community loss was a theme which united the diverse approaches of the classical sociologists Marx, Weber, and Durkheim (Turner, 1988). In Durkheim's case, it was the disruption caused to community ties by industrialization and urbanization and the search for new sources of solidarity which were a central focus to his work. In a development of Durkheim's ideas, urban sociologists of the Chicago school linked city life with social isolation and disorganization arguing that 'slum' areas could not be communities but were simply alienated areas of transition (Wirth, 1938; Bell and Newby, 1971).

More recently, aspects of a growing privatism identified in Britain back in the 1960s (Goldthorpe et al., 1968), resurfaced and were popularized in America as 'cocooning', retreating to the domestic hearth when the outside world is perceived as unsafe or uncertain (Popcorn, 1992). Academic discourses locate the sources of disengagement in a shift of dominant political ideologies in the direction of neo-liberalism, along with an erosion of societal moral values and their replacement by aggressive consumerism and selfish individualism. Communitarians, for example, argue that the political and moral pendulum, rather as Durkheim (1952) had reasoned, has swung too far from collectivism towards individualism, and that liberal freedoms need to be balanced with a new sense of social responsibility. The remedy is seen to lie in restored communities (Etzioni, 1995). Other contemporary writers – most notably the political scientist Robert Putnam – have identified an increase of atomization alongside a decline in social capital (Putnam, 1995, 2000). Social and political commentators have turned to the concept of social capital to explain social phenomena and social change, while the work of both Etzioni and Putnam have influenced the political philosophies of political leaders and their policies on both sides of the Atlantic and across the political spectrum.

Though a complex (if not entirely new) concept, social capital is generally viewed as a phenomenon embodied in social relations, a resource produced when people co-operate for mutual benefit (Putnam, 2000). Two main strands can be identified. The first, with its theoretical antecedents in de Tocqueville's *Democracy in America* (Tocqueville, 1968) is concerned with individuals' participation in local and national associations such as clubs or voluntary groups, political organizations or activities, with civic engagement. Its most recent embodiment can be found in Prime Minister David Cameron's political perspective of the 'big society'. The second embraces conceptualizations of co-operative communities. Focussing on local social networks and reciprocal aid this dimension of social capital resonates with the community studies literature of the mid-20th century. In Britain, for example, Young and Willmott's classic study of family and community ties in the working class area of Bethnal Green in East London (Young and Willmott, 1962) is amongst the most familiar of these; in America, the Lynds' seminal study of 'Middletown', which documented small town life in the 1920s, became a template for what 'community' was all about (Bell and Newby, 1971). Links from social capital to an older political and philosophical tradition are not hard to discern. Ralph Miliband (1994a), pointed out that we have inherited optimistic beliefs about human capabilities from the enlightenment, the belief for example that human beings are capable of organizing themselves into co-operative, egalitarian and self governing communities, ideas which were sustained in the work of the 'utopian socialists' William Morris and Robert Owen and in the guild socialism of G.D.H. Cole. For Owen, for example, co-operation was the moral basis of social life, while Morris believed that 'community' happened when competition gave way to co-operation, a co-operation amongst equals (Harrison, 1969; Morris, 1979). The ethos of community and democratic participation, along with ideals of solidarity, equality and social justice, remain central to certain contemporary philosophical discussions on 'the common good' (Sandel, 2010), and to progressive political ideas on the 'good society' and the vision required to achieve it.

The trends identified by contemporary writers and commentators towards increasing isolation – involving variously a reduction in collective activity, more individualistic lifestyles, or deepening self interested attitudes, as well as the damaged social relations identified as a consequence – are seen as affecting all groups in society. But it is the disengagement of the poor, and not better off groups, which has become the prominent focus of academic and policy concern. Ironically, whereas it was once the growing affluence and 'embourgeoisment' of the working class which was linked to the allegedly home centred lifestyle and individualistic attitudes of *The Affluent Worker* in the 1960s (Goldthorpe et al., 1968), it is the experience of poverty and social exclusion, particularly in areas of 'concentrated poverty' which have since become most closely associated with a dislocated community life. For some social analysts, these are trends which have developed alongside the growing irrelevance of social class (Saunders, 1990); the break-up of 'traditional' working class communities following decline of the manufacturing sector, and, as Hobsbawm (1981) had argued, the erosion of traditional forms of solidarity and class consciousness and their replacement by capitalist values.

By the 1980s and on through the 1990s, certain neighbourhoods, particularly those located in the inner cities or peripheral housing estates, had become identified with 'degeneration', not simply of the built environment, but of the social, and for some writers, of the moral environment also (Harrison, 1983; Faith, 1985; Campbell, 1993). Whilst these analyses were generally sympathetic to the plight of disadvantaged people, theoretical or policy approaches to 'community' which problemize poor neighbourhoods and place excessive stress on their 'social disintegration' and dysfunctional elements can not only obscure what is valuable, but can have the effect of pathologizing the urban poor and stigmatizing their communities. Illegitimacy, crime and unemployment are seen to reinforce each other in small communities, producing a geographically concentrated underclass for example, and a culture of welfare dependency (Murray, 1984, 1994) ideas which find their most recent apotheosis perhaps in the public encouragement of censorious attitudes towards the vulnerable on the part of post 2010 policy makers.

The bleak landscape of isolation and lack of connectedness may have been overdrawn, but the present interest in community and social capital needs nevertheless to be viewed against a backdrop of growing poverty in Britain in the 1980s and the 1990s; of poor but also wealthy households becoming increasingly geographically segregated from the rest of society in recent decades (Dorling et al., 2007), and in the context of the British Government's policy objectives in the first decade of the 21st century to erode child and pensioner poverty, regenerate deprived areas and encourage resident involvement using targeted initiatives such as those associated with the New Deal for Communities Programme. Policy makers began to acknowledge during this period what bodies like the Joseph Rowntree Foundation have consistently argued, that the disadvantage of both poverty and place must be tackled. Levels of poverty are disproportionately high amongst social tenants on housing estates (Hills, 2007), for example, as is dissatisfaction with the area where they live.

If we have become increasingly disconnected from each other and from the places we live in, as social capitalists amongst others maintain, what are the implications for health and well-being, particularly as experienced by those in disadvantaged circumstances? It was the sociologist C. Wright Mills (2000) who first identified the central feature of social science research as the exploration of the relation of personal troubles to public issues of social structure. Amongst the many factors which most closely affect us are those concerned with or which impact upon our sense of well-being, our physical and mental health, or our quality of life. Recognizing some of the public issues which impinge on the lives of individuals and their communities and identifying the processes involved in their effects is essential if political responses and interventions for positive change are to be effective. The central subject matter of this book is a study of relationships between three linked phenomena: people living in deprived circumstances, their neighbourhood based communities, and their health and well-being.

Despite a substantial literature on the relationship between poverty and reduced health chances, on deprived places and poorer population health, and on the protective influence of social networks involving support, participation or other forms of collective and co-operative activity on health and well-being, the nature of the relationship between them is complex and uncertain. There is still much to learn, for example, about people's everyday understandings of poverty and its effects, about the value of community and the meanings that local ties hold for people and what the implications of these are for their well-being. Related issues concern the effects of the local context on social relations and social networks as well as their more direct impacts on well-being. An enhanced understanding of these issues is needed if we are to gain, not only a more effective purchase on social processes involved in health and the social patterning of health inequalities, or on links between poverty and place, but also a greater comprehension of the stratagems people adopt to challenge or cope with social and economic difficulties and resist or overcome their deleterious effects.

Poverty, inequality, place and health

Following publication of an early study on social class and mental illness (Hollingshead and Redlich, 1953) and the later and revolutionary Black Report (Black, 1980) on social inequalities in health which demonstrated that individuals from unskilled and semi-skilled occupations had a greatly increased risk of premature death when compared to professionals and managers, research and official statistics have shown that men, women and children from lower socio-economic groups have disproportionately higher rates of physical and mental illness, disability and premature death (Whitehead, 1993; Acheson, 1998; Graham, 2007; Gray et al., 2009; De Maio, 2010; The Marmot Review, 2010). The consequences of early disadvantage for health can start at birth and persist throughout the life course (Davey-Smith, 2003); adults raised in poor families have been found to be 50 per cent more likely than those from more advantaged backgrounds to suffer from limiting illness (Hirsch and Spencer (2008).

Two contrasting approaches to explaining patterns of health inequalities can be mentioned at this point as they are illustrative of a theme running throughout this book. It relates to relationships between aspects of human agency, encompassing culture, values, action, and behaviour, and structural and material factors like social class, the social and geographic distribution of resources, services and facilities, and the economic and policy climate. The first involves a certain degree of choice; the second refers to matters over which the individual has little control. One of the most contentious explanations put forward for the persistence of social inequalities in health focused on cultural influences on patterns of consumption involving alcohol, diet and smoking. Although factors like these are clearly important to health outcomes (DOH, 2010), some political advocates of cultural explanations, commenting on a North/South health gap, appeared to be placing blame on the poor themselves for their ill health, a position paralleled by political discourses which sought to individualize the causes of poverty itself. Sir Keith Joseph writing in the 1970s for example, had identified 'a cycle of deprivation' involving the intergenerational transmission of cultural traits allegedly associated with poverty, while Charles Murray's moralizing propositions on 'underclass' found fertile political ground in the 1990s (Joseph, 1972; Murray, 1994). Like Joseph, Murray insisted that it was the cultural practices of those on the margins which were largely responsible for perpetuating their poverty; as satirical commentary of the time put it, they chose to be poor. Questions on intergenerational continuities and lifestyle choices tend to resurface in policy circles (Deacon, 2002); contemporary Conservative Party thought on 'broken Britain' which identifies family breakdown, educational failure, economic dependence, indebtedness and addiction as pathways to poverty (Duncan Smith, 2006), has been criticized for confusing the causes of destitution with its effects and for applying 'brokenness' exclusively to the poor (see for example Toynbee, 2006; Gentleman, 2010).

The principle mode of explanation for persistent and growing poverty has focused squarely on structural determinants, on economic restructuring, unemployment, and 'bad policies' (see MacGregor and Pimlott, 1991) as well as on underlying systems of social stratification involving inequalities of class, ethnicity, and gender. Research indicates that those most at risk of being in a 'work poor' household for example include members of certain minority groups, people with disabilities, low qualifications and skills or living in areas of weak labour demand, and people in their fifties. Older pensioners are more likely to be in poverty than younger ones, while teenage motherhood and being a single parent are both associated with a high risk of poverty (Berthoud, 2003; Berthoud et al., 2009; Kemp et al., 2004; Gingerbread, 2009; DWP, 2010), as is living in certain parts of Britain. London, for example, despite having the greatest proportion of households in the top tenth of the income distribution, also has the biggest share of the country's low-income households: the capital has been identified as the most unequal city in the developed world (MacInnes and Kenway, 2009; Dorling, 2010). Earlier work which focused on East London and the Lea Valley showed that unemployment was exceptionally high in most parts of a region hit by the collapse of manufacturing industry, and that despite job growth, well-paid local jobs were not going to local residents (Cattell, 1997). Even with a minimum wage work may not always in itself be enough to lift poor families out of poverty (Cooke and Lawton, 2008; Joseph Rowntree Foundation and New Policy Institute, 2010), but the effects of unemployment can be long lasting nevertheless. The significance of unfavourable structures for the continuity of poverty across generations is illustrated by a study which found that adults who grew up poor in the 1980s and entered work at a time when unemployment was high are suffering greater disadvantage in mid-life than those who grew up poor in the 1970s (Hirsch, 2006). We could now be faced with the repetition of intergenerational progressions like these as already record breaking youth unemployment figures in 2011 are expected to escalate as a result of economic stagnation and policy changes involving the withdrawal of certain job related initiatives targeted at this group.

Work addressing health inequalities between social groups directs attention principally towards what one of the most influential writers on poverty in the second half of the 20th century, Peter Townsend (1987), referred to as 'material deprivation'. Income, housing and employment status and conditions, along with educational opportunities, have been found to have a critical influence on physical and also mental health and illness indicators (Graham, 2001; CSDH, 2008). Children living in disadvantaged families are over three times as likely to suffer from mental health disorders for example as those in well off homes (Hirsch and Spencer, 2008). The concept of 'health inequality', whilst it refers to the unequal distribution of these determinants according to socio-economic status, gender or ethnicity (Acheson, 1998) is more than simply descriptive. Scott-Samuel's definition centres on 'unjust or unfair differences' in health determinants or outcomes (Scott-Samuel (2004: 1); normative and political dimensions which are further emphasized by a report from the World Health Organization: 'Putting right these inequities – the huge and remedial differences in health between and within countries – is a matter of social justice' (CSDH, 2008: ii).

A notable development in epidemiological work on health inequalities involved a positional shift from interest in the direct effects of disadvantage to the influence of the experience of inequality itself. It was demonstrated that the healthiest societies in the developed world are not the richest ones, but those with the most egalitarian income distribution (Wilkinson, 1996; Le Grand, 1987; Wilkinson and Pickett, 2010). A two-fold explanation was offered. The first, and one which I shall be returning to later, is that income inequality is detrimental to health through individuals' perceptions of inequality and inferiority. The second, is that healthy, egalitarian societies are richer in social capital or more socially cohesive (Kawachi and Kennedy, 1997; Wilkinson et al., 1998). From a sociological perspective the hypotheses raise a number of questions. Firstly, for example, the direction of these relationships has been questioned (Saunders, 2010); secondly, we could ask whether the processes described would be apparent across different contexts of time, place and culture. Strong perceptions of inequality, along with political or union activity, appeared to co-exist with the solidarity and mutual aid – the one a source the other a form of social capital – evident in some traditional working class districts of the last century (see for example, Dennis et al., 1956). Different processes might well have been in operation here. A related difficulty is that potential problems concerned with the scale of analysis are not always made explicit. Wilkinson and Pickett have acknowledged the problem of scale and suggested that studies of income inequality in large areas are more supportive to their ideas than those covering smaller geographic areas (Wilkinson and Pickett, 2006).

The relationship of place to health is an issue which has been assuming increasing importance in the literature on health inequalities. Poorer health outcomes are unevenly distributed spatially as well as socially (Curtis, 2004; Dorling et al., 2007). District NHS profiles for 2009 indicate that men in Blackpool live on average 10.5 years fewer than their counterparts in Kensington and Chelsea, while women in Hartlepool have the lowest female life expectancy in Britain (www.healthprofiles.info). Essentially, as the aptly titled 'Grim Reaper's Road Map' (Shaw et al., 2008) makes clear, death rates from most causes are higher in those towns in Britain where people are poorer. London's record is especially alarming: the proportion of men dying before the age of 65 is much higher in inner London than in any other region in Britain (MacInnes et al., 2010).

The research emphasis on locality echoes a much older tradition of mapping poverty: Booth's classification of London's poor districts is a prominent example (Booth, 1889–1891). Frederick Engels, writing in the earlier part of the 19th century, used official reports to identify differences in life expectancy between deprived and better off English towns and streets within towns. He explained the variation he found in terms of the poor living, working and environmental conditions and bad diet available to working class people, and built on his material explanation by adding a strongly political dimension. Engels accused the authorities, that is, the government of the day, factory owners, landlords, and local officials, of 'social murder': 'Society in England ... commits ... social murder, that it has placed the workers under conditions in which they can neither retain health or live long, and so hurries them to the grave before their time...society knows how injurious such conditions are to the health and the life of the workers, and yet does nothing to improve these conditions' (Engels, 1987/1845:

128). A contemporary Engels might be justified in persisting to make accusations of callous indifference, of social murder, if he or she were to consider the part played by multinational companies in the perpetuation of poverty and high rates of illness in developing countries along with inadequate remedial action on the part of international organizations. Townsend for example argued that bodies like the World Bank, the International Monetary fund, and the World Health Organization could and should take a prominent role in reducing inequalities (Townsend, 1993; Walker and Walker, 2009: 18). At the national level however, Britain's recent policy climate has been self evidently different to what it was in the 1840s. New Labour pledged to eradicate child poverty for example 'within a generation' and health targets, in common with other European countries, reflect commitment to improve health and reduce inequalities between disadvantaged and better off areas as well as narrow the gap in life expectancy and infant mortality between rich and poor (National Audit Office, 2010; Euro Commission, 2009). In 2008 Prime Minister Gordon Brown re-iterated his Government's concerns: '... we believe that everyone, children, men and women, no matter their birth or background, no matter where they live, should have the best chance to enjoy a healthy life (Boseley, 2008).

By 2005, the Department of Health (2005) was able to highlight gains made in reducing the health gap, but acknowledged that on certain measures it remained stubborn. Whilst it needs to be acknowledged that policy change may take many years to show a serious beneficial effect on the health or deprivation statistics (Stronks, 2002; Fordham and Lawless, 2003), Britain is nevertheless amongst those countries where disparities between rich and poor, on some measures at least – adult and infant mortality, heart disease and some mental health indicators – appear even to be increasing (Shaw et al., 2005). It isn't that we are becoming unhealthier as a nation, the reverse is the case. But despite steady improvements overall, the gains made are unevenly distributed (www.healthprofiles.info). A Report of the House of Commons Select Committee on Health (2009) states that health inequalities [as measured by life expectancy] between the social classes have widened over the last ten years, by 4 per cent amongst men, and by 11 per cent amongst women, a result, the Committee acknowledges, of the health of the rich improving more quickly than that of the poor. Some interventions may actually widen health inequalities (Wanless, 2004), an example relates to objectives to encourage people to adopt healthier lifestyles: evidence suggests that richer groups respond better to health promotion messages (cmselect/cmhealth/286/28603.htm). But these are not necessarily or predominately cultural issues; contributory factors include restricted opportunities for those less well off to lead healthy lives.

Since New Labour's introduction of a Minimum Wage; Working Families Tax Credit; Income Support changes; Minimum Income Guarantee, Pension Credits and Winter Fuel Payments for Pensioners as well as programmes in schools, expansion of free nursery places, employment measures connected to the New Deals and Pathways to Work Schemes, and programmes aimed at poor neighbourhoods, real progress was made in tackling child, family and pensioner poverty (Sutherland et al., 2003; Toynbee and Walker, 2010). The well-being of young people benefited for example (Waldfogel, 2010), and older people reported some relative freedom from financial worries (Hill et al., 2009). Levels of poverty fell after 1997, but flattened off after 2005 when spending was reduced, to improve again by 2008/9 (Hills et al., 2009). Analyses like these which relate interventions to changes in levels of disadvantage underline the non-inevitability of poverty: work by the IFS for example found that households in the bottom half of the income distribution did better under Blair and Brown; those in the top half gained under Thatcher and Major (Elliott, 2010). Successes were also achieved in narrowing the gap between rich and poor: Britain experienced the fastest growth in income and wealth equality among the worlds 30 richest countries between 2000 and 2005 (OECD, 2008). But the country still remains one of the most unequal in the developed world and there appears to have been a small widening of income inequalities since 2005 (ONS, 2010). The statistics indicate some ambiguity nevertheless. Hills et al. (2009) maintain that overall the U.K. did become a more equal society after ten years of a Labour government; the problem lay in very rapid growth in the income of those at the very top, while incomes of the poorest tenth grew more slowly. Not until 2011 did the current leadership of the Labour Party begin to acknowledge that their Government's relaxed attitude to wealth had been mistaken.

Egalitarians, as Roy Hattersley (2007) notes, have always insisted that equality is a defining characteristic of the good society. Townsend consistently argued that the problem of poverty is a problem of riches, class and privilege, inequalities that are not easy to overcome (Townsend, 1979). Governmental ineptitude in tackling runaway top salaries and paralysis in halting the growing power of finance capital can have serious implications for health: international studies suggest that it is not poverty itself but income inequality that poses the biggest risk.

Americans, for example, living in a wealthier, but more unequal country than Japan, die on average five years earlier than the Japanese; average life expectancy in Britain is less than that for some similarly developed countries, including Sweden, Canada, Italy and Australia (Wilkinson and Pickett, 2010; CSDH, 2008), and mental health problems are more pronounced in countries like Britain which have high levels of income inequality (Friedli, 2009).

More egalitarian income distributions have been related to anomalous findings between countries on relationships between poverty and deprivation and poor health. Countries with low median incomes like Kerala, Sri Lanka and Costa Rica, for example, achieve life expectancies comparable with Europe (Sen, 2001). Cuba is another interesting case, with a narrower health gap in age at death between the better off and poor than that in many Western counties. Yet these are complex issues; different factors can be expected to contribute to poor health in different places. Townsend (1979) preferred to use the concept of 'resources' in his work on poverty rather than 'incomes' as it shifts attention to the reasons for unequal distribution of total resources. Because it identifies income inequality as the chief driver of health inequalities, the Wilkinson thesis on inequality and health has been critiqued for allegedly minimizing the confounding effects of additional factors and their spatial variation (Coburn, 2000; Lynch et al., 2000), and evidence on public services provision lends some weight to these arguments. In Cuba, for example, intensive community oriented social work and community oriented primary care are recognized as important contributory factors in protecting the health of the poor and maintaining a narrow health gap between the lesser and more advantaged (Beckworth, 2009; Dresang et al., 2005). Cuba's achievements via progressive social and health policies need nevertheless to be seen alongside the country's markedly different political and economic regime and narrower income inequalities relative to the West.

Income distribution may well be (in part) a marker for the distribution and nature of public services and other societal characteristics, nevertheless the strength of the available evidence is such that income inequalities cannot be discounted as an important element in patterns of causation. For Wilkinson (2000), it is *perceptions* of both relative income and social status which are privileged as having the greater influence on health inequalities. While we could expect perceptions of relative deprivation to exert a strong influence on the social patterning of health across the British population as a whole, they seem less likely to be able to account for variations between smaller geographic areas. If it were the case, then what Sir Michael Marmot (2004) has termed, 'status anxiety' would be more acute and have a more debilitating impact on the health of the poor in mixed income settings than it would in more demographically homogeneous places. Similar issues have also been addressed in the literature on poverty and exclusion, where questions have arisen on whether it is worse to be poor in a poor area than one that is socially mixed (Atkinson and Kintrea, 2004: 438). Yet Marmot's studies of civil servants indicate that the risk of ill health is not only heightened for poor people living in lower income areas, but that perceptions of social position are enhanced by living in a more affluent area, and further deflated by living in a poor one (Marmot, 2005: 10). Additional or alternative explanations will need to be considered.

Understanding social and contextual influences on health

Work setting out to further understandings of social and economic influences on health has focused on two explanatory issues in particular in recent years: one concerns the relative importance of compositional and contextual effects, the other gives prominence to identifying psychosocial pathways between determinants and health status.

(i) The neighbourhood context

Amongst questions frequently addressed in the literature on social inequalities in health are those centered around the difference that places can make, independently of, or in interaction with, the socio-economic characteristics (including class, income or ethnic group) of those living there (Cummins et al., 2007; Stafford et al., 2005; MacIntyre and Ellaway, 2009; Parkes and Kearns, 2006; Frohlich et al., 2007). Opportunities to lead healthy lives are more restricted, studies have demonstrated (as did Engels), in poor areas compared to better off places (Sooman and MacIntyre, 1995), and poorer access to good primary care may be a continuing factor for people living in some poorer places (CBI, 2007). But what of anomalous variations between similarly poor and deprived or advantaged areas themselves? Despite the strength of the relation between poverty and ill health, some places in Britain have been shown to have better population health and mortality rates than their similarity deprived counterparts (Phillimore and Morris, 1991; Drever and Whitehead, 1995).

A prominent example of the difference places can make to health can be found in a case study which appeared to suggest that aspects of community life and residents' social networks could play an active role. 'Roseto', a small American town with a largely Italian population, consistently produced considerably lower mortality rates than neighbouring – and similar in terms of the income and occupations of their residents – places until the 1960s, when social changes in the direction of 'Americanization', or individualism, took their effect (Wolf and Bruhn, 1993). Roseto was distinguished by population stability, ethnic and social homogeneity and strong family ties, as well as by a high degree of participation in local clubs and associations, and cohesive and supportive community relationships. Local culture and values centred on Catholicism and church activities and local co-operative norms strongly influenced community life (Egolf et al., 1992). More recent work has highlighted the significance of the neighbourhood or community context to the generation of health enhancing social capital (Lomas, 1998; Gatrell et al., 2000; Blaxter and Poland, 2002; Subramanian et al., 2003; Veenstra et al., 2005; Carpiano, 2007; Mohnen et al., 2011). While it has been suggested that growing income inequalities are associated with reduced social capital in poor areas, the Roseto case illustrates that that not all such areas necessarily suffer from impoverished social ties and a lack of social capital. Many of the features characteristic of Roseto are ones we associate with the 'traditional' British working class communities documented during the middle of the 20th century. Classic studies included 'Ashton' a Yorkshire mining town (Dennis et al., 1957), and Bethnal Green in London (Young and Willmott, 1962) a poor working class district identified for its patterns of close knit supportive networks and for strong community loyalties. In these communities, social capital – though then not labelled as such – was an intrinsic element of the local culture. Nevertheless, communities like these could be marred by exclusion and parochialism (Westergaard, 1975); for today's heterogeneous, work poor and sometimes divided neighbourhoods we need to identify contemporary conditions which generate potentially health-enhancing co-operative social networks, but which can also encourage a more inclusive community life as well.

(ii) Social and psychological pathways

By the beginning of the noughties work on understanding health inequalities had taken a polarized form in the epidemiological literature between explanations which focus on perceptions of inequality and their health damaging psycho-social mechanisms, and accounts which place emphasis on structural causes and the direct effects of material influences (Wilkinson, 2000; Lynch et al., 2000). For Richard Wilkinson shame, disrespect, social anxiety and perceptions of inferiority induced by interacting with people of higher social status are the important pathways involved. Referring to studies of non-human primates to aid understanding of the effects of social structure on modern human societies, he argues that people are especially sensitive to differences in social status involving hierarchal relationships of dominance and subordination (Wilkinson, 2000, 2001). A critique from a neo-Marxist/materialist perspective took issue with what they saw as the severance of income inequalities and perceptions of status in his work from the wider societal, political and economic context (Coburn, 2000; Muntaner and Lynch, 1999) but based their central argument on the idea that interpretations of links between income inequality and health must begin with the structural causes of inequalities rather than people's perceptions of them (Lynch et al., 2000). Whilst both causal models have made major contributions to the epidemiological literature, they could be seen to share some limitations in regard to social processes involved in relationships between macro and micro levels of analysis. A sociological understanding of social influences on health and well-being can be enhanced by re-asserting the value of the work of C. Wright Mills (2000), for whom establishing connections between public and personal issues requires, essentially, an emphasis on process. This may involve using the more fluid concept of 'well-being' (discussed in Chapter 2) which sits more easily with investigations of process than harder measures of health. It also entails exploration of the complex interrelation of structure, context, meanings and health outcomes (Pearlin, 1989).

The neo-materialists' avoidance of processional issues and the role of meanings which people attach to experience, can be contrasted with Wilkinson's psycho-social explanation of the trends he identifies. Consideration of the model from an interactionist perspective however, would require us to be sensitive to variation. People's understandings of the inequality they experience are subject to some fluidity, and open to contextual influence. Participants to a recent survey for instance while believing 'deserved' income inequalities to be fair, by 2008–9 were adjusting their opinions along with the onset of the financial crisis (Bamfield and Horton, 2009). We might expect perceptions of inequality to vary also with forms of social consciousness: the numerous influences they are subject to may rest on daily experiences in local social settings (Lockwood, 1966), but also on wider societal forces. In the present national context, public questioning of hefty bonuses in the financial sector for example is indicative of the potential role of economic conditions in prompting changes in ways in which the structure of inequality is perceived. If perceptions of inequality are dynamic, then mechanisms involved in relationships between such understandings and health outcomes are likely to be subject to various permutations. We might question whether individuals are persistently engaged in making the kind of social comparisons which give rise to feelings of inferiority as Wilkinson suggests, for example, or that such feelings dominate the everyday experience of people living in deprived circumstances.

Elucidating the complex and multi-faceted nature of influences on our health and well-being may also require a shift in emphasis from building uni-directional structural/functionalist models to developing explanations which acknowledge the role of subjective human agency (see also Popay et al., 1998; Williams, 2003). Fears that by addressing agency we may divert attention from underlying structures, or 'resurrect a discredited individualism' (Deacon and Mann, 1999: 431), are real. A more effective purchase on processes – involved in social exclusion, in the decline or resilience of community life, in relationships of health and well-being to poverty and place – will, from the perspective being developed here, need to incorporate a sociological focus on the structure/action dynamic. Doyal and Gough (1991) contend that the impaired agency of the poor should be the focus of our moral concern, while Wilson's (1996) studies of poor neighbourhoods in America with high levels of unemployment led him to view structure and culture not as mutually exclusive, but as phenomena which closely interact. The approach taken in this book is to explore dynamic relationships between place, poverty and health and well-being through a focus on the mediating role of social networks.

Social networks

There are many reasons for choosing to emphasize the part played by social networks in relationships between poverty, community and health. Social networks are an expression of experience; they reflect (and can also affect) for example, involvement in local life and work or feelings of community attachment. They embody personal biographies, changes to our lives and to where we live and work; at the same time, our lives may be changed by the social ties we form and access. Being poor or wealthy has significance for the extent and nature of our social connections, the connections themselves for our health and well-being. Developments to the concept of 'well-being' now feature an emphasis on positive social relations. An examination of social networks can also facilitate a focus on positive dimensions of deprived neighbourhoods along with negative ones, and can help discern some of the effects of differing and changing community contexts. The essentially organic nature of social ties is one of the features which emerge from later chapters.

A social network refers to the social relationships that surround an individual, the characteristics of those ties, the connections between them and the value of the tie to the individual (Berkman and Glass, 2000; Brown and Harris, 1978). Not all social relationships are experienced as positive, they can sometimes be perceived as oppressive rather than supportive, or as burdensome by those providing help (Oakley, 1992; Crow, 2004), or may have a malign influence on behaviours which influence our health (Kunitz, 2001; Kirke, 2006). Drug taking, dietary habits and consumption of alcohol are common examples. Nevertheless, in most circumstances, being part of an extensive social network is beneficial to the health of individuals across social groups (Blaxter, 1990; Berkman and Breslaw, 1983; Kawachi and Berkman, 2001; Valente, 2010). Approaches to explaining these relationships focus on the many functions or benefits afforded by membership of a network. Social ties are seen as acting either as a buffer against stressful life events and a protection against depression, or as exerting a more direct influence, through strengthening immunity to disease for example (Lynch, 1977; Cohen and Syme, 1985). Social support – practical, instrumental or emotional aid – has been consistently shown to have a positive influence on health and well-being (Cohen and Syme, 1985; Stansfeld, 1999; Hildon et al., 2008). More generally, studies have shown that social networks, as well as providing opportunities for companionship and sociability, have the capacity to confer social esteem or a feeling of belonging, or contribute to positive self identity and a sense of coherence (Wellman and Wortley, 1990; Allan, 1996; Swann and Brown, 1990; Antonovsky, 1987). Strong work based social networks can be a source of greater worker control and empowerment (Blauner, 1964).

The Durkheimian concept of 'social integration' has been used to explain the better health chances found for people with extensive social networks. The Health and Lifestyles Survey for example, demonstrated a strong relationship between high integration of individuals (as measured by household situation, frequency of contact with friends and family, working status, length of local residence, attendance at a place of worship, involvement in community work, and feeling 'part of the community') and both physical and psychological self assessed health (Blaxter, 1990). People who are more involved in the local community tend to be more positive about where they live than those who are not (Halpern, 1995), while participation in formal and informal organizations and leisure activities for example have been shown to carry advantages for health (Hawe and Shiell, 2000; Wakefield and Poland, 2005; Almedom, 2005; Szreter and Woolcock, 2004; Abbott, 2010). Policy drives which place emphasis on encouraging participation in local civic life, in voluntary organizations, public services or area regeneration initiatives and which aim to devolve greater control over decision making to local people might be expected, where successful, to benefit the well-being of those individuals involved. People are not passive recipients nonetheless; they give, as well as receive support for example, or may choose to act collectively to achieve common goals. While supportive networks can help us to cope with long term problems like poverty or from short term crisis, some ties may, as Wellman and Wortley suggest, help to effect transformations, provide 'social capital' to change status, homes, jobs, spouses, or change the world (Wellman and Wortley, 1990). Ways in which individuals' social networks enhance coping strategies and strengthen resilience are explored in later chapters; so too are means by which communities actively resist and challenge disadvantage and inequality.

Making the links

Retaining what C. Wright Mills calls 'a sociological imagination' requires us to seek links between the seemingly diverse areas of study that concern us (Nettleton, 2007). A focus on social networks, as protective factors, can help clarify what it is about some individuals and some neighbourhoods which make them resistant to the negative effects of adversity, but adopting a network perspective is also expedient for seeking analytical purchase on processes involved in relationships between socio-economic position and health, and place of residence and health. The approach adopted here, in which social networks are explored as key linkages between the topics under consideration, can be justified with broad reference to meanings, structures, and processes.

The literature on poverty includes examples of qualitative studies which, by exploring the meaning of poverty to individuals and identifying some of its effects, provide insights into some of the potential mechanisms involved. Studies demonstrate that difficulties like a low income, poor housing, debt, under resourced or stigmatized neighbourhoods, fear of crime, as well as struggling to manage and cope with them for example, can be potent sources of stress, anxiety, and defeatism, as can the reality of restricted opportunities for changing their situation (Graham, 1993; Lister, 2004; Dominy and Kempson, 2006). The experience of poverty is sometimes expressed as feelings of powerlessness, stigmatization and damaged self esteem; it can be associated with a lack of hope or with fatalistic attitudes (Cohen et al., 1992; Flaherty et al., 2004; Beresford et al., 1999; Wilson, D., 1993). Not unexpectedly perhaps, certain of these, like low perceptions of control or esteem, have also been linked to negative outcomes by health researchers (Brown and Harris, 1978; Wheaton, 1980; North et al., 1993; Stansfeld and Candy, 2006). What is especially interesting here is that certain features – enhanced perceptions of self efficacy and raised esteem – are, as noted earlier, recognized as amongst those advantages which social networks can bestow.

A social network perspective can aid understanding of what Bourdieu referred to in relation to social capital, as the processes by which social and economic inequality are reproduced (Bourdieu, 1986). Like many resources, access to productive social networks varies across social groups. As Pearlin explained: 'And just as the distribution of wealth, power and status are unequally distributed in societies, the extensiveness and resourcefulness of ... [social] networks are unequally distributed too' (Pearlin, 1985: 44–5). Some studies have suggested that people with more household income include more non-kin in their networks and are more likely to report adequate support than those on lower incomes (Willmott, 1987), while the social networks of unemployed people tend to be more restricted than those of the employed (Gaillie et al., 1994; Morris, 1995). Similarly, social capital is an asset which is inequitably distributed across social groups and between areas (Hall, 1999; Coleman, 1990). The barriers to involvement in voluntary activity for example are greater for those on low incomes, who may be deterred by any costs involved, the formality of meetings, or lack of confidence and requisite skills (Brownhill and Darke, 1998; Taylor, 2000).

What is essentially the oppositional nature of the relationship between poverty, social networks and well-being needs to be more widely addressed. For people living in poor and deprived circumstances, and who face a myriad of problems in their day-to-day lives, social contact and access to social capital may be especially valuable assets for protecting their health. Those more advantaged will have many coping resources of different kinds from which to draw. There have been some indications for example that practical and emotional support may have a particularly substantial protective impact on the psychological health of those in the poorer sections of society (Whelan, 1993), and that contact with friends is more important for the mental health of people living in deprived households than for those who are better off (Stafford et al., 2008). Just as Tudor Hart identified an 'inverse care law' in relation to a mismatch of needs and provision of health care (Mercer, 2007), then so too perhaps might an 'inverse social networks law' be recognized. The poor need health protective social networks more than the non-poor, but part of the problem of being poor can, for some people and in some places at least, be a reduced ability to access them. Nevertheless, we should be wary of over-generalizing: studies of working class communities, as noted earlier, remind us that this is certainly by no means the case in all contexts.

To be poor nevertheless can involve being deprived in more than a material sense. Work on social variation in health chances has, in the main, explored individual risks related to material resources, but Townsend's concept of 'relative poverty', sometimes alluded to in this literature, embraces social as well as material elements. 'Social deprivation', for example, describes a person's lack of integration, their inability to participate in the normal life of the community or to access ordinary social customs, activities and relationships (Townsend, 1987: 86). Approaches to 'social exclusion' resonate with the concept. For Room, for example, social exclusion focuses primarily on inadequate social participation, lack of social integration and lack of power (Room, 1995); interpretations also embrace multiple aspects of deprivation, or the role of neighbourhood. Some look to citizenship and structural issues, to exclusion from economic and political systems, others to cultures, while yet others highlight processional issues and dynamics over time (Walker and Walker, 1997; Lister, 2004; Hills et al., 2002; Byrne, 1999; Scharf and Smith, 2003; Levitas et al., 2007).

Interpretations of social exclusion operationalized in surveys during the 1990s put little emphasis on social relations however (Levitas, 2009; Walker, 2009). An exception was the 'Poverty and Social Exclusion in Britain' study (Gordon et al., 2000), which confirmed a strong association between low income and other dimensions of social exclusion, yet appeared also to indicate that social isolation and support could be exceptions to the general trend (Bradshaw, 2000; Lister, 2004). Later chapters will help address this anomaly by describing circumstances under which people with low incomes and living in poor communities are able to readily interact with others, access supportive ties or become involved in local activities.

An individual's social networks, if impoverished, are a key dimension of their social exclusion; by contrast, social capital, generally recognized as beneficial to health and well-being, implies thriving and productive ones. Identifying features which impinge on people's ability to access, develop and sustain productive and co-operative social ties are essential if we are to gain greater knowledge about ways in which the health gap between disadvantaged and advantaged groups and neighbourhoods is to be reduced and to identify preventative strategies. The emphasis in 'Poverty, Community and Health' is on face-to-face ties, as these can be more therapeutic than those more distant (Putnam, 2000), and on locally based social relationships. Despite arguments that, in general terms, social networks are becoming independent of locality (Wellman 2001; Pahl, 1996) or that the notion of community has lesser relevance to the modern world (Giddens, 1990), the local arena can be expected to have continuing and especial relevance for people on low incomes whose day-to-day experience may be lived out within relatively narrow spatial boundaries.

Similarity and difference: Social network characteristics

Social networks have been treated here so far as relatively simple, one dimensional constructs, but they can be differentiated in a number of ways. By their degree of formality, by the type of relationship, involving family, friends, colleagues or neighbours, or by the social and demographic characteristics, including age, employment status, gender, ethnicity or social class, of those who make up the network (Willmott, 1986; Pahl, 2000; Peren et al., 2004). Social networks can be considered in relation to aspects of their internal structure, by features such as extensiveness, geographic proximity, frequency of contact and density, that is, the degree to which network members know one another, what has been referred to as 'close knit' or loose knit' (Bott, 1957). They can also be assessed by their strength, by the importance of the ties to the individual. Social network analysts, and more recently social capital theorists, have categorized social ties as either bonding or bridging, involving 'thick' or 'thin' forms of trust. Bonding (strong) ties involve supportive relationships amongst similar people such as family members or members of an ethnic group, and bridging (weak) ties connect individuals to dissimilar groups and more diverse resources (Putnam, 2000; Granovetter, 1973).

A social network perspective which draws attention to their inherent features has salience for matters connected with both well-being and community integration and cohesion. Strong ties can be beneficial but in some cases can be controlling (Crow, 2004) for example, or may adversely affect health-related behaviours. Bonding ties can also act to 'bolster our narrow selves', and re-enforce social divisions (Putnam, 2000: 22–3). Dense, closely knit networks of neighbours and kin and the reciprocal aid associated with them were recognized as the defining characteristics of the traditional working class occupational community; in such settings opportunities to form new contacts outside the group were restricted (Lockwood, 1966; Bott, 1957). Arguments on the loss of community were generally centred around the loss of dense ties; social capitalists cast the net wider to focus on looser ties and the decline of associational involvement. While social forces can transform the ties we make, it is not generally clear which kinds of networks – made up of strong or weak ties, homogeneous or heterogeneous contacts – are most effective in sustaining health or promoting well-being. Work in network analysis however indicates that varying degrees of network density can be helpful in different circumstances (Hirsch et al., 1990; Granovetter, 1973). Strong, mutual exchange networks for example are essential to help people in poor areas to cope (Stack, 1974), but despite real benefits in terms of support and identity, the tendency to associate with your own kind can result not only in some being excluded from patterns of support, but may be of limited value for accessing additional resources like specialized information or job opportunities, where looser ties can be more advantageous (Cattell, 1995; de Souza Briggs, 1998; Calvo-Armengol and Jackson, 2004; Afridi, 2011).

If social networks are a productive resource, examination of factors which shape, constrain or provide opportunities for their maintenance is clearly important, but there are also some pertinent questions connected to the conscious creation of social ties. While Durkeim (1952) recognized the importance of social interaction for social integration and solidarity for example, he tended to see these relationships as uni-directional. But what motivates the decisions which people make on whom to include, exclude, mix or identify with? What part is played by values and attitudes in network formation, of, for example, tolerance, solidarity, or perceptions of inequality? The chapters which follow look at the social production of a sense of community in the context of deprived neighbourhoods, at structural and cultural influences on patterns of networks differentiated by strength and homogeneity and at corresponding forms of social capital. They will also consider the implications of differing network characteristics both for well-being and for community integration and cohesion. Amongst the questions addressed are: 'Can the neighbourhood be a source of organic solidarity?

Are there distinctive forces at work in new as well as old features of urban life and are they relevant to our well-being? The book draws from a number of community studies I've conducted in East London, a region described in 1890 by Frederick Engels, as 'the largest working-class district in the world' (Young and Willmott, 2007: xiii). The studies are located in areas where a history of poverty stretches back over centuries.

This chapter began by drawing attention to some of the historical variations on the theme of community decline in Britain and America. It went on to introduce issues and research questions arising from the literature on poverty and deprivation, social and spatial inequalities in health, and social networks and community participation. The literature was discussed alongside the current and recent context of poverty and health inequalities in Britain and policy responses to it, and in relation to tensions between aspects of individual agency and structural/material constraints and opportunities. Key concepts were identified – some of which, like social exclusion, can imply impoverished social networks or, like social capital, thriving and productive ones – to serve as heuristic tools in approaching a study of the linked themes of poverty, community, and health and well-being. The chapter argued that a research focus on social networks has heuristic value for uncovering influences on both the inclusion of individuals and the integration of groups, for deepening understanding of the social patterning of health inequalities and inherent processes, and for increasing knowledge on what makes individuals and their neighbourhoods thrive. 'Poverty, community and health' suggests a pivotal role for social networks as key mediators and moderators between structural constraints and opportunities and individual's health and well-being.

By addressing these interconnecting issues the book makes a timely contribution to the present political and economic context. Rising unemployment, cuts to housing benefit and to local authorities' budgets, changes in childcare credit, unemployment benefit and VAT, along with curtailment of initiatives like Sure Start, Educational Maintenance Allowance, and the Job Fund mean that life for vulnerable individuals and communities is becoming increasingly harsher. These are changes which carry a real and alarming danger of an exacerbation of health inequalities. Community involvement is being encouraged under the mantle of the 'big society', but it is a society to be achieved via a diminished state, depleted public services and a reduction in funding for the very voluntary and community groups who might be expected to help achieve it. Sadly, the prospects for community life in working class areas are looking bleaker than they have for a generation.

The book's coverage

Beginning with William Morris's vision of ideal communities and with the work of the ethical socialist Richard Tawney, Chapter 2 discusses social and political concepts with utility for understanding relationships between poverty, community and health – inequality, solidarity, well-being, participatory democracy and social capital – and touches on some of the ways these ideas have been addressed by policy makers. The chapter critically considers notions of 'community' and begins to evaluate the potential of placed based communities for well-being, social solidarity, and the good society.

Drawing on classical sociology and theories of the middle range, Chapter 3 outlines briefly the theoretical and methodological framework for the qualitative research. Features include the development of a social network typology used to assist analysis of narrative data and identify social processes involved in the relationships under consideration. The chapter closes with a brief description of the setting for the East London studies.

Rather than viewing place based communities as an irrelevance in the modern world, following chapters show that people continue to express their continuing desire for localized manifestations of community life and the advantages they entail. Based on residents' own perceptions and experience of their neighbourhoods, Chapters 4 and 5 contrast the distinctive features of two housing estates, discuss their implications for well-being and demonstrate ways in which the locality exerts a powerful influence on community and family life. As well as considering factors which bear more directly on health and well-being such as poverty, the built environment or the neighbourhood's reputation, historical and contemporary features are identified which have helped shape the community and its degree of social inclusion, conferred a sense of belonging and identity, and provided opportunities for developing social networks and accessing social capital.

In Chapter 4 structural and cultural characteristics are highlighted which have contributed to perceptions of the 'Dock Lane' estate as a largely traditional working class neighbourhood; factors contributing to the norm of reciprocity and to the strong 'bonding' and at times exclusive ties which typified this still resilient estate are explored. Looking at life in the second study area, the 'Bridge Street' estate, Chapter 5 critiques 'victim blaming' and pathologizing approaches to poor areas and examines reasons why alienating conditions on Bridge Street had made it harder for the resilience of positive perceptions of community, of trust and of cultures of mutuality. The chapter demonstrates nevertheless the co-existence of a thriving, participatory and dynamic community and shows how it was actively and collectively created alongside the demoralized one.

Chapter 6 compares theoretical approaches to social capital and contextualizes the concept by looking at influences on its different forms and its key sources – population stability; social inclusion; integration; self interest, solidarity and class consciousness – across several urban neighbourhoods. It introduces the case of 'Canal View', and explores how it came to be a neighbourhood unusually rich in both a culture of reciprocity and of local involvement. A key question for this chapter concerns the potential of the local arena as a source of more inclusive social networks, less conditional social capital and wider solidarities, as opposed to a setting for conflict and division. The chapter identifies circumstances in which there is potential for the development of new forms of community consciousness whilst continuing to embrace and build on valued elements of the old.

Beginning with questions on the extent to which growing individualism in society has damaged well-being and happiness and taken its toll on co-operative community life, Chapter 7 draws attention to people's varied understandings of well-being and happiness. It shows that people derive happiness from diverse sources; these include aspects of individualism as well as collective activity. Along with identifying the many ways in which community life and a neighbourhood store of social capital are beneficial across age groups, the chapter looks also at some of their social and therapeutic limitations, and at particular groups excluded. It underlines the importance of local resources and services for meeting the many and diverse needs which people associate with maintaining health and well-being, and for the attainment of an equitable balance between independence and interdependence.

It is not generally clear which kinds of networks, made up strong or weak ties, homogeneous or heterogeneous contacts, are most effective in protecting health or promoting well-being: Chapter 8 looks closely at individual cases to identify social processes involved in relationships between social ties and health and to consider ways in which different network formations are able to maintain well-being and boost resilience to adversity. Beneficial or harmful aspects of individual's lives, the resources drawn on to help withstand or overcome stressful experience, and the coping strategies adopted are considered here through the prism of social network models grounded in the lives of the people studied. Whilst models capture structural constraints and opportunities and the social richness or impoverishment of lives lived, they also embody aspects of human agency. In this way, social networks are shown to perform a dynamic role in processes involved in health and well-being.

What are the prospects for the well-being of people living in poor neighbourhoods in today's rapidly changing political and policy climate? Chapter 9 draws together concluding themes from previous chapters and examines the implications of post 2010 policy agendas for poverty, community and health. The book's conclusions are discussed within the context of current political ideas on the 'big society' from the right, and on the 'good society' from the left and centre.

2
Utopian Dreams

Introduction

Twentieth century London was once described as a city peopled by extraordinarily healthy, happy and long lived men and women, a London of small communities where all were addressed as 'neighbour' and where strangers were welcomed. There was useful non-alienating work for all, goods were made for use and pleasure, not profit, and consumption was low. These were, above all, self governing, co-operative and egalitarian communities, without poverty, and without riches. Factories were run as co-operatives; central government had withered away. It was, of course a futuristic, imagined London, William Morris's utopian dream: 'News from Nowhere' (Morris, 1890/1974).

Had Morris, in giving expression to his vision of a better society found a key to healthier lives as well? His assertion for example that fellowship is life, and that lack of fellowship is death, reflected his fervent belief that fraternity, and the co-operation which he believed sprang from it, were indispensable requirements for leading a fulfilled and happy life (Morris, 1888). Morris's fictional Nowhere story can readily be dismissed as a mere fantasy of little relevance to the real world, but this is not the view taken by his biographer the historian E. P. Thompson, who writes: 'Never for long, in News from Nowhere, does Morris allow us to forget this sense of tension between the real and the ideal ... We are made to question continually our own society, our own values and lives' (Thompson, 1977: 694). Artists and environmentalists are returning to Morris's work to uncover lessons for the greening and sustainability of London in 21st century, but it is the social and political content of his work however which is of particular interest here.

Equality, solidarity and vision

A little utopian dreaming may be no bad thing, whether for an individual's hopes and well-being, or for governments whose policies impact upon them. But first, it is a simpler task to describe what (with caution) could be called an *unhealthy* community; little imagination is needed. Morris's co-operative, participatory communities would co-exist with egalitarian and solidaristic forms of social relations, but relationships between social and cultural groups in society today are defined, to no small extent, by relationships of inequality; in some places, by division rather than cohesion. The poorest, as Coates and Silburn (1970) once expressed it, suffer from a multitude of deprivations and inequalities, not only of a material nature, but also of a social and political kind. Their poorer health record is a casualty of their experience. Whilst some commentators on the political right have at times questioned the very goal of equality in health, believing it to be at best unobtainable, or at worst unnecessary (IEA, 1988), societies in which health inequalities persist are generally considered unjust, unfair societies; their continuation into the 21st century an aberration. Successive Health Ministers in the noughties explained their commitment to tackling health inequalities by emphasizing their dedication to values of fairness and social justice. Social justice as fairness, for analysts like Hutton (2010), as it was for Rawls (2001) is the basis for a good society.

The principle of social justice, argued Runciman, owes its existence to all three of the major political ideologies in Britain, if interpreted in very different ways. Though demarcations may now be less clear cut, to Conservatives, social justice referred traditionally to a social hierarchy governed by a stable social system of interconnected rights and obligations; to Liberals a socially just society is one in which positions are achieved through competition, and not through dependence on social position, and to Socialists, social justice is linked to goals of maximum social equality (Runciman, 1965). The ethical socialist, Richard Tawney, writing in the 1930s, had provided a vision for reformers in the immediate post war period. Equality was elevated as *the* crucial goal. His book was an appeal to tackle the iniquities of the British class system, a system which was based not only on the inequitable distribution of wealth and other material resources, but of power, privilege, culture and opportunity too (Tawney, 1931). Debates concerning the relevance of class under conditions of late capitalism have tended to focus more on its alleged death than on its continuing saliency (Lawler, 2005; Saunders, 1990), but the tenacity of class as a system of inegalitarian distribution of both resources and opportunities is difficult to refute given the strength of evidence on, for example, social inequalities in health and a growing gap between the incomes of the very rich and the very poor, as well as on the constricted and slowing opportunities for social mobility in Britain (Milburn, 2009) demonstrated recently. Changes in class identity and consciousness, an historical relationship, which, E. P. Thompson (1968) argues, happens when some people identify shared and collective interests, are however, more complex and mutable. Whilst some sociologists maintain that ideological differences associated with class persist, or that class co-exists with other forms of social identity, others contend that the breakdown of occupational communities in particular has led to the undermining of working class identity (Martin, 2010; Mackenzie et al., 2006; Savage, 2000; Bottero, 2004).

Key dimensions of Tawney's ethical socialism were captured in the hope, the vision and commitment to achieving a better society which influenced an administration whose policies improved the lives of the poorest, benefited health and reduced inequalities of various kinds despite a massive national debt in 1945. The political ethos which gave rise to the post war welfare state has been contrasted with that of the recent Labour Government who are criticized for neglecting the tradition of ethical socialism and loosing the vision of the good society. Labour, argue Cruddas (2009) and Cruddas and Rutherford (2008), for example, must re-establish its belief in equality, and resurrect the idea of fraternity, while the pressure group Compass seek to reconnect the party with its traditions of mutualism and association (www.compass-group.co.uk). More widely, evidence of a growing consensus among some philosophers and political scientists on the need for a radical alterative to the ideology of neo-liberalism and culture of what Sampson (2004) refers to as capitalist triumphalism, prevalent for three decades and widely understood as socially damaging, is becoming increasingly apparent. Michael Sandel for example presents the case for a new politics of the common good, necessary he believes, if we are to achieve a just society. He argues that we must challenge purely privatized notions of the good life and cultivate civic virtue. A just society, for Sandel, will require a sense of solidarity and mutual responsibility (Sandel, 2009, 2010).

Tawney recognized the social harms inflicted by inequality. He believed for example that inequalities were inimical to fellow feeling, to fraternity, and that they vulgarized and depressed human relations (Phillips and Taylor, 2008). Social solidarities, what Durkheim (1893) conceived of as relationships of co-operation and interdependence, can be damaged: too great a gap between rich and poor, as Sandel (2010) acknowledges, undermines solidarity. Nevertheless, success in the achievement of egalitarian goals in the immediate post war period in itself appeared to rest on preconditions which included the spread of solidaristic values. The Beveridge Britain of the 1940s was, as Richard Titmuss described it, a country where a visionary belief in the possibility of the creation of a better, more egalitarian society had caught the popular mood. In turn, the universalistic social policies adopted by the incoming government re-enforced those solidaristic values. Social, economic and fiscal policies were expected to play a key role in the realization of a socially cohesive society (Titmuss, 1987). Solidarity, the child of interdependence, argues Baldwin, requires some form of collective identity and an awareness of shared needs and risk. Beveridge's universalistic, egalitarian approach to social policy rested on an appeal to the self reliant as well as the poor (Baldwin, 1990: 33). Similarly, Horton and Gregory (2009) contend that whilst policy changes at this time were driven by shifts in public attitudes to welfare, they also owed their success to changes in how people viewed the poorest in society. The distribution principle involved in welfare policies played a significant role in shaping attitudes, in the sense that '... policies with wide coverage align interests and identities so that we are in this together' (Horton and Gregory, 2009: xix). Contrasting the 1940s with the noughties, they argue that New Labour failed to win public support for tackling poverty and inequality. The post 2010 coalition government has prioritized gaining support for their welfare policies, but they are policies which are in essence inegalitarian. Moves designed to reduce the economic deficit and which are widely understood to place a greater burden on the poor and unemployed have been rendered acceptable through the promotion of a blame culture effecting a distancing of the less fortunate from the rest of society. There have been many constraints on the growth of universalistic values and commitment to others in recent decades, the dominance of free market neo-liberalism and the decline of countervailing forces in the form of Trade Union membership, for example, not least amongst them. But governments from Prime Minister Margaret Thatcher's onwards have been especially adroit at creating perceptions of division and thus hindering the development of perceptions of interdependence. The ideological creation of a feckless 'underclass' for example has been a key weapon of cleavage. Now, divisive stratagems which once more equate poverty with moral failings help ease the path for regressive welfare and fiscal policies.

A significant feature of British society in the 1940s decade is an evident confluence of some of those elements, which, in his vision of an ideal society, Morris expected would enhance our health and happiness. A socially integrated and more egalitarian post war British society was to be achieved and administered centrally, however. There was little emphasis at this time on certain additional factors which were core components of Morris's vision: minimal interest in small scale units for example, in co-operation and participation at the local level, essentially, in communities, after 1945.

Community

In public policy the term 'community' is loosely used to mean all the people in a given neighbourhood, town, estate or parish, or refers to a network of people with other strong interests in common (DCLG, 2006: 13). In sociology, the term may be elusive and vague; but the concept's popularity shows no sign of lessening (Mayo, 2000; Pahl, 1996). It is not surprising that Raymond Williams once described community as a warmly persuasive word (Williams, 1976: 76). Definitions commonly convey notions of fellowship, harmony, and shared identity based upon interweaving social relationships (see for example Bell and Newby, 1971). Day (2006) suggests that definitions like these make real cases appear to fall short of an ideal, thus community becomes a mere philosophical dream. Less esoteric approaches include those which, like Wellman's (1979), give prominence to social networks and their role in the provision of support, feelings of belonging and social identity. The classic 'community studies' literatures generally employed the term in relation to social connections in place based communities. Many of these explored the experience of working class neighbourhoods; some, like 'Coal is our Life' (Dennis et al., 1957) looked especially at ways in which the local and regional economy shaped community life. A contrasting and more subjective interpretation of community focused instead on the feelings and understandings of community members themselves (Cohen, 1985). Peter Willmott's 'attachment community' provided a bridge between some of these perspectives, and placed emphasis on solidaristic elements (Willmott, 1989).

Yet 'community' remains a highly contested term. Critics believe that it has become overly romanticized and conservative (Mayo, 2000; Pahl, 1996) or that there is undue emphasis on assumptions of 'sameness' (Bauman, 2001). A strong sense of local attachment may be based on exclusion and invoked to establish distance from others (Lockwood,

1966; Cohen, 1982, 1985). The 'Communitarian' take on community (which had strongly influenced Prime Minister Blair's (1996) political outlook) has been the subject of particularly vigorous critiques. Communitarians regard people as essentially social beings, rooted in families and communities, but its proponents add strongly moralistic overtones to this innocuous interpretation. Etzioni for example defines communitarianism as a social movement aiming at shoring up the moral, social, and political environment (Etzioni, 1995: 245). The concept has been judged as authoritarian and conservative: Etzioni seeks to reassert the norm of the heterosexual two-parent family for example (Bell, 1993). But it is the idealized, unproblematic idea of community supporting shared meanings and values together with a disregard of conflict, denial of social difference and avoidance of issues of freedom, autonomy and inequality, however, which has drawn the bulk of the critics' fire (Sayers, 1995; Young, 1990).

Community loss is a recurrent theme for urban sociologists. The idea that urbanization damaged community life was a persistent thread running through the Chicago school studies of the earlier part of the 20th century for example. Contemporary social theorists now look to modernity and globalization, not to detail the disintegration and erosion of community life, but to question the validity of spatial aspects of community, arguing that the important ties, for example, may be those unconnected to locality; that the local arena is simply less significant in the lives of most people (Wellman, 2001; Giddens, 1990). Bauman (2001) for example, referring to 21st century social conditions such as greater fluidity, fewer restraining influences and increased freedom of choice, argues that these can be seen as incompatible with the constraints of community. Nevertheless, there remain valid reasons for retaining the idea of 'community' and its associations with particular places as a conceptual tool for meaningful social analysis. The local arena is likely to have greater significance for the lives of the poorest for example than it has for the more advantaged, as will mutually supportive relationships amongst neighbours. Research has indicated for instance that social tenants spend more time in their neighourhood than home owners (Scottish Homes, 2000). Conceptualizations of community which stress its processional and active qualities or which continue to elevate social networks as key elements appear especially constructive. Day and Murdoch (1993), for example, overcome the dichotomy between community of place and interest group by identifying 'community' as the interaction of different social networks in specific contexts.

We have seen a shift in emphasis in accounts of local life to incorporate not only kinship and other local networks as important sources of help but also to include more directly political elements (Willmott, 1989). Janowitz and Suttles (1978) argued that the local community provides a milieu in which the civic ideals of democracy (in a pluralist sense) can flourish. 'Community' was also used in connection with community development activities for example which aimed to increase participation in local decision making and foster shared interests and identities (Willmott, 1989; Croft and Beresford, 1992). Abrams' 'Neighbours' (Bulmer, 1986) provided a bridge between traditional community studies and contemporary approaches which have local involvement and volunteering at their centre. Today advocates of progressive politics in the main wish to see an expanded role for civil society, largely in the form of increased civic engagement. Approaches to the 'good society' or to the 'big society' for example are variant, but share a common language of empowerment (White, 2009).

Community participation

A recognition that the most vulnerable may have little influence in the political process is illustrative of one aspect of long term unease concerning the efficacy of systems of representative democracy. The focus on participation at the local level is another. Participation, though generally considered as an essential component of democracy, has also nonetheless been judged as antithetical to democracy, and linked to political instability and compulsion (Hayek, 1960; Schonfield, 1969; Orwell, 1949). Advocates of a return to the ideals of participatory democracy look to a wide spectrum of liberal and socialist political and social thought. For John Stuart Mill, for example, participation was the most effective way of promoting self interests, safeguarding freedoms, and providing political education. By contrast, Rousseau's ideal participation was co-operative, communal and altruistic (Pateman, 1970; Miliband, 1994a). Rousseau, and much later, the ethical and associational socialist G.D.H. Cole, looked forward to a society of small collaborative units where near universal participation would be the norm. Cole was nevertheless sensitive to the dangers of excessive collectivism and loss of freedom (Cole, 1919; Hirst, 1990). Marx's contribution was more challenging: he saw political potential in the processes of participation. Although insisting that state power had to be crushed before participatory democracy could flourish, he nevertheless acknowledged that class consciousness could be nourished by participation within the existing political system (Evans, 1972).

Concerns voiced in the middle of the 20th century from the political right about anti-democratic tendencies of the interventionist state became later expressed as a critique of 'top down' policies adopted after 1945 which allegedly served to disempower citizens and weaken self help and co-operation. Following appeals for a return to classical democratic ideals (Lukes and Duncan, 1963), participation, in various forms, was widely seen as an antidote. By the turn of the century participatory ideals had become co-opted by policy makers: encouraging involvement was a key strategy in area regeneration initiatives for example (SEU, 2000; Batty et al., 2010) and a new Department for Communities was set up to encourage active citizenship. The community empowerment white paper (DCLG, 2008) placed emphasis on plans to give people more control in relation to local services. Conservative led government plans for the 'big society' go further in relation to both the form and level of participation anticipated: communities are to be empowered to run their own services and take over control from local authorities (Maude, 2010). While anti-statist features of big society ideas are questionable, there are many reasons to welcome nevertheless the current policy emphasis on encouraging volunteering, not least its potential to benefit the health of participants. The aims of the 'new localism', which the ODPM for example identified as to empower, socially include, challenge discrimination, strengthen community cohesion and build social capital (ODPM, 2005b: 7), are clearly laudable, but the encouragement of involvement via local initiatives is not without its problems. There have been long term concerns about accountability; the representativeness of participants in relation to neighbourhood demographics, and constraints on the agency of the most deprived sectors of the community (Willmot, 1989; Taylor, 2000). In any case, in a free society there will also always be individuals, from a variety of backgrounds and for a variety of reasons, who do not choose involvement.

A political desire for voluntarism may, or may not be congruous with other political ideals, such as greater equality or the attainment of social integration. Potentially negative implications for social justice have been identified for example. Wakefield and Poland (2005) warn that interventions undertaken to build civic engagement may be regressive rather than a progressive; that encouraging participation may strengthen already uneven power relations between different sectors of the community. Re-iterating some essential problems associated with the participatory democracy tradition, Walker argues that, because participating individuals, groups and communities can be motivated by self interest rather than a desire to contribute to the common good, their action does not necessarily secure equal access to resources. Progressive policies, social justice and egalitarian goals, he argues, are best achieved by a strong, centralized, interventionist state (Walker, 2002). The current climate of austerity brings additional dangers: responding to funding restrictions placed upon them, moves by local authorities to encourage volunteering and thereby shore up local services are more likely to be effective in better off areas than in poorer. Finally, it is not necessarily self evident that social cohesion is advanced by resident involvement in local initiatives. Intolerance or exclusivity amongst some participating groups may be exacerbated in the present highly competitive climate for funding, though limitations like this are not always seen as intractable. Opportunities are needed for people with different identities to work together, to develop common bonds, form alliances, and to identify their own well-being with that of their neighbours (Atkinson, 1994; Taylor, 2003; MacGregor and Lipow, 1995). The political project for the democratic left, for example, as Cruddas and Nahles (2009) identify it, is one of democratic renewal; it is to build the good society around ideas of democracy, community and pluralism.

Community and the potential for solidarity

There is some blurring of the boundaries between Durkheim's concept of organic solidarity, a form of cohesion based upon relationships of exchange, co-operation and interdependence between unlike social groups (Giddens, 1971; Allcorn and Marsh, 1975), and the form of solidarity involved in Marxian notions of class identity and class consciousness. Traditional working class communities were clearly a source of solidarity, if in a bounded sense, but strong community solidarities may it has been argued, inhibit wider solidarity. For Westergaard, the two essential preconditions for radical class consciousness, that is identification and a recognition of common interests with people outside the immediate locality or occupational community, are solidarity and vision, but parochial limitations and demands of immediate need act to constrain them (Westergaard, 1975). The sources of solidarity, he argues, lie in the wider society and not the local community. If becoming socially, politically and class conscious is a learning process however, then local conditions may once more be advantageous. Social theorists have identified the potential of place based communities as locales for the active building of new forms of community, identity and consciousness (Harvey, 1989; Castells, 1997; Freire, 1996). Communities are now regarded as potential sites for political mobilization and the achievement of social change, not via top down initiatives, government schemes and formal involvement, but through grassroots activity amongst less powerful groups, or, in Freire's case (Cooper, 2008), via radical community development. Day, in a comprehensive review of the literature, draws attention to the emancipatory potential of Raymond Williams's vision of community and compares it to the more conservative, communitarian approach. Whilst Etzioni wishes to re-instate old forms of community and the disciplines it imposed, Williams, Day argues, sees it as a means through which people can seize control of their own destinies (Day, 2006: 18; Williams, 1988). Conceptualizations of community which, as well as acknowledging its negative aspects, embrace positive dimensions of community and recognize its transformative potential, can sit comfortably with the use of a social model of health. The World Health Organization used the concept of 'well-being' to describe 'positive health' (WHO, 1948: 100). It enables a focus on what promotes and protects health, rather than on what causes illness (Blaxter, 2004; Bowling, 1991).

Community, health and well-being

Issues connected to the causal pathways that influence people's subjective perceptions of their well-being (as opposed to objective measures of health, illness and disease) are gaining prominence across academic disciplines. Some contemporary approaches define the concept in relation to the satisfaction of human needs: for eco-psychologists, these include social and emotional needs, and needs for self actualization (Pickering, 2001); for human geographers, they can refer also to security, to feelings of identity, material wants, or aesthetic pleasure (Gesler, 2003). Interpretations which stress the social dimensions of well-being are of particular interest: the focus for positive psychologists for example is on 'flourishing' or feeling good, not only about ourselves, but about our social relationships, within families, between peers, and in communities (Keyes, 2002). Ideas on 'happiness', a term which to some extent is supplanting 'well-being' in sections of this literature, place a similar emphasis on positive social relations. For Haidt (2006), for example, human beings thrive when they connect with somebody or something outside of themselves, while the economist, Richard Layard, advocates a concept of happiness which stresses our social being (Layard, 2005). A new movement named 'Action for Happiness' was launched by Richard Layard, Geoff Mulgan and Anthony Seldon in 2011 with the aim of encouraging kindness and promoting a culture based on the happiness of others (http://www.actionforhappiness.org). Taking the concept in a slightly different direction, happiness, argue Fowler and Christakis (2008) is not only a function of individual experience but is also a property of groups in the sense that the well-being of one member affects that of others in the group. This biological model aside perhaps, it is not hard to see parallels between some of the current variants on the themes of well-being and happiness and the work of William Morris, where the emphasis is on fraternity and fellowship, but they also bear comparison to aspects of Marxian theory. Marx (1844) understood the antithesis of well-being as alienation, that is, separation from others, from our social being, and dislocation from our species being, our true selves, within a capitalist system, as well as the more familiar notion of detachment from the products of our labour.

Consideration of influences on health and well-being (however defined) in community settings presents some challenges. A very real difficulty associated with the use of terms like 'healthy community' and 'unhealthy community', especially where poor neighbourhoods are concerned, is that such designations carry with them the baggage of the past. They can conjure images of eugenicists' notions of purity and contamination or intellectual degeneracy; invoke categorizations of 'deserving' and 'undeserving' poor (MacNichol, 1987; Lawler, 2005), or lean heavily on conformity and the imposition of authority. Concerned with what they considered the 'social disintegration' of town life, the focus of the Peckham Health Centre for example, established in the 1930s, was on the encouragement of 'healthy social relations'. The very poor were excluded from the facilities however, and for the centre's founders, the notion of a healthy community was essentially conservative, emphasizing hierarchy, control, and the family as the leading unit of society (Lewis and Brookes, 1983).

Fear and demonization of the poor and the denigration and stigmatization of the areas they live in has had a prolonged history. Stedman Jones (1976) describes how in the 19th century the poorest parts of London were frequently described in the most derogatory of terms, as engines for depraving and degrading the population for example. Parts of the capital were especially feared for their supposed contagious effects. Ideas of contagion and contamination were not restricted to the spread of illness however. Whilst notions of well-being today frequently rely on a social model of health, in these historical examples by contrast a medical disease model was appropriated to scrutinize social problems and expound on moral issues. It was believed that 'demoralization' and unemployment, for example, could be caught. References to a miasma or 'social contamination' effect common in much 19th century commentary on poor areas resurfaced in recent years amongst the work of those who, like Charles Murray, believed that the social costs of poverty grow disproportionately with the rate of poverty in an area, but were also taken up more widely in mainstream work and commentary alluding to the 'problem' of 'concentrated poverty'.

Negative attitudes to poor areas are difficult to eradicate. Conceptualizing relationships between communities, social relations and health and well-being requires approaches that are not invariably predicated upon a presumed decline of community in deprived urban areas but instead on positive forms of social engagement, and which consider communities as potential sites for the nurturance of positive well-being. Research studies on relationships between place of residence and well-being include work in environmental psychology for example which focuses on mechanisms involved in stress recovery and which has identified restorative benefits of places in such 'community' related features as place identity, a sense of attachment and residential satisfaction (Korpela et al., 2001). From a sociological perspective, well-being has been linked to what Giddens termed 'ontological security', a sense of belonging or identity and feeling comfortable with one's world (Dupois and Thorns, 1998). Our social being as reflected in neighbourhood based social ties and social interactions are factors generally associated with benefits in terms of health, well-being and quality of life. Chapter 1 indicated that they can provide access to 'social capital', for example. A number of studies have explored relationships between social capital and physical and mental health and in most cases found beneficial effects (Macinko and Starfield, 2001; Kawachi et al., 2008; De Silva et al., 2005).

Social capital

Although on one level social capital could be seen as a re-working of older concepts, 'community' for example, 'co-operation' 'social integration', 'participatory democracy', or even 'solidarity', perhaps the very advantages of the newer concept lie in its readiness to absorb strands of these various ideas. Social capital has been defined by Putnam as those '... features of social life – networks, norms of reciprocity and trust – that enable participants to act together more effectively to pursue shared objectives' (Putnam, 1995: 664). He sees membership of clubs, co-operatives, and voluntary associations as its prime source (Putnam, 2000). Coleman (1990), the concept's principal theorist, identifies several forms including obligations and expectations of mutual aid, information potential, and norms and sanctions associated with informal social control. For Jane Jacobs, whose work pre-dates much of the current interest in social capital and yet has been undeservedly neglected in contemporary discourse, social capital refers to cross-cutting social networks which provide a basis for trust, co-operation and perceptions of safety. Trust, an 'unconscious assumption of support' is 'a resource in time of personal or neighbourhood need' (Jacobs, 1961: 65).

Given that co-operative social networks and community participation are at its heart, William Morris might have felt some affinity with the idea of social capital. Yet, whilst Morris insisted that the kind of community life he imagined would exist within conditions of economic, social and political equality, egalitarian issues do not, in the main, feature in most theoretical approaches to social capital. An exception can be found in the work of Pierre Bourdieu (Bourdieu, 1986; Leonard, 2004), who, in adopting a structural, class analysis, recognized that economic capital strengthened social or cultural capital, but the concept of social capital more generally has been critiqued for underplaying material, economic and political dimensions (Lynch et al., 2000; Woolcock, 1998; Coburn, 2000). It has also been found wanting for the circularity of its arguments; because access to its benefits can be exclusive, and, in common with appraisals of 'community', for the insufficient attention given to its negative, darker, or unproductive side (Portes, 1998; Foley and Edwards, 1998). Some of these difficulties arise however from how it has been used rather than from features intrinsic to the concept itself. Firstly, for instance, Coleman treats social capital as neutral, he recognized that its effects could be both positive and negative. Secondly, research on social capital and health has been charged with using a conceptualization of the concept which ignores divisions in society (Lynch et al., 2000), marginalizes class relations and instead 'blames the community' (Muntaner and Lynch, 1999). Thirdly, research utilizing social capital has tended to obscure social, political, and economic contexts (Blaxter and Poland, 2000), yet context was highlighted by two of the topic's major exponents – Coleman and Jacobs – as highly significant in social capital's generation. The specific context in which social capital is embedded can be seen as central to its processional qualities. Empirically, however, social capital has been frequently treated as something lacking in particular communities rather than as an analytical device for uncovering social processes (Morrow, 1999; Leonard, 2005). The advantages in utilizing social capital lie in its relational approach which '... requires us to look at social phenomena from different angles simultaneously ...' (Schuller et al., 2000: 29). As such, the concept has value for developing understanding of relationships between poverty, communities, and health and wellbeing.

Conclusion: In pursuit of the health giving community

It is doubtful whether the term 'unhealthy community' can be used with any degree of tranquility. It slips too easily into the language of victim blaming, or resonates with 19th century notions of pollution and contamination. Unhealthy communities are, in an obvious sense, simply communities in unequal societies. Ideas on a 'healthy community' for the 21st century would need to engage creatively with notions of participatory democracy, and acknowledge re-distribution of resources as a key condition. It would also take into account diversity in cultures and freedom to choose patterns of living, something which, perhaps unexpectedly, William Morris considered. According to Thompson: 'In both News from Nowhere and [Morris's] lectures, the emphasis is upon communal life. But ...in a society which fostered true variety, he knew that different men would choose to live in different ways' (Thompson, 1977: 686).

Excessive 'community', nonetheless, whether in the form of supportive ties or involvement in organizations and activities, may also be detrimental to health and well-being. Durkheim's work on suicide drew attention to relationships between the degree of social integration in a society and psychological health. Suicides were identified as either 'egoistic', that is caused by a lack of integration and meaningful social interaction, 'anomic', which he related to weakening of the moral codes that normally regulate individuals, and 'altruistic' which occurred where individuals were too closely integrated into the values of their society. In the latter case, individual action and autonomy are crushed (Durkheim, 1952; Giddens, 1971). The language may have changed, but the nature of current ruminations around the need to replace the dominant paradigm of individualism with something approaching the 'good society', and what governments can do to help deliver it, are indications of the longevity of Durkheim's ideas. His interest in the influence of underlying societal 'moral forces' especially has continuing saliency: a sense of well-being is generated he believed, in social orders in which there is a balance of both egoism and anomie (individualism) and altruism and fatalism (collectivism) (Taylor and Ashworth, 1987). Whilst the leader of the Labour Party, Ed Miliband (2010) has alluded to a vision of a society where self interest and shared interest go hand in hand, more often they are seen as oppositional in contemporary discussion.

It would be mistaken to give pride of place to localism as the only form of community life of value. Supportive 'bonding' ties are an essential resource for helping people living in poor areas to cope with everyday difficulties. Critiques of community (or indeed of social capital) which focus on its 'dark side' are generally referring to less appealing dimensions of strong, dense ties. But just as there are dangers in giving undue prominence to a rosy notion of community entailing unity, harmony, and shared values, there are problems in over-emphasizing the community-as-conflict model. It can leave us with the sense that social relations under late capitalism cannot resemble anything other than a competitive Hobbesian dystopia. Social networks made up of strong and weak, homogeneous and heterogeneous ties, could be amongst key factors for identifying characteristics of health giving synergetic communities and for assessing their contribution to the good society.

3
Researching Poverty, Community and Health

Introduction

Having begun to pull together diverse strands of influence on health and well-being this chapter will build on the foregoing discussions to briefly outline the theoretical and methodological framework for the East London studies drawn on in later chapters. It has been suggested that to advance understanding of health inequalities we need to look beyond social epidemiology to sociology and social policy (Graham, 2001: 298) and, because social problems do not confine themselves to the pigeon holes of academic departments (Mills, 2000) the study has recourse to a wide social science base encompassing in particular sociology, social and public policy, and politics. Ethnographic methods were adopted for the empirical research, but, as Nettleton argues, observations on the minutiae of social life 'always need to be understood in relation to broader debates about the current state and changing nature of the contemporary social world' (Nettleton, 2007: 2410).

Throughout the book, contemporary ideas on social capital and social exclusion have been utilized, but reference is made also to ideas from an older tradition: the social administration heritage of Titmuss and Townsend, the ethical socialism and commitment to equality of Tawney, the emphasis on the value of community life from the co-operative and 'utopian' socialists Morris and G.D.H. Cole. Their ideas are amongst those discussed in Chapter 2. The most durable influences on the development of my approach come, not surprisingly perhaps given the nature of the enquiry, from classical sociology. I was interested, for example, in Emile Durkheim's focus on the search for the conditions which foster organic solidarity, on the role of mediating institutions in generating it, and on the importance for health and well-being of social integration and a societal balance between individualism and collectivism (Durkheim, 1893, 1952/1897). At the outset, I adopted a broad, loosely classical perspective: material and Durkheimian approaches to explaining social influences on health have tended to be treated as mutually exclusive (Popay, (2000). Endemic to epidemiological models of health inequalities are assumptions that certain conditions determine certain outcomes, and that processes involved are uni-linear. For the purposes of my own enquiry, in which social networks in poor communities are a primary focus, a perspective informed by Durkheim and which does not neglect a Weberian focus on meaningful social action, is not necessarily in conflict with a materialist or neo-Marxist perspective. Sociologists do not always treat the major strands of classical sociology as wholly distinct in any case, prominent examples of synthesis have come from Habermas, who argued for a reformulated Marxism integrated with action theory (Habermas, 1989) while Giddens', structuration theory uses the concept of the duality of structure as part of a unified social theory (Giddens, 1984).

A basic Durkhemian approach to community and health has been overlaid here with an emphasis on the importance of the distribution of resources derived as much from Richard Titmuss and Peter Townsend as Karl Marx, and by a recognition of the tension between structure and action from both Marx and Max Weber and between structure and values from Weber (Gerth and Mills, 1970; Marx, 1852). The recognition that, despite structural constraints, social actors can alter social outcomes evident in the work of Weber is also acknowledged by Marx, who, whilst recognizing that historical and material circumstances act as constraining influences on action, nevertheless argued that man is a producer as well as a product of the social relationships of which he forms a part (Giddens, 1971). As he puts it in the familiar passage from the 18th Brumaire: 'Men make their own history, but they do not make it just as they please; ... but under circumstances directly encountered, given and transmitted from the past' (Marx, 1852: 360). A broadly classical, triadic approach to Durkhemian, Marxian and Weberian constructs together with structuration theory inform exploration of process in the East London studies, and facilitate the moving away from the determinism (if sometimes exaggerated) inherent in Durkheim (Taylor and Ashworth, 1987), for whom society's influence on groups and individuals was the central concern of his social enquiry and not individual agency.

Some 'mid range' theorists must also be mentioned at this point. It was consideration of some of the ideas of Robert Merton, Elizabeth

Bott and William Julius Wilson for example, which prompted me to question the analytical approaches of some epidemiological studies, as well as contributing towards the development of my own approach. Though more usually considered appropriate to a study of deviance than to health, Merton's work on 'relative deprivation' and the American dream (Merton, 1957) seemed nevertheless to have relevance in this context in that the focus is on individual action – the response to poverty, deprivation and inequality – and on the underlying influence of reference groups which affect the extent to which people will see themselves as deprived. Elizabeth Bott (1957) also used the term 'reference group' in her work on social ties, and linked them to the formation of identity and values. Finally, the American sociologist W. J. Wilson, taking a less oppositional view on structural and cultural determinants of poverty to those outlined in Chapter 1, argues that consideration of both is crucial for understanding change (Wilson, 1996).

Research methods

A key feature of this book is a focus on complex social processes. It is generally recognized that different layers of influence interact in complex relationships to affect health (Acheson, 1998), but mechanisms are not well understood. A theoretical model for enhancing understandings and elucidating processes was begun to be developed in Chapter 1 by adopting an approach which pays attention to both macro and micro levels of analysis, to structure and social action in context, and by hypothesizing a critical role for social networks in dynamic relationships involved. The methodological framework adopted for empirical research aiming to explore ideas further would need to have potential for advancing the perspective through enhancing understanding of the interplay of various factors under consideration, but it would also need to be flexible to allow for the generation of new hypotheses. With this in mind, a number of research imperatives were considered.

The research design should be capable, for example of focusing on both the individual and the setting; of addressing complexity and capturing variability, what Willis and Trondman (2000) refer to as the irreducibility of human experience. A holistic approach to looking at people's lives and the places they live in would be needed, capable of embracing a broad range of individual experience. To retain a 'sociological imagination' (Mills, 2000), the research should not neglect aspects of individual's past lives which may have implications for their present well-being, and should be sensitive also to historical features of the setting. At the same time, research stratagems would need to uncover processes by which people maintain a sense of community and have capacity to reveal the meanings they attach to social phenomena and their effects on health. When researching social ties, for example, a problem with network measures used in quantitative research is that they do not provide information on the quality of the relationship involved, or on how the adequacy of support is perceived by those receiving it (Stansfeld, 1999; Brown and Harris, 1978). Nevertheless, the production of descriptive data through empirical research is insufficient in itself for advancing the perspective outlined here. Ideally, the research must be designed so that it can facilitate development of an analytical framework with relevance outside the setting (Willis and Trondman, 2000).

Despite the affinity of the construct with the sociological concept of 'community', major studies on the relationship between 'social capital' and health have tended, like those on health inequalities, to rely on the use of survey data. Given the complexity of the territory, this has perhaps been a limitation in the literature. Whilst illustrative of general trends, the statistics can explain little about how they happen (Popay et al., 1998). Critics of work involving the integration of survey derived data with psycho-social theories for example point out that using such data to develop social explanations on the relationship between income inequality, social capital or social cohesion and health is flawed because it cannot capture complexity, context or meaning (Forbes and Wainwright, 2001). Ethnographic and other in-depth qualitative methods are generally considered the most appropriate method for exploring processes (Hammersley and Atkinson, 2005; Pearlin, 1989). Key attributes of in-depth qualitative research include an emphasis on social and historical context, on interpretative understanding, on seeing social life as processional rather than static, and stem from interactionist theory (Mathews, 1977; Plummer, 1983). Such methods are particularly suited to a perspective which treats people as both the subjects and objects of action. Nevertheless, viewing phenomena from the standpoint of those being studied reflects only one element of the research perspective developed here; it needs to co-exist alongside a recognition that experiences and attitudes are located spatially and temporally in wider structures, and embedded in networks of relationships (Plummer, 1983). Although qualitative research methods are seen as less rigorous in terms of representativeness and reliability than quantitative methods their use is justified in sociology in that procedures reflect the nature of theoretical concerns in the discipline, such as those involving social relationships and social interaction (Bulmer, 1984).

Our knowledge of processes involved in social influences on health can benefit from a focus on real people and real communities (Blaxter and Poland, 2002). Investigating the tension between people and places, and the close correlation between the way we live and our well-being can be examined fruitfully through comparative community case studies. A comparative approach based on localities was expected to provide a better understanding of the role of place; intensive on the ground qualitative research a more effective purchase on mechanisms involved in relationships between poverty, community, social networks and health and well-being.

Secondary analysis of official statistics was used to identify deprived wards and to map the wider spatial and temporal context in which the communities selected for study were located. Official statistics and local authority and health authority data were gleaned to provide a profile of the region and to identify changes occurring within it; the earlier of these was published as 'London's Other River' (Cattell, 1997). Using a range of regional and local documentary evidence and discussions with service providers, practitioners and others with local knowledge, neighbourhoods (all housing estates with high proportions of social housing), were chosen for study on the grounds of similar poverty levels and dissimilar opportunities for local involvement. Documentary evidence, observation and interviews with people whose work took them into the area helped to build up knowledge of the neighbourhood, but in-depth interviews with residents (along with focus groups in the second set of studies) were the main research tool. Community studies of this kind are used to illustrate the meaning of macro level trends for people's lives, can facilitate holistic treatments of social relations and are recognized as an especially effective medium for the development of sociological arguments (Crow, 2000: 173).

Qualitative research in East London

The methodological stratagems adopted at this stage of the research were influenced by the advantages of the method but selection was based on more than technical suitability: listening to the views of poor people is seen also as a political choice (Cohen, 1992). Whilst ideas espoused in the Chicago School research literature stressed the individual's subjective interpretation of a situation as paramount, I was satisfied that the ethnographic methods adopted could sit comfortably with Marxist as well as interactionist perspectives. Cornwell for example, argues that '... ethnographic material will bear witness to the part each person plays in shaping the course of his or her own life without losing sight of the fact that they do so in conditions that are not of their own choosing (Cornwell, 1984: 204). Following Cornwell, I decided not to abstract health and illness for study but attempted to treat them as part of ordinary, everyday life.

Mindful that neither poverty, community nor health are static experiences, and because an individual's past experience of poverty and deprivation can have implications for their current state of health, I considered taking a life history approach to the research. It is recognized as a useful means of exploring process (Becker, 1966); it can provide a way of looking at the impact of structural change on the individual (Thompson, 1978) and shows compatibility with Marxist approaches, and, as Brannen and Nilsen (2006) note, can be used to transcend tension between structure and agency. Incorporating aspects of an individual's life history into the research endeavour has been shown to be particularly fruitful when researching health. Cornwell found that when people told stories about their experiences, illness was understood as a product of a causal chain of action and reaction which takes place over time (Cornwell, 1984). Like Cornwell, however, I did not take a straightforward life history from respondents, but instead adopted interviewing methods in which past experiences could emerge as integral to people's accounts and understandings of their current lives and of their communities.

Fieldwork

The fieldwork strategies outlined here relate principally to the first set of studies (described below); they were replicated with minor adaptations in the later pieces of research. Within an interactionist perspective the primary purpose is to generate data which can give an authentic insight into people's experiences; unstructured open ended interviews are one of the main ways to do this (Silverman, 2010). I opted for a semi-structured interview schedule however as it facilitates greater comparability than the completely unstructured interview, but allows people to answer more on their own terms than the standardized structured interview permits (May, 2010). In selecting people to interview, an inclusive approach to social and demographic groups and to forms of deprivation was adopted: the tendency in analyses of poverty to focus on the plight of people living in particular circumstances such as old age, sickness, large family size, single parenthood, and low pay, amounts, argue Westergaard and Resler, to a fragmentation of research in inequalities, a reluctance to acknowledge the common source of class division (Westergaard and Resler,

1976: 19–20). Selection was via participatory observation, through key contacts, and by snowballing. As well as aiming to reflect the demographic make up of the neighbourhood, efforts were made to include the less active, less confident, as well as the more participatory individual.

Researchers have an obligation to those who participate in the research. In qualitative research this can include a willingness to empathize with those being studied. Michael Young's approach to interviewing for example involved a profound respect for the individual respondent whose beliefs, attitudes and sentiments were being explored (Runciman, 1995). Developing trust and establishing rapport are essential preconditions for the successful interview, but there may still be an element of exploitation, especially where potentially unequal power relationships are involved (Finch, 1984). To overcome this problem, I encouraged interviewees to tell stories where this was appropriate, a stratagem which allows the story teller a greater degree control than they would have when answering direct questions (Cornwell, 1984). Essentially however, my interviews with residents were deliberately informal and conversational. I was influenced by feminist approaches to interviewing which advocate Oakley's less structured research strategies in which interviewer and interviewee interact in a non-hierarchal relationship (Oakley, 1981: 44).

Interviews looked holistically at how residents experience, interpret and respond to various influences on their lives, and at ways in which they take an active part in shaping them. Reflecting a Simmelian approach concerning the sociological significance of ordinary social interactions taking place in mundane settings, discussions explored everyday lives, routines, and changing experiences. They focused especially on perceptions of neighbourhood and community life; making ends meet and other difficulties; social ties and support given and received, and local formal and informal involvement. They also covered perceptions of self and political efficacy; hopes for the future, and attitudes to mixing with others, along with impressions of the wider society and understandings of fairness and inequality issues. British sociologists in particular have tended to use data gleaned from interviews as a means of eliciting people's own versions of their values and world views, especially when focusing on working class or under-privileged groups (Savage and Burrows, 2007: 894). Health was explored from the quality of life, well-being and happiness perspective discussed in Chapter 2, and reflected the social model of health adopted. Nonetheless, to approach core issues from different angles, some more directly focused questions were put which relied on self reported health status and common sense understandings. Questions designed to cast a wide net in relation to stressors and coping strategies as well as individuals' needs, resources and social networks included variants on the 'describe a typical day' format which I'd used with effect when conducting earlier research for the College of Health (one of several community organizations set up by Michael Young in Bethnal Green). After piloting, I discussed the interview schedule with the late Peter Willmott, whose very helpful suggestions on the wording and order of topics and prompts were incorporated. The schedule was nevertheless used as an aide-memoir: to some extent I allowed those I interviewed to direct the course of the interview, whilst at the same time tried to cover the broad topics of interest in general terms.

An understanding of people's social networks is an essential feature of this work. I anticipated that a flexible semi structured interview approach would be able to provide information on features central to the inquiry without resorting to the exact measures and techniques adopted by network analysts, who map linkages to establish density for example. I was fortunate to be able to discuss this issue with the sociologist Janet Foster: we decided that precise questions on network structure were inappropriate within this framework, and that they would interfere with the flow of conversation I was seeking. Abrams, in his seminal work on 'Neighbours', provides an additional justification. He recognized that, by giving equal weight to all links in the network, network analysis neglects the significant content of relationships (Bulmer, 1986). I would expand the point to cover the schedule topics as a whole: adherence to a precise set of questions can distort the data produced by obscuring distinctions between the significance of some topics for certain individuals and their lesser import for others.

Analysis of interview data

I relied on a grounded theory approach to analysis. Although previous stages of the research had formulated ideas to be explored in interviews, I wanted to avoid the pitfall of selecting field data to fit a preconception of the problem (Fielding and Fielding, 1986). Grounded theory places emphasis on induction and openness, analysis is grounded in the people studied and analytical categories are expected to emerge in the course of analysis (Glaser and Strauss, 1967). The method has been criticized however for failure to acknowledge implicit theories which guide the work (Silverman, 2010), and in practice a recursive process is involved. A particular advantage of grounded theory methodology is that it is designed to guide the production of conceptually dense data which it does interactively, through facilitating engagement of concepts in interplay with the data itself. These relationships are embedded in a thick context of descriptive and conceptual writing (Glaser and Strauss, 1967: 31–2). When interpreting the East London material, I aimed to maintain a balance between cross cutting themes, context and illustration of processes throughout the analysis. The research produced rich data: people talk of their day to day lives, about the problems they face and how they cope with them; they relate stories about the past, about times when they enjoyed life and times which were difficult. Residents (their identities are anonymized) discuss their working experience; their social ties involving relationships with family, friends, neighbours and others, as well as experience of reciprocal aid and involvement in formal and informal organizations. The conversational style and open-endedness of the interviews themselves meant that cultural issues, the values individuals hold and their attitudes to the wider society and political system are interwoven with these accounts of their experience, as are perceptions of the factors which they believe influence health and quality of life.

To avoid minimizing the effects of wider social, economic and political structures or ideologies on people's lives and social networks; ignoring variation in human experience, or obscuring the role played by human agency in network formation, I needed to find a mode of analysis for developing understandings of processes involved in social and spatial influences on health and well-being with relevance outside the studies' immediate context. Theme analysis may not always be wholly sufficient for facilitating progression from description to explanation. Investigating the potential role of social networks for capturing interplay between macro and micro levels of analysis for example poses problems for conventional methodologies and necessitates an innovatory approach to the analysis of qualitative data. I wanted to move towards a form which retained individuals in their time and place and yet allowed comparison with other cases. Presenting individual case studies was an attractive option, particularly as the method would facilitate uncovering processional links in the chain between individual experience and well-being, but a major drawback was that important themes could be submerged and the production of any generizable explanation difficult. I opted instead for the ethnographic technique of model building, or the construction of typologies. This is an abstract way of presenting the relations between social phenomena and simplifying and understanding social mechanisms (Hammersley and Atkinson, 2005). By emphasizing certain defining traits they represent an attempt to form Weberian ideal types, abstract constructs which are not necessarily normatively desirable (Gerth and Mills, 1970).

During early stages of analysis, it became clear that there seemed to be an emergent pattern in residents' narratives relating to the categories of people that made up their social networks and other key themes, such as attitudes and values, or social support and coping strategies. There were also nascent patterns connected to the degree of density and homogeneity of residents' networks. As a first stage, I looked simply at certain structural and compositional elements of the network, with a view to developing more sophisticated categories later. Bott's concept of 'membership groups', the groups an individual belongs to, was adopted as a means of categorization (Bott, 1957). Membership groups were a useful analytical tool to use with the East London data because they provided a way of bringing together characteristics, structures and functions of networks for analysis.

Strategies for the development of a network typology were both conceptually informed and grounded in the data. Building on the concept of 'membership group' I derived network models from the data. These were developed in stages, reflecting structural characteristics then cultural elements; analysis progressed to assess their explanatory value in relation to health and well-being and incorporate conceptual links. The models referred initially to the degree of homogeneity or heterogeneity in a network, estimated with reference to the range of membership groups within it. Groups identified from residents' accounts of their social ties include family, ethnic group, neighbours in the street/block, people in the wider community, school friends, people connected with present and past work, clubs, churches and mosques, voluntary organizations and local initiatives. The typology was then further developed in a way that reflected issues associated with agency. For example, it also relates to interviewees' positive or negative reference groups, introduced as a way of understanding issues around identity and values. Categories which emerged from the data like social class; ethnic group; rich/poor; East Enders/outsiders and older/younger people, helped to differentiate people in terms of their attitudes to mixing with and co-operating with similar and dissimilar others. Bott (1957), suggested that individuals will adhere to the norms of a positive reference group, but not to a negative reference group.

Working closely with individuals' accounts of their life experiences, social contacts, and involvement in community life, the typology was further developed in a way which reflected some additional cultural issues. Norms and values espoused by residents appeared to have some basis in their experience of, and attitudes towards community life; social network models were then named with regard to approaches to 'community' evident in the literature. Individual's narrative data was assigned a network type: *Socially Excluded; Parochial; Traditional; Pluralistic, or Solidaristic.*

Most respondents slotted quite easily into models, others did not present a totally accurate fit; where this occurs, I note the variation, grounded theories are very fluid. Within the models, processes involved in health and well-being are explored and embody four dimensions: psycho-social pathways; norms and values; action and coping responses, and perceptions and meanings. Individual case studies are used in Chapter 8 to demonstrate how different social network formations can mediate poverty and health and well-being. Certain health protecting or damaging attributes and attitudes for example are shown to vary with network type, as are ways in which people are resilient, how they are able to cope (or not) with life's difficulties. Some of the key themes addressed by the book are discussed later within this methodological framework.

East London

The community studies took place in East London, a region which contains places which are amongst the poorest and most deprived in England (ODPM, 2004; Cattell, 1997; MacInnes et al., 2010). Following chapters refer to three pieces of qualitative research, involving five cases. The first study (located in 'Dock Lane' and 'Bridge Street') was undertaken as part of my ESRC funded doctoral research into poverty, social networks and health and well-being (Cattell, 1998, 2001, 2004). For the second study, on perceptions of neighbourhood for the Joseph Rowntree Foundation (Cattell and Evans, 1999), Dock Lane was researched a second time and compared to 'Canal View', itself the later focus of a second, Health Development Agency funded study on social capital and health (Cattell and Herring, 2002a, 2002b). Along with observation, resident focus groups and discussions with people whose work took them into the localities, the three projects involved in-depth interviews with residents, 226 in total. Occasional comparisons are made also with a fourth East London study, again funded by the Joseph Rowntree Foundation, which focused specifically on relationships between public spaces, social relations and well-being (Dines et al., 2006; Cattell et al., 2008). Overall, the empirical research spanned an 11 year period.

Located in three adjacent East London boroughs, the neighbourhoods selected are housing estates, named here as Dock Lane, Bridge Street and Canal View. Although there is no clear delineation between the boundaries of the East End and East London, the first two can certainly be described as 'East End' neighbourhoods, while the third – Bridge Street – is located in a district once, but no longer, associated with plentiful job opportunities in manufacturing. Both Dock Lane and the district where the Canal View estate is situated have suffered historically from a stigmatized public reputation linked to poverty and 'anti-social' industries, and, in the case of Dock Lane, criminal activity. In contrast, the wider Bridge Street district escaped the experience of a historically maligned image; the Estate's poor reputation at the time of the research was more localized, and of much more recent origin.

All the neighbourhoods were experiencing high levels of unemployment and economic inactivity when researched, with a relatively high proportion of residents in receipt of benefits and children eligible for free school meals. Reflecting a pattern common to low income areas, older people, young families, and children were over-represented within each locality, each of which had fewer adults of working age than the London average. Semi skilled and unskilled occupations were predominant in all three, and skilled workers were a little more numerous on Canal View than on the other two estates. Although the demographics of Dock Lane were changing, it was nevertheless home to a higher proportion of white residents than one would expect given the diverse make up of the borough. Canal View and Bridge Street were more ethnically mixed, with black Africans, Afro-Caribbean's and Turkish people for example well represented on Canal View, and South Asians, Afro-Caribbeans and Black Africans on Bridge Street. Single parents made up an unusually sizeable proportion of families in all three areas, higher than that of the already high London average. Loan parents are at a higher risk of poverty than any other family type (Gingerbread, 2009).

Acknowledgements

The book is largely a development of my doctoral research (Cattell, 1998, 2001, 2003, 2004), and I would like to thank the Economic and Social Research Council for funding the doctoral work. I have also drawn from my subsequent research: I would like to thank Mel Evans and Nick Dines for their contributions to the empirical research undertaken for the second and fourth studies, both funded by the Joseph Rowntree Foundation, and I gratefully acknowledge the contribution made by Rachel Herring to the Health Development funded project drawn on in Chapter 7. I would also like to thank Susanne MacGregor for her support during the doctoral work, as well as Janet Foster, Hilary Graham and the late Peter Willmott. Thanks are also due to Jack Cattell for valued computer assistance. I also very much appreciate the generosity of East London residents and people whose work took them into the study areas for sharing their thoughts, insights and experiences.

4
Community Resilience

Introduction

In 1904 Joseph Rowntree identified what he believed were Britain's worst social evils: poverty, war, slavery, intemperance, the opium trade, impurity and gambling. Along with poverty, drugs and crime, respondents to a recent survey identified the decline of community, family, and values as amongst today's ten great evils. Community, it seems, had weakened, fallen victim to the growth of individualism and greed (Watts, 2008; Mowlam and Creegan, 2008). Even allowing for the possibility of a perceptions gap operating here, a tendency in surveys for us to express satisfaction with our own families or neighbourhoods while at the same time insisting that family and community life are declining elsewhere (Taylor, 2008), this disheartening and pessimistic general assessment of life today stands in sharp contrast to a familiar appraisal of a British locality made 50 years ago. Michael Young and Peter Willmott described community life in Bethnal Green (now in the East London borough of Tower Hamlets) in the 1950s thus: 'Poor, Bethnal Greeners may have been ... But if they were, their poverty was accompanied by a sense of family, community and class solidarity, by a generosity towards others like themselves, by a wide range of attachments, by pride in themselves, their community and their country and by an overflowing vitality' (Young and Willmott, 2007: xv). Richard Titmuss (1962), writing in the preface to their classic study, was concerned that the flowering of British community life which they recorded would be short lived, that town planning of the 1950s and 1960s would destroy it. By the 1980s certain areas of social housing had become identified with 'degeneration'; anxieties which were followed later by a discourse on community decline which shifted the focus of concern onto housing allocation systems and changes in the principles underpinning welfare policy. Michael Young (1996) himself suggested that, because tenants for new social housing in Britain are now chosen according to their needs rather than for their family or community connections as they once were, that the principle of equality has triumphed over fraternity in welfare provision.

It is not clear nevertheless that individual needs and community needs are necessarily and inevitably oppositional; it may be more appropriate to consider them at least in some ways as interdependent, and ask how East London residents themselves assess the underlying influences on community life. Other than housing allocation policies, these might be expected to cover a wide array of issues. Economic change in Britain's former industrial and manufacturing areas left many communities especially vulnerable. David Widgery, a Bethnal Green GP, described the effects of change as little short of catastrophic: 'what is being lost is precious, that sense of neighbourhood, community and mutual solidarity which has given London its special character' (Widgery, 1991: 38). Referring to the loss of the collective strength and solidarity intrinsic to union life he adds: 'I'm watching something die and I wish I wasn't' (Widgery, 1991: 38). This chapter looks at the everyday lives of people living in a former occupational community – the Dock Lane estate – to explore ways and processes by which the sense and practice of community is sustained or diminished. At the same time, a purpose is to draw attention to the implications of community as a social reality for our understandings of health and well-being. The interpretation of community used is largely influenced by those definitions which privilege its social and cultural dimensions: social networks providing mutual aid, sociability, identity, and social capital, for example, and by Willmott's (1989) notion of 'attachment community', where social interaction and solidaristic relationships revolve around a common locality and 'community spirit' is a key dimension of people's subjective understandings.

Dock Lane

Closely knit networks emphasizing mutual aid were the hallmarks of the traditional working class community (Lockwood, 1966; Bott, 1957). Occupational communities like those which had grown around mining and dock work are the clearest examples (Bulmer, 1975). Until the mid-1970s, when containerization precipitated decline, the Dock Lane estate had been a typical occupational community. Described as a 'whole way of life' by people living and working there, the docks and the dockside factories were the economic and social backbone of the area. In common with former industrial regions across Britain, the once plentiful demand for manual labour has ceased. A woman who was born and bred in the area described some of the changes: 'When the docks were going, there were ship repairers, chandlers, riggers, and factories which processed the raw goods the ships brought in. The shops were busy too. Closure was so rapid. Everyone knew the jobs were going, what must it have been like for those who'd always worked? By 1977, there wasn't a docker left. Now, I know people who've never worked'. The closure of the docks was reportedly a blow from which the area has never fully recovered. Economic decline is believed to have had an impact on local life on par with World War 2 bombing and the post war slum clearance housing programmes. According to a man whose family had lived near to and worked in the docks for generations, all three have historically had some effect on population movement for example. The new Dock Lane estate was built to replace the ravages of the Blitz and expanded in later decades. Residents whose families had moved in at this time suggested that the new estate encapsulated the spirit of early post war Britain; the hope, shared beginnings and optimism for a better future.

Dock Lane (not its real name) is a generic term covering several small scale council developments. Bounded by major roads, railways and docklands, the area is, in common with the Canal View estate featured in later chapters, relatively physically isolated. There is a mix of housing styles and ages: solid post war and later terraces, low rise maisonettes and flats, and the later built and less popular towers. Some of the latter replaced the notorious Ronan Point and similar blocks where in the 1960s unsafe prefabricated building methods resulted in the skyscraper collapsing dramatically like a pack of cards. The borough in which Dock Lane is situated remains largely a working class district; unlike pockets of some adjacent East London boroughs, it has not gone though a process of gentrification. Most of the accommodation on the estate itself remains as social housing. The majority population is white, but long-established residents include black East End families who settled here after the First World War. The estate is located in a highly deprived area; when researched, it had experienced considerable difficulties in recruiting GPs and in encouraging them to stay.

Pea soup, rice and cups of tea

A difficulty with discourse on 'community' is that it can be used to refer to what only appeared to exist in the past, whether with regard to social theory (Turner, 1988), or the images of community constructed by residents themselves. On one level collective representations can appear as something of a caricature, steeped in a cosy nostalgia (Cohen, 1982, 1985; Pahl, 1996), yet we need to acknowledge the influences of the past on contemporary communities and what they mean to people: as Bourdieu (1986) argued, the social world is accumulated history. Dock Laners' own perceptions of community life frequently make reference to the neighbourhood of the past, but these are narratives not necessarily blinkered by memories of an imagined golden age. People repeatedly alluded to coping with poverty for example, and to the role played by others in the process. A local businessman who spent his childhood in the area recalled that: 'In the 1930s people were brought up to cope, and people looked after each other then. People like 'Pea Soup Jack' who always had a bowl of soup and a piece of bread for anyone who was hungry. There are old people still alive now who owe their lives to him'.

Most frequently people reminisced about co-operative practices to share scarce resources, or about expectations that support could be relied on when needed. A resident recalling her childhood before the Second World War for example talked about her father's employment. Like that of the dockworkers, it was insecure: '[this area] was beautiful when I was a child. Dad was a labourer on the roads. When he was out of work neighbours would come in and feed the children'. Another woman told a similar story: 'Dad was a tally clerk in the docks, and Grandad worked the grain boats. We were very poor, it was struggle to pay the rent, but [she added with satisfaction] Mum always found hers. We had three rooms downstairs and another family lived upstairs. When the woman upstairs died my mum looked after the children, she just automatically took over, and did his washing too. They all helped each other then'. Goods as well as services were freely exchanged, the form of which was to some extent influenced by the nature of local work. She continued: 'We always had plenty of rice, because of Dad and Grandad's work, so we always gave neighbours rice, and another man gave us vegetables'. In close knit communities like these, an additional source of reciprocity was derived from the solidarity associated with union membership. A man recalling his childhood in the 1950s in an area close to Dock Lane remembered vividly the food parcels which were brought round when his father was on strike, and which helped to keep the family healthy. In these East London cases, an essential source of reciprocity was integration into an occupational community and its shared values, but the norms were also honed by necessity. Memories of deprivation were not altogether swamped by affection for the old ways. Poor housing and living conditions before the estate was built were frequently mentioned, or starting off married life in one or two rooms at mother-in-laws and the lack of privacy such excessively dense networks entailed. The grinding poverty of the times was a recurrent and prominent feature of their stories. If people managed to keep their heads above water despite the odds being against them, it was a circumstance which their families remember with pride. A resident recounted for example that although her mother could not read; she could count, and made sure that 'the coal man didn't rob her'.

Anecdotes about mutual aid when times were difficult were interlinked in residents' understandings of community with memories of more intensive social interaction and tightly knit networks. A sense of enjoyment derived from everyday social interaction and shared activities in local streets also featured in some of these memories. Recalling the terrace where she had lived as a younger woman a resident explained: 'You just had to stand outside your front door and soon you'd be talking to someone'. In this way she easily became, as Richard Hoggart (1957) had described it when writing of the importance of the street to working class life in Britain back in the 1950s, part of the neighbourhood, but it was also something she remembered with a great deal of pleasure. Providing a contrast to the lives of today's children, of whom only a minority play in the street near their homes (Play England, 2010), examples also touch on ways in which children were socialized into a co-operative and enjoyable street life. As another resident recounted: 'We all mixed in then, women used to turn ropes for the children's skipping games in the street. I miss them days'. Memories like these can create for the individual a sense of belonging and nurture a sense of 'ontological security'; for Giddens (1990) a psychological need which is founded on the establishment of trust relationships, particularly in childhood.

Despite some inevitable romanticism in older persons' recollections of the co-operative cultures of their younger days, their perceptions were, nevertheless, grounded in specific temporal contexts. Accounts illustrated how the norms were embedded in social, economic and demographic structures, and nurtured by physical features of the local environment. Population stability, intergenerational continuity and family proximity for example – themselves underwritten by local work opportunities as well as the practice of 'speaking for' adult children to landlords – together supported integration of the individual into co-operative life on Dock Lane. The three generation household for example was common. A resident described succinctly how it operated, and in doing so effortlessly linked demographic and household structures to the shared neighbourhood practice of 'keeping an eye' on the children: 'The daughters always took the old girls in. You'd find them all sitting in the front windows, watching us play, and shouting for a cup of tea'. The reciprocal aid and altruism of these stories have their present day equivalents on the estate, but some residents (as they did in all three neighbourhoods) felt keenly that those aspects of local community life which were meaningful to them, such as localized co-operation and trust, had declined. Yet a generational deficit in the generation of social capital can easily be overdrawn. There were many contemporaneous examples of supportive and reciprocal relationships among young mothers for example on this estate, as well as those involving older people. More generally, there were still elements of the old East End community spirit, even if, as some older residents suggest, it was not quite as strong or as obvious as it used to be. Despite the closure of the docks, the traditional norm of reciprocity and the expectations and obligations of mutual aid which it engendered to some extent survived changed conditions. What Jacobs (1961) had referred to, in her classic book on city life, as the eyes on the street, may have been fewer, but neighbours still 'look out' for other people's children.

Factors contributing to people's sometimes contradictory understandings of community life involving both its decline and resilience, can be explored by considering 'community' both as structurally influenced and as socially constructed by conscious human actors. While there are circumstances under which, as I show later, a strong sense of community and local attachment is not always the sole prerogative of long term residents, a degree of population continuity is required nevertheless to maintain the stability of the social structure needed for the viability of community life, and which for Coleman (1990), for example, is a necessary pre-condition for the maintenance of social capital. Successive generations of families living on Dock Lane remain a salient and enduring feature of the district, and one which many residents are eager to perpetuate. Continuity in this form, while central to their understandings of community is also something which has implications for well-being. Giddens further delineates ontological security as the confidence that human beings have in the constancy of their social, as well as material, environments (Dupois and Thorns, 1998). Decline of the local labour market and changes in social housing allocation policies which gave priority to the homeless, have made it much more difficult for those adult children who wish to remain on their parents' estate to do so. 'They have to do something dodgy to stay' one man explained. Nevertheless, a degree of intergenerational continuity survives, even if in some cases, it takes a different form. There are many young families – particularly loan parents

– on Dock Lane who do have parents living nearby, and who rely on them, particularly their mothers, for day-to-day support and help with childcare. Some were able to circumvent housing allocation rules by accepting accommodation in a local hostel in the hope of eventual re-housing on the estate.

While population stability supported reciprocal aid between neighbours on many parts of the estate: 'There's a good dozen on this square who are great friends and who you can call on for help', for example, not surprisingly, a sense of community and everyday social capital involving co-operation and trust were less evident where tenancies were short term, or where, as tenants alleged, the council were moving 'outsiders' into the area. Dench et al. (2006) argue that an unintended consequence of privileging the most needy when allocating social housing in Britain has been the marginalization of the white working class and racial conflict. Here in Dock Lane, racist attitudes were certainly evident yet there were nevertheless many residents (across ethnic groups) who, rather than discuss demographic changes in terms of the ethnic characteristics of newcomers, instead focused on the break in continuity of the local population and its consequences for community life. They referred to the dislocation of social activities like street parties for instance, or about individual's needs for family support. The general feeling was not only that an allocation system which did not put locals first made little sense and was palpably unfair, but that it damaged the estate's culture of reciprocity, something of which they were immensely proud. As one long term resident expressed it: 'The council say it is not an equal opportunities policy to [house people] who know each other in the area. Yet it's rubbish. If your mother needs you, it's not racism, it's just not fair. And this is a black person telling you'. Others recognized that the allocation system did little to help create a welcoming climate for immigrants: 'The Council and the Social make you prejudiced', or 'It provides fuel to the BNP'. Whilst certain housing allocation policies have hampered residential stability, others in the past have had the reverse effect, and assisted the perpetuation of social capital in the 'thick trust' form involving tight knit, mutually supportive social networks of neighbours or kin, if also a degree of insularity. The Housing Department had at one time operated a popular policy of re-locating old neighbours together: 'I've lived in this house for 20 years, before that I was in a tower block. It wasn't too bad in the tower block because it was filled with local people who had all moved out of the old houses together. The block was friendly; we all knew each other already. Then we all moved to these houses here, our children have grown up together, we've all helped each other over the years, and we're still here'.

Despite locating their experience in specific structural contexts like those described in preceding paragraphs, when asked directly, residents nevertheless frequently attributed a perceived decline in co-operation, trust and local involvement to issues of agency, to normative change for example in the direction of increasing materialism or selfishness. For others, although generally unsure of the mechanisms involved in a breakdown of trust, its decline was reported alongside an increase in crime, drugs, anti-social behaviour and a perceived decline in parenting skills, characteristics which they associated with the lifestyles of younger people in particular. Yet altered behaviours, including the growth in supposedly dysfunctional parenting, can be readily linked at least in part to local structural issues, to features connected, for example, to a declining street life. Co-operation involving childcare, while a regular feature of everyday life on many parts of Dock Lane in places where the housing design and street layout supported neighbourly interaction, was in other places more difficult to establish. A middle aged resident critically reported: 'When my children were young we used to be all out there [on the green behind the flats], keeping an eye on the children. Now they just sling them out'. Contributory factors appeared to be related to the sub locale however: a high population turnover in the block along with few opportunities to mingle with fellow residents (there was no outdoor seating at this time for example) created difficulties for casual exchanges or the establishment of co-operative norms. It was felt by some people living in isolating blocks that newcomers simply needed neighbourly contact, help and advice 'to learn our ways'. This was a reference to the culture of reciprocity around childcare, and also to maintaining a pleasant environment – like taking turns to clean the common areas – which a young parent identified as a feature of other, more stable parts of the estate and which had the added advantage of more appropriate housing for the needs of families. Children too were expected by residents to benefit from more community involvement and contact with adults. The trusting relations established in childhood between children and adults alluded to by older Dock Lane residents when children would 'run messages' for older people to the shops (or the bookie) and adults would supervise street games, were striking examples of the kind of socialization which used to be more common.

'A whole way of life'

Along with stories of mutual aid and intense social interaction, an equally prevalent aspect of residents' understandings of community life took the form of comparisons made between the resources and facilities which once characterized the area, and their subsequent decline or loss. Some referred to the withering of social, commercial, and community facilities like youth clubs, community centres, and shops, others recalled the local leisure venues, the cinemas and dance halls that had once dotted the local landscape. Whilst the de-localization of certain facilities has been a national trend, their loss is felt most keenly by people whose personal and financial circumstances mean that they spend a greater part of their time in their local neighbourhood and are dependent on what it can provide. One of the most salient features of these narratives on Dock Lane however was work, local work, its availability in the past, and the lack of it now. Not all accounts of working experience were positive. Some were critical of the low horizons fostered in their generation for example, others talked about the monotonous nature of the tasks, of the direct dangers to health of factory work, or the insecurity faced by dockers or skilled tradesmen employed in the ship repair industry at a time when men were laid off when work was slack, and taken on again when the supply improved. Conditions like these would have done little for people's well-being as 'ontological security'.

These important caveats aside, localized work was clearly the bedrock of the community and a pivotal factor in facilitating the development of a neighbourhood culture of social capital. As well as a key source of social contact, it helped encourage residential stability and intergenerational continuity. To gain dock work, sons were introduced to employers by fathers, and the many dockside factories provided a plentiful source of local work for others. Classic occupational community studies of heavy industrial areas were largely based on male experience, but here, carrying on the family tradition was not restricted to men: 'Once you became 14 you either went into Silvers, Keillers or Tate and Lyles [rubber goods and marmalade manufacturers, sugar and syrup refiners]. All of my Aunts worked in Keillers so I went there', explained an elderly woman. Getting a job was an important rite of passage, as well as a much needed boost to the family income. For some, gaining employment furthered their self esteem, and enhanced feelings of pride or identity. The young person was able to play their part in reciprocal arrangements within the family itself: 'Before the war, when I started work at 14, I gave Mum my wages, and she gave me pocket money back. I didn't mind, it meant so much you see. You were proud because you were bringing something into the family'. It was the role played by local work in community life however which was an especially unmistakable feature of these stories. Even the collective use of residential streets on the journey to work cemented local relationships and helped to forge the dense and overlapping ties so typical of an occupational community. A former dock worker described one of the ways it operated: 'In the old turnings on top of the docks, when the hooter went, everyone got up out of bed, put their boots, coats and hats on, and walked out of the door, and they all met up with one another, and went to work with one another. Then they all came home together ... a whole society was built around living in the dock area'.

Durkheim contended that the occupational sphere performed a 'solidarity' function (Khattab and Fenton, 2009), while a long sociological tradition originating in humanistic Marxism has linked feelings of unhappiness to lack of involvement with people at work (Marx, 1844). Here in Dock Lane, being young, and being employed were happy times for many, not least for the companionship and everyday solidarity they derived from the workplace. It was the social dimension of work which emerged in retrospective accounts as the dominant aspect of their working lives, particularly (but not exclusively) amongst some of the middle aged and older residents. It was suggested that the enjoyment derived from good social relations in the workplace was instrumental in protecting well-being through strengthening people's resistance to the negative effects of some of the harsher aspects of their day-to-day experience. For example: 'I worked in a factory when I was 15', said a resident, 'I loved it, being part of things, and we all stuck up for each other. There was music going and singing all day'. She added 'For all their problems they enjoyed being there'. Work also gave people experience of organizing collectively, not solely through union activity (and this had been a strongly unionized area with a long history of struggle for better conditions), but also via involvement in work based social clubs. For instance: 'I was 30 years in Knights soap factory, and my husband worked in the docks. When I retired, they still had social evenings and outings for ex workers ... the ex workers organize them.' Accounts like these provide an illustration of ways in which work, community and leisure experience were not only intertwined, but remained so for some people after retirement.

The accounts people gave of their working lives illustrated what were for them, some of the properties of work which helped promote their well-being; at the same time the supportive friendships they made continued throughout life. Yet a culture of reciprocity may well have been less robust without a degree of continuity of the social ties involved. The next section looks at some additional dimensions of community and social capital showing resilience on Dock Lane across age groups, and considers the contribution made by a number of underlying structural and cultural factors.

Local attachment and a sense of community

Definitions of 'community', embracing social, geographic, and cultural elements, are many, various, and frequently contested, but are generally centred around the notion that people have something in common, either place of residence or shared interest or culture. Reflecting, in part, social constructionist interpretations of community as essentially subjective (Cohen 1985), Peter Willmott (1989) used the term 'attachment community', a concept richer than the more frequently used 'place attachment', to give prominence to the extent and density of people's social relationships but also to a sense of identity with a place or group and solidarity with their fellows (Willmott, 1989). Different strands of 'attachment community' can each have implications for well-being. The part played by the density of social ties in coping with life's difficulties are themes explored in more depth in Chapter 8; here, more amorphous features of Willmott's concept can be addressed.

Variation in the spatial scale of the locality which people are attached to, or detached from, is an issue frequently used to question the validity of notions of communities of place. Reflecting Willmott's recognition however that most people have more than one idea of the size of their local community, Dock Lane residents used several different territorial markers to establish their own interpretation of community, and at the same time distanced themselves from any negative reputation attached to the wider area. While community is by no means disembedded from place, it was the distinctly social elements which for many people nevertheless were much more central to their assessment of the neighbourhood and its community life. Their understandings attest to the continuing relevance of the work of the classical sociologist Georg Simmel, who emphasized that such boundaries are sociological not spatial facts (Lechner, 1991). The elements which make up Willmott's attachment community can be understood as a set of evolving and interactive relationships. For example, positive perceptions of and engagement with local people on Dock Lane attach individuals to the neighbourhood, at the same time, a strong sense of local attachment fosters the development of localized social networks. I was struck by the extent to which commitment to local people shone through many of the representations on what community means to residents. 'The people', sometimes referred to as 'the community' were singled out as reasons why many of those interviewed wanted to stay on the estate. Affective ties, emotional attachment to people and place can be consolidated over time, and are understandably stronger amongst those with long term roots. Nevertheless, strong community sentiments showed potential for continuity, appearing capable of transmission in some circumstances to those who arrived on the estate without local connections. A young woman who had lived there for only four years said for example that she would hate to move out because: 'I'd miss the people round here so much'. People tended to explain the strength of their fellow feeling for others in terms of what are perceived as traditional East End virtues: locals' conviviality, their sense of humour and capacity for not letting life get them down, as well as their generosity and willingness to help each other when needed. A resident who had moved onto the estate a few months before I met her described her impressions of those she'd met: 'They take things in their stride, they don't let things get on top of them. They have a great sense of humour, but they swear like dockers – and that's just the women'. A resident born and bred on the estate expressed especially strong positive feelings: 'The people here are brilliant. You can have a laugh and a joke with them, and [referring to the help and sympathy available when needed] they are good to you'. Comments also emphasize the extent to which the value of fraternity, of togetherness in good times and in bad, is held in high esteem by working class people here. The same resident intimated that these cultural characteristics were instrumental in the resilience of local people themselves, despite the odds being against them. She added: 'Think how even better they'd be if they'd been given half a chance'.

The strong community sentiments found here are both an indication of, and a partial explanation for, the neighbourhood's collective resilience to an externally imposed and stigmatizing image (see also Evans and Cattell, 2000). Local people resent hearing their estate rubbished by outsiders and despite the criminal element (crime dynasties are reportedly settled in the area) the majority of residents are recognized as decent, respectable, and, when work is there, hard working people. Given that the negative public image of the estate tends not to be internalized by residents, we would not expect the deleterious health impacts associated with places perceived as unsafe. The challenge to stigma is boosted by the strength of local – and to some extent class – identity, and also by a robust sense of what has been referred to elsewhere as 'collective efficacy' (Innes and Jones, 2006), which here refers a belief that people can sort out local problems themselves. A middle aged resident who was active in local civic life described an experience which illustrates how the local approach to 'looking after your own' can operate: 'My life was threatened three months ago by some drunks. One of them came to my house and threatened to blow it up. I didn't contact the police; the locals went after him and dealt with him. A few weeks later I saw him and he apologized. He'd been warned off'.

On one level the local culture involving a closing of ranks indicates a conditional identity, a partial solidarity limited to insiders, but the sources of identity and commitment on Dock Lane are complex. This is the old East End: here attachment to the area, its work and its traditions is inseparable from class identity and a fierce and shared pride in its collective history. Stories were recounted for example about the East London dockers resistance of Mosley's Black shirts during the 1930s, others made reference to the area's industrial history, or the sense of self respect derived from manual work. As a resident in her thirties told me for example: 'People round here are proud to be working class, they tell you that Dad was a docker, and Grandfather was a docker. They don't want to be anything else'. A strong sense of history, born of pride but also of shared experience and suffering, has in no small part contributed to the strong sense of community still evident. Work based struggles through union activity played a part of course, so too did the perilous effects of the Second World War on the immediate locality. Most of the area was flattened during the blitz, only a church and a few pubs remained. Hundreds of children and their parents waiting for transport to evacuate them to safer areas were killed when a school took a direct hit. The casualty rate in this area was very high indeed. A resident reported for example that she lost a whole family of her relatives when the school was bombed. These memories exert a powerful influence on those who remained in the area, the bombed school, now a flourishing primary, is still referred to by some residents as 'the tomb school', and the iconic church became a powerful symbol of survival.

Stories like these are a striking and yet ubiquitous feature of residents' narratives, and are important for comprehending the relative resilience of community spirit in a neighbourhood experiencing considerable social and economic change since the 1970s. What is especially significant however is that such sentiments were not, as we might expect, solely confined to older respondents, some younger individuals (albeit perhaps an a-typical minority), who included newcomers and people from minority ethnic groups, were in the process of developing their own commitment to the area and were enthusiastically maintaining and perpetuating the oral history tradition. Residents like this were people who had quite rapidly become included in neighbourhood life since their arrival; they had got to know longer term residents through having opportunities to meet them in neighbour-friendly streets and communal areas close to flats or in some cases through involvement in local associations; they were also people who possessed a strong personal commitment to belong. Post modern social theorists tend to stress the weakening of the significance of place in people's lives and to their choice of social ties, but here, some residents were consciously choosing to immerse themselves in a local culture that attracted them.

Where the labour market no longer provides a foundation for local social relations, the perpetuation of a culture involving shared identity, positive perceptions of community or a shared sense of history, requires, in no small part, appropriate and ample opportunities for social exchange and engagement; the same features needed for a culture of reciprocity to flourish. Variation in patterns of neighbourliness across the estate can readily be explained by higher population turnover in the less desirable housing creating difficulties for maintaining social relationships, but also because traditional housing design generally does not create barriers to everyday casual social interaction in the way that some modern blocks can. A good proportion of the original estate had managed to escape replacement by high-rise forms of development. Several of those Dock Lane residents interviewed living in small closes or low rise blocks set round squares, some with a patch of green, and where there is space to sit and be sociable, describe these casual meeting places as one of the most gratifying things about living in the neighbourhood. For example: 'In the summer the children play out on the green together, and we adults sit outside together. It reminds me of a caravan holiday'. Favourable housing design was helping to sustain the norm of co-operative childcare, while watchful eyes in neighbourhood spaces meant that parents felt secure that their children could play outside without coming to harm. In contrast, mothers in Dock Lane tower blocks, as elsewhere, led more unhappy and isolated lives. At one time, living in them could be a much less alienating experience nevertheless: community centres attached to certain blocks of flats had helped compensate for their social limitations. Residents, of all ages suggested that resources like these, where locals could relax and share a joke, have played a major role in maintaining community spirit. For some East Enders, the closure of the community centres was as significant a blow to the life of the community as the closure of the Docks was to others. Their loss was particularly keenly felt as they were the last of the localized leisure facilities to go.

Meeting places, of various kinds, whether high profile settings as in the example above, or the more mundane and ordinary – are critical to the life of a community and have salience for the health and wellbeing of its residents, topics which are taken up in later chapters. Dwindling resources like social clubs, pubs and small local shops meant that there were fewer meeting places on Dock Lane at this time than there once were. Remaining facilities however continued to have everyday significance; even a local undertakers' premises, it was claimed, met some of the social functions once provided by the corner shop. But it was the more socially vibrant arenas, in this case a market within walking distance of the estate, which occurred most regularly in conversations with residents. The stalls and surrounding shops provided endless opportunities for casual conversation and the exchange of information; a regular user described how she gained immediate restorative benefits from a trip to the market when she was feeling low: 'I never feel isolated. If I feel fed up I'll just take myself off down to the market where I see lots of people. You stop worrying about your own problems, because everyone has a tale to tell. You hear some good gossip, you keep in touch with what's going on. It's not all believable, but you sort out fact from fiction'.

There is no guarantee that all casual meetings will be pleasurable experiences, Conradson (2005) argues for example that settings are not intrinsically therapeutic, but are experienced in different ways by different people, while incivility in public spaces can have a detrimental effect on mood (Airey, 2003). Most people, none-the-less, valued and gained benefit from this kind of social engagement. It was generally reported by East Londoners that even simple gestures such as nods and smiles were experienced as reassuring and cheering. On the Canal View estate (explored later) people experiencing the consequent loneliness of recent unemployment mentioned the casual encounters that brightened up their lives: the little 'hellos' and chats at the bus stop, the doctors and in the local shop.

Cultures of exclusion and exclusionary structures

The mutual aid and neighbourliness of the Dock Lane estate, a traditional working class area, is tempered by insularity and a certain amount of exclusion. A strong sense of belonging and the associated social closure of social ties could create difficulties for new residents without roots in the area. The tendency to associate with your own kind, with 'people like us', can result in some being excluded from those components of community deemed protective to health and well-being. Perceptions of division between insiders and outsiders were beginning to blur however and interpretations of community as a closed entity starting to weaken in some cases. For a minority of settled informants, especially, but not exclusively, people in minority ethnic groups, understandings of 'community' embraced efforts to get to know newcomers. Some were convinced that their own potentially integrative actions were necessary to strengthen the resilience of the East End community life they very much valued.

Perceptions of a strong sense of community, in these cases, motivated people to adopt inclusionary behaviour. Nevertheless, the more dominant local culture was one which involved a more exclusionary outlook: there were many people in Dock Lane at this time who tended not to welcome newcomers, trust outsiders or embrace other cultures. Racist attitudes were noticeable, the worst aspects reportedly brought in from outside, by the BNP. Prejudice has a longer history however: just as there is some evident continuity between positive aspects of community life in the past, and a reciprocal culture in the present, so too can we trace the long term nature of a darker side to community life. Some elderly residents for example, recounting the stereotypical attitudes to difference which were commonplace when they were children, acknowledged aspects of local history in which there is less evident local pride. Yet simply not being local appears to hold as much, or more significance in terms of distrust and suspicion than ethnic background in this community. A black British woman working nearby had experienced racist behaviour from fellow market traders but nevertheless believed racism to be much less of a problem for black East Londoners like her own relatives who were brought up locally. It can certainly take some time for a new resident to be and feel, accepted. A young (white) woman who had moved to Dock Lane a few years previously from the North of England felt strongly that the local culture of 'you look after your own' had been instrumental in her exclusion from patterns of support between neighbours: 'They don't care about anyone else round here, only their families and immediate friends. You are either in or out here. They stick up for each other, for their own, right or wrong'.

Community is limited in accounts like these, a conditional cohesion which can take time to overcome, or for some resourceful individuals, has to be worked at. Milly for example moved to the estate as a child with her family 21 years ago: 'When we first came here there was only one other black family in the street. We had a brick thrown in our window, but we stood up for ourselves, defended ourselves, and so we were quickly accepted. If you stand cowering behind the door, you become a victim'. A white incomer from another part of East London told a similar story: 'When I moved here, it was two months before anyone spoke to me. Older kids said to my kids "you don't belong here." But I made myself heard, I mouthed off a bit, and said I'm staying. I came here as an outsider, and was made to feel it. Now I'm accepted'. A desire to be integrated into the community on the part of some recent arrivals however can be held back by negative images of the local neighbourhood. Its stigmatized reputation in public (though not local) perceptions, for crime, racism, and being 'rough' (which includes the use of bad language) for example, places constraints on human agency, can dampen motivation to belong and may slow the pace of integration. Some newcomers recounted however that even perceptions of insularity can change on greater acquaintance. As one said: 'Once you start talking and they know you're no different from them, you get a different side to it all'. Diminishing opportunities to meet and talk to others are clearly especially significant for the inclusion of newer residents into the community.

Social capital's vulnerability

Despite those aspects of a traditional working class community involving close knit networks of strong 'bonding' ties and a culture of mutuality continuing to thrive locally, another key form of social capital had been less resilient. Participation in local associational life was limited. The local culture of 'looking after your own' and distrust of outsiders appeared to combine with a robust tradition of avoiding co-operation with the authorities to make involvement less likely than it might in other parts of London. Dock Lane in this sense is not untypical of the kind of relatively isolated industrial community which Lockwood had associated with a 'proletarian' form of social consciousness, where a mechanical solidarity towards 'us' co-exists with hostility towards 'them', the wielders of power (Lockwood, 1966). Factors contributing to the persistence of these attitudes many years after the demise of the docks were related to a number of factors, lingering bitterness over loss of local jobs along with perceptions of exclusion from the benefits of nearby regeneration at the time of the research, for example. At the same time, frequent changes in council personnel meant that in practical terms trust was difficult to establish. Nevertheless, decline in civic engagement in Britain as a whole can be largely explained by reduction in those opportunities generally acknowledged as the preserve of the working class, trade-unions especially (Hall, 1999), and the Dock Lane area was no exception. Reflecting localized industrial decline as well as national trends, traditional forms of political participation through political parties or trade unions were certainly a less prominent feature of life on Dock Lane than they once were, while few alternative forms of engagement had emerged to fill the vacuum. At the same time, the effects of neo-liberal welfare policies adopted in Britain during the 1980s and 1990s had eroded people's confidence about what could be achieved. As a chair of a tenants' association on the estate, anxious not to pinpoint blame on locals themselves for their relative inaction expressed it: 'People here feel helpless. You can't take away from people and then expect them to help themselves. If you are poor there is only so much you can do'. Her words could be considered as especially prescient in the present political and policy climate: British people are being urged to participate in local services and voluntary organizations to create the 'big society', whilst at the same time, grants to local community groups are being axed and people in poor areas face a severe curtailment of their local services.

Putnam has suggested that social trust and civic engagement are highly correlated (Putnam, 1995). On Dock Lane, however, resistance to becoming involved comes not from lack of trust of fellow residents. The expectation that 'you look after your own' is both evidence of social capital – of the 'thick trust' kind – and a block to wider social trust. Yet whereas on one level the particular form and culture of community could be seen as inhibiting formal participation, local norms can also in certain contexts encourage it. People will join local groups or initiate campaigns where the issues at stake have particular meaning or historical significance for them. On Dock Lane grassroot activities could be seen to blossom where they resonated with the strong sense of emotional attachment to people and place which characterizes the neighbourhood as a whole. When people got together, with support from community development officers, to defend a valued landmark, the 'Cathedral of the East End', against the threat of demolition it was pride in their collective history (the church was one of the few local buildings which survived the Blitz) as well as personal associations which motivated action. They mobilized to defend community as they knew it. Just as a strong local identity and shared sense of history were instrumental in the resilience of community spirit, they motivated participation in a campaign to retain physical evidence of it.

Conclusion

A range of economic, social, demographic and physical as well as cultural characteristics and historical features contributed to perceptions of the Dock Lane estate as a largely traditional working class neighbourhood, where longer term residents especially (but not exclusively) display strong community loyalties, a strong sense of place, and a shared sense of history. The norm of reciprocity and the strong, dense and supportive 'bonding', but at times exclusive ties involved typified this still resilient community. Community in East London is as much about conviviality as it is about attachment, as much about sociability through casual exchange as about social support or civic engagement. The Dock Lane setting takes on many aspects of an 'attachment community', components of which nurture health and well-being through meeting needs for a sense of local identity and belonging, for feelings of safety, and for access to mutually supportive relationships. Solidarity with fellows (if here conditional) also affects individual contentment, while shared memories of community life have a role to play in the maintenance of a sense of 'ontological security'.

In common with those studies on post mining and steel working communities which have shown that, contrary to expectations, well established social networks can continue to provide support long after the work from which they sprang disappeared (Mackenzie et al., 2006) the substance and sense of community on Dock Lane, though less strong than it was, had been sustained into the end of the 20th century and beginning of the 21st. But just how sustainable is the social organization of the area? Strong positive perceptions of community held by residents suggest that the estate had been remarkably resilient in the face of neglect, but that it would be unlikely to remain so without considerably more resources. Middle aged and older people had experienced plentiful local jobs, clubs to get involved in, local leisure facilities and more meeting places of various kinds when they were young. A strong local culture will weaken unless the norms continue to be capable of transmission to newer residents and younger people now that local industry is no longer providing the base for settled social relations and interweaving ties.

5
Community Demoralization and Resistance

Introduction

For British working class families sharing in the optimism and egalitarian climate of the post war years, a council home, as it had been for residents on the then newly built Dock Lane, was something to hope for and aspire to. Council housing had been celebrated by the reforming Attlee administration as means by which social inequalities could be ameliorated and the 'New Jerusalem' (Hennessy, 1992) brought into being. By the latter decades of the 20th century however, council estates had come to symbolize much of what was wrong with British society. Social research identified a 'concentrated poverty' effect in which certain areas, usually the most unpopular housing estates, were becoming increasingly the domain of the very poor. Echoing W. J. Wilson's work on processes in American cities in which he identified increasing social isolation of the very poor from mainstream norms (Wilson, 1987), estates were seen as home to a growing 'underclass', and associated with a fear of social breakdown (see for example, Power and Tunstall, 1995).

The proportion of people living on housing estates who are unemployed has increased in recent decades (Hills, 2007); Britain's uneven experience of economic restructuring during the 1980s and 1990s will have helped to make this more likely. At the same time, 'Right to Buy' policies, along with poor maintenance of housing stock in some places led to the residualization of social housing as accommodation for those with little choice (Taylor, 2003). But 'concentrated poverty' theories on the whole give little weight to structural explanations like these. Whilst Wilson located increasing polarization between impoverished and better off areas in America in population movement and the uneven spatial growth of unemployment, the more dominant 'underclass' thesis was a pernicious development of those cultural approaches to explaining poverty which, rather than seeking explanations that lie outside an individual's control, look instead to the behaviour and values of the poor themselves (Piachaud, 1997; Pierson and Worley, 2005). This perspective of disadvantage (and it's one which is being politically re-visited and honed in the 2010s) lays blame on the moral and behavioural delinquency (Levitas, 2005) of the disadvantaged, and puts the spotlight on worklessness, dysfunctional parenting, anti-social behaviours, feral youth and criminal activity. Rather like their counterparts in 19th century London, proponents adopt a disease model, identifying a strong place based 'contagion effect'. For Murray (1984, 1994), an intense clustering of poor people for example leads to a concentration of social and economic problems.

In the policy arena, New Labour, in addressing the push to ensure that no one is disadvantaged by where they live, were not exempt from overall tendencies to negative labeling. The Social Exclusion Unit for example, slipped into a pathologizing medical and biological metaphor when discussing 'neighbourhood decay' (SEU, 2000), while both Conservative and Labour area regeneration programmes of the 1990s and 2000s, responding to what is perceived as a deterioration in generalized features of urban life, tended to adopt 'deficit models' of urban neighbourhoods (see for example, Whitley et al., 2005). When deprivation is too closely associated with certain geographical areas, there is a tendency, as Peter Townsend consistently argued, to: '...misrepresent national problems as area problems, with the effect of minimizing their extent, and scapegoating whole communities' (Townsend, 1991: 93). He recognized that the location of problems '... has to be traced back repeatedly to differences nationally between the social classes and especially to the social distribution of incomes...employment, industry, wages, rented and owner occupied housing, public transport, and the rest' (Townsend, 1991: 122). In contrast, it is the redefinition of social problems as problems of the individual, as Cooper (2008) argues, which has been a defining feature of the neo-liberal order. Whilst poor people and poor areas were regularly vilified in the right wing press, the growth of equally insidious processes of stigmatization of council housing itself were taking place. Hanley (2007) attributes the origin of this aspect of negative labeling to former Prime Minister Margaret Thatcher's equation of social housing with individual failure.

By examining distinctive characteristics of particular housing estates along with residents' experience of and responses to local conditions, I hope here to avoid the tendency to victim blaming at times just beneath the surface of commentary on 'deprived' areas or in discussion on social capital and community life. The latter can appear to apportion blame to communities themselves for social capital's withering for example. Communitarian perspectives which place emphasis on people taking responsibility for reviving local life themselves are acquiring a harsher edge in the contemporary political arena, where substantial cuts to services are being made under a cloak of building the 'big society'. The focus of attention in this chapter is on life in the second study area, Bridge Street, an estate with a very different history to Dock Lane, and, because it was undergoing radical physical regeneration at the time of the research, an estate in transition; a community in the process of re-constitution.

Bridge Street

Although an outer London borough, the area where the Bridge Street estate is located shares many of the characteristics more commonly associated with inner London. The estate is located in a heavily built up area; at the time researched there was little green space available other than a nearby cemetery. The population at this time included people on short term tenancies. Bridge Street is a very poor estate in a very poor ward, and levels of health attainment, as indicated by official statistics, are generally poor. According to health and education professionals, few children on the estate had holidays away (something they shared with youngsters on Dock Lane), and many appeared to be poorly fed. Despite many similarities in the profile of residents in terms of poverty, household composition and unemployment, Bridge Street is a very different estate to Dock Lane in many respects. A key differentiating feature especially significant for the viability of community life and the genesis of social capital concerned a great deal of movement on and off the estate. It is difficult to maintain the trusting relationships necessary for the development of a culture of reciprocity for example, in conditions where the social structure is unstable. Implications for individual well-being could also be expected: national attitude surveys have linked living in a place you don't want to move out of with happiness, for example (MORI, 2004).

Physically, the area covered by Bridge Street is smaller than Dock Lane, although there was something about the uniformity and drabness of the buildings before re-development which made it *appear* unending, to the outsider at least. Plentiful and meaningful social interaction in a shared locality is generally recognized by sociologists as the raw material of community life (see for example, Bulmer, 1975; Frankenberg, 1966), but one of the most striking features of Bridge Street at this time was its apparent lack of a localized street life. Few people stopped to greet each other on its streets, walkways or landings. To the observer, the most immediately visible difference between the two neighbourhoods lay in the design of the housing. Unlike Dock Lane, where traditionally designed post war homes were still relatively numerous, the brutal modernism of Bridge Street's housing stock took the form of wide, low rise blocks, as well as more conventional towers. The external appearance of the housing could only be described as ugly and alienating, the elongated low rise blocks, especially so. Residents understandably found the environment both alarming and oppressive, likening it to a prison for example, a term which emerged as a metaphor for Bridge Street and used in different ways in several accounts of community life here. Even the numbering system of the flats was bewildering and contributed to the general unease: 'I lived here for a year before I could find my way around' said a resident. At the time of the research the estate was undergoing radical physical redevelopment: a few of the old tower blocks had been demolished and replaced with new terraced houses built to a traditional design. Nevertheless the majority of tenants were still occupying the old housing.

Despite this generally inauspicious backdrop, the estate was not without resources. It was better provided with community initiatives than many neighbourhoods of a similar size. There were certainly more opportunities available and a higher degree of involvement in tenants' organizations, activities such as community festivals, and various small scale projects than were evident on other estates undergoing regeneration within the same borough. Historically, the area had benefited from sustained and effective community development work, as well as from long term activity on the part of local voluntary organizations. A great deal of work went on in Bridge Street to break down some of the isolation which it soon became apparent was endemic on the estate, and to encourage people to develop their social networks. Projects included childcare groups; Somali support; a children's breakfast club; a community computer resource; childminders' drop in sessions and a credit union. A women's' project directed at low income and ethnic minority women provided free courses on childcare, cooking, and developing employment skills, while the local educational visitor carried out intensive outreach work to encourage people to come along to facilities like a toy library. Estate residents were targeted for activities like these, but the experience of living in this particular locality discouraged some from involvement. The estate's stigmatized reputation appeared to be having a stultifying and demoralizing effect on individual agency.

Bridge Street residents had been on the receiving end of scapegoating and of pathologizing attitudes which had influenced some earlier policies directed towards the disadvantaged. As a taxi driver remarked to a resident: 'Oh Bridge Street estate, that's where you can buy an ounce of coke in the sweet shop'. Its poor reputation was reportedly derived from high crime levels, anti-social behaviour and from an influx of what had once been referred to as 'problem families' who were 'dumped' there during the 1980s. 'Dumping' was a process of allocating empty property in unpopular estates to anti-social or non-coping households (Seabrook, 1985). The stigma attached to these residents appeared to have then spread rapidly to embrace newcomers as a whole. A local police officer explained that once a poor reputation was established, people had little desire to stay, and the cycle of decline became entrenched. Only those who had no choice were left or ended up there. He added: 'If you have a problem, whether its social, economic, or a criminal record, then the only place you are likely to get a flat is on the Bridge Street estate'.

Fear of crime was to emerge as a salient feature of life here on Bridge Street. While people were understandably worried by rumours circulating at the time about criminals, particularly paedophiles, being housed in flats near families, feelings that the estate was not a safe place to live were not solely derived from negative perceptions of fellow residents. Alarm for personal safety was very much exacerbated by physical features of the locality, by the design of the old blocks for example, which were felt to be 'eerie'. Gaining access to the flats in these streets in the sky was certainly an alarming experience; the visitor was faced with long tunnel-like windowless corridors on the ground floor, for example. The split level arrangement and location of the flats was also problematic: if tenants were unfortunate in having troublesome or noisy neighbours, it could be very difficult to know with certainty who they were, where they were located, and consequently who to like or to avoid.

Whilst Bridge Street residents had seemingly internalized views perpetuated by the media that disadvantaged housing estates like theirs were places where dysfunctional behaviours and welfare scroungers were the norm – and such beliefs can be detrimental to mental health, through lowering mood and self esteem or altering behaviour (MacIntyre et al., 1993; Halpern, 1995) – not everyone accepted these derogative views of fellow residents. A minority who included people active in local projects felt able to challenge victim blaming attitudes. As a woman participating in the local tenants' organization insisted, people on the estate may have had problems, but this did not make them problem families. The struggle to cope with poverty could be overwhelming; some informants drew links between the difficulties faced by parents in bringing up a family on a low income, for example, and the unruly behaviour of their children. A man living and working on the estate described a situation which he believed was typical of many: 'A lot of people live on the edge. Some mothers are struggling [financially]. Some find it difficult to cope with their children. Poverty gets them down, parents whose kids don't come in at the right time, they don't go looking for them, and they just give up'. Although the new houses (a small minority of the homes at this time) were providing much improved living conditions, regeneration could bring added financial difficulties for families. Rents had increased and family income further depleted by the installation of water meters. Getting into arrears with rent was commonplace on the estate, and moving into a new home led to some householders incurring additional debts. Quick to exploit the needs of newly re-located tenants, inducements in the form of catalogues advertising furnishings were left at the door. Consequently, as a young resident explained: 'Even those in the new houses are depressed. Its lack of money ... They may be living in a nice house, but they have less money and more worries'. The intention of the present coalition government not to renew funding for schemes helping households to stay free of debt is a decision which could have serious effects on the well-being of people like these struggling to survive on low incomes.

The experience of hardship is highly debilitating, but damaging factors not directly connected to family and personal circumstances but related instead to the physical and social context of Bridge Street could also be readily identified. Residents themselves put particular emphasis on stressful conditions on the estate and their perceived effects not so much on physical health, which might be expected given that they were living on a building site, but on their mental health and general sense of well-being. 'A lot of people are depressed here. It's such a depressing place', said one. The dismal visual quality of the built environment on Bridge Street was seen as a direct causal factor: 'I hate coming home to this grim grey mass', for example, but just as frequently the experience of stress was linked to isolation. A lack of social connectedness was something which appeared to have characterized the estate for decades, affecting people across all age groups. Lack of trust of fellow residents inhibited mixing as I show later, but features of the physical environment itself also created obstacles. People felt 'cooped up' in their garden-less homes, and there was little to tempt them outside onto the estate and the immediate surrounding area. With no green spaces or other small scale opportunities for lingering nearby, there were few chances at this time for people to escape from the effects of their debilitating surroundings, to retreat from pressures or stresses at home or simply to gain enjoyment from mingling with others.

Yet there were many very positive aspects to life on the estate. Whilst on one level, with so many difficulties stacked against them, people could feel powerless to address day-to-day problems, improve their personal circumstances or challenge anti-social behaviour on the estate, at the same time, a strong sense of collective efficacy shone through. Residents, albeit a minority, came together to challenge and resist the decline and neglect of their neighbourhood. It was their collective action (with help and support from various individuals and agencies, including the Local Authority, local MPs, a member of the Royal Family and, importantly, Community Development workers), which led to eventual redevelopment.

Community, alienation and social capital

On several counts Bridge Street presents almost a mirror image to the nature of 'community' and forms of social capital associated with it presented in the last chapter. With no tradition of very localized heavy industry or of intergenerational continuity of residence for example, and little of the neighbourliness we associate with such areas, there was not much about Bridge Street to suggest a traditional working class community. Although commitment was stronger for residents involved in formal activities, amongst most people there was little evident sense of pride in the neighbourhood or identification with fellow residents, and even little curiosity or concern with the area's history. It could be expected that a strong sense of collective history would be less likely to be found here than in more settled neighbourhoods, but even amongst older, long term residents, there were those whose estrangement was such that there was a sense in which they appeared ready to distance themselves from the area's past as well as its present. It is difficult to find elements of Willmott's 'attachment community' here. Unlike earlier generations, people were not choosing to live in Bridge Street, nor were they 'hoping to go up in the world' as the motivations of aspirant East Enders moving into this part of East London had been described earlier by Willmott and Young (1960). Indeed, many people – of all ages – would rather have lived elsewhere. Some for whom this option was blocked could turn to desperate measures, setting fire to their flats the most extreme example recounted. A sense of powerlessness, while reflected in the actions some felt driven to take, was also evident in the imagery people used to describe living in this neighbourhood. As one quipped: 'I call this estate Alcatraz 2: easy to get on, difficult to get off'.

On Dock Lane, positive perception of local people were a major source of commitment and residential stability, but in Bridge Street, residents' narratives indicated that rather than neighbourliness and trust there was distrust and suspicion, family dispersal and strain rather than a local supportive extended family, anomie rather than strong local culture and values, alienation rather than attachment to the community. As a mother with school age children insisted: 'There is no community spirit at all ... There's a lot of mistrust, you worry who you talk to ... You have to be careful the way you look at some of the neighbours'. It was certainly noticeable how unhappy many people appeared to be. Newcomers on Dock Lane had to work hard to be accepted into the local community; on Bridge Street, new arrivals recognized little 'community' to become part of. Their early impressions were largely negative, and focused for example on their alarm at the physical appearance of the estate, unease over what they soon recognized as a lack of connectedness and general sense of isolation, and on their own growing feelings of entrapment, any of which could impact negatively on well-being. Making comparisons with local life in their countries of origin, some recent immigrants found some features of life here especially disturbing and felt very lonely.

Residents nevertheless felt able to acknowledge the dual nature of collective life on Bridge Street. While reluctant to identify anything approaching a sense of belonging, relationships of trust between neighbours, or day-to-day reciprocal exchange, they spoke with more enthusiasm about available opportunities for more organized community involvement and the contribution these made to local life. An everyday friendliness deficit was recognized alongside '... opportunities to get to know people if you want to, if you are a joiner that is'. Whilst regeneration activities and community development aided projects were acknowledged as doing much to re-build aspects of community life on Bridge Street, it became apparent during interviews nevertheless that even residents who were socially included in the sense that they participated in local organizations, or had begun to establish friendship networks locally via children's play groups or courses for example, did not appear to know their neighbours. 'I'm doing a first aid course', said one, 'I've met people on the course who have lived on the estate for as long as I have but I didn't know them! It's a shock when you realize that they've been here just as long as you'.

Lack of connectedness impacts negatively on well-being; one of the means by which it does so lies in the critical implications for social relations and social capital, a social entity involving co-operative and trusting social networks, reciprocal aid and participation in clubs or organizations, along with perceptions of safety. Sources of distrust were complex, residents responded to Bridge Street's reputation for crime or anti-social behaviour for example, by 'keeping themselves to themselves' and retreating inwards into the home, but structural issues like high population turnover coupled with poorly designed blocks, also discouraged neighbourly interaction and acted to exacerbate feelings of distrust. Negative perceptions of neighbourhood safety can be damaging in ways other than the discouragement of sociability among residents. Living in a locality believed to be dangerous has been shown to adversely affect health for example (Ziersch et al., 2004). Fear of crime emerged as a constant undercurrent to life on Bridge Street. Whilst it can sometimes be difficult to judge whether a fear of crime and distrust of fellow residents is justified, Innes and Jones (2006) point out nevertheless that people's perceptions and beliefs about disorder and crime are as important for neighbourhood decline as actual crime and disorder rates. Negative neighbourhood perceptions can also impinge on behaviour. A teenage boy on the Canal View estate (introduced in the next chapter) who had previously lived in a highly deprived and stigmatized neighbourhood expressed it as: 'If you live in an ugly environment, sometimes you act ugly'. On Bridge Street it was not only fear of crime but the experience of serious crime, as a victim or witness, which damaged community relations and acted as a block to community cohesion. A worried mother provided a not uncommon example: 'I didn't want to get involved in the estate, I heard about the violence and the trouble, and my daughter [a child] saw a shooting, so I kept myself to myself'. One resident I spoke to was in a state of shock having witnessed an attempted murder on the estate the night before when hanging out washing on her balcony. Ironically the incident did bring residents together, people were gathered in huddles discussing it on the streets the next morning, but the effect was short lived. For some vulnerable men and women, the negative repercussions were longer lasting: the incident acted to further increase their fear and isolation. Another young woman reported for example: 'Mum has become phobic, she won't go out on her own, and the man being dropped from the fifth floor has made her even more frightened'.

Such experiences are clearly damaging in a number of ways, affecting the well-being of both individuals and their communities. It was not surprising that some residents deliberately chose to have as little to do with the place and the people in it as possible at this time, taking avoiding action to cope with what they perceived as a hostile environment and thereby excluding themselves from potentially mutually beneficial local relationships. A middle aged man explained that he was glad that he lived on the edge of the estate: '... because you don't have to walk through it to get to the station or the shops'. People on Bridge Street could be so alienated from one another that even immediate neighbours were not above suspicion of criminal activity. On Dock Lane people were generally proud of their own blocks and terraces and 'stuck by' the people in them, but not on Bridge Street, where they were quick to impose negative categories. As Jacobs (1961), a chronicler of community life and social capital in American cities had observed, suspicion and fear of trouble will often outweigh any need for neighbourly help. A resident who understood drug dealing to be taking place on her floor, described the situation in her block of flats: 'People don't trust each other ... two doors away a woman was burgled while she was away, but she never asked me whether I'd seen anything'. Lack of neighbourhood trust hampers people's ability to access or offer support in times of need, but its negative impact on individuals can also take more direct routes. It can add to a mother's financial problems, for example, and have implications for the health of herself or her child. A single parent explained: 'It's difficult to manage, but if your child doesn't look smart someone might call the social services in and say the child is being neglected. So if you buy winter shoes for the child, you may have to go without food'.

The sociologist Georg Simmel argued that social relationships are reproduced through the very ordinary facets of life, via the social interactions taking place in everyday social settings for example (Lechner, 1991). Taxing aspects of the physical environment such as poor housing conditions and overcrowding have long been known to have a detrimental effect on physical and mental health, while physical improvement to the housing stock has been shown to have positive effects (Candy et al., 2007; Clarke et al., 2007). But less attention is generally given to the social effects of housing and estate design. Widgery, alluding to Young and Willmott's classic study, recognized the damage that some forms of housing and 'slum clearance' schemes could have on the health and well-being of working class people when he described, with some sadness, the changes he'd witnessed while working as a GP in a neighbouring borough: 'The old terraces may have been unhygienic, but they provided endless locations for social intercourse, gossip, courtship and news gathering ... [while now] tower blocks froze people into well upholstered isolation' (Widgery, 1991: 38). 'Gossip' while recognized as an important factor in defining community (Frankenberg, 1966) is also, as we saw in Chapter 4, something which people can find cheering.

Bridge Street residents had the misfortune to live in some of the most unprepossessing and socially isolating housing in the country. They were highly critical of the social effects of the design of the (un-regenerated) dwellings for example, where flats with entrances on the same walkway would lead to upper, lower and middle decks. 'You can't really talk about neighbourliness in the low rise' explained one young man, 'because it's difficult to know who your neighbours are'. While for some people the decision to avoid fellow residents was a deliberate choice, constraints associated with the physical environment meant that an individual may have little option but to 'keep themselves to themselves', a phrase used repeatedly to describe the lacuna in community life on the estate. Nevertheless, it would be misleading to over-emphasize the importance of housing alone as a source of chance meetings. Few casual meeting places of any kind at this point in Bridge Street's history put severe limitations on residents' ability to interact with others. Some people were resourceful however; a cafe just outside the estate had become a regular place of association. Informal meeting places like this, where people feel comfortable to linger, and spend time 'laughing and joking' with others are especially valued where the immediately surrounding environment is so alienating. Opportunities for casual engagement need to be appropriate nonetheless. Regeneration had provided a smart new social centre in the middle of the estate, but there were indications amongst residents at this time that it may not be meeting their needs for socializing: 'There's no where you can go for a coffee and a chat. They don't cater for us; it's just the voluntary organizations in there'. Elsewhere, in Birmingham, a community teashop run by volunteers and set up to meet just such a demand is well used, and by a wide range of ethnic and social groups (Manzoor, 2011). On Bridge Street, a bench just outside the centre was proving popular however, and a prime source of chance encounters. In some cases people using it were finding themselves chatting to their own neighbours for the first time as they passed by.

Key aspects of Coleman's conceptualization of social capital include the potential for exchange of information inherent in social relations. Although those involved in associations and projects were relatively well informed on local issues, for most people, lack of trust, 'keeping myself to myself' and the diminished social interaction they engender impact negatively on this particular form of social capital. Information is not circulated; village gossip, of the kind still found on parts of Dock Lane, where 'everyone has a tale to tell', just does not happen here to the same extent. As a consequence, it could be difficult for residents, especially those new to the area, to find out basic information they needed, how to locate a GP, for example, while organizations such as a local Disability Resource Centre experienced problems in trying to track down potential members living on the estate. In a situation where making new contacts is difficult, the quality of existing relationships assumes greater importance. But negative features of life on Bridge Street appeared able to impair the social networks of residents not only by reducing contact with other locals, but in some cases, by affecting personal and familial relationships as well. Bonding, supportive ties that might have been expected to be protective to health and well-being, either directly, in promoting contentment, or indirectly, through modifying the effects of stressful circumstances, were themselves being compromised by a febrile local context. Our ability to 'flourish' (Keyes, 2002), to feel good about oneself and one's relationships can be undermined by any number of circumstances, but here residents felt strongly that having to cope with a run-down and hostile environment was damaging. As one explained: 'Nine out of ten people on this estate have relationships which don't last. There's too much tension and pressure here'. Another put it more graphically: 'Health on the estate is poor, because it's very stressful here. People would move in happy, and three or four months later would be chasing each other with hammers'.

While living in a deprived and distressed urban environment might be anticipated to test relationships between partners, another, and less expected consequence, was the effect on wider family networks. Trends like family breakdown in Britain have been generally singled out in some quarters for eroding social connectedness, but the socially disconnected Bridge Street appeared to be taking its toll on family life itself. In some cases relatives even refused to visit. A young mother explained how poor design features interacted with the estate's discredited reputation for crime and drugs to consolidate and heighten feelings of danger: 'My mum won't come and visit me here, it's the design of the place, the dark lifts, the horrible corridors, and it's so intimidating. You don't know who is going to jump out on you. Mum doesn't like the people here either; she says it is too rough'. Even in a remote sense, given that local extended families are not a feature of the area, perceptions of Bridge Street as unsafe contribute to a situation in which mothers and daughters like these can have little reliance on the day to day reciprocal aid which was once a strong feature of East London life, and which was still evident on Dock Lane. Conditions on Bridge Street could have a markedly negative impact on the well-being of those in one of the poorest and most vulnerable groups, single parents, some of whom led very isolated lives.

Collective mobilization and community dynamism

It would be quite wrong nevertheless to portray life on Bridge Street at this period in its history as one of unmitigated misery as earlier pages may have implied. 'Community' is more difficult to categorize in some ways than on Dock Lane. On Bridge Street, people put questions of coping much more to the fore, not simply of coping with poverty, but coping with a stigmatized and dangerous neighbourhood. In these circumstances, people create community in different ways, through becoming involved in local projects, participating in tenants' or self-help organizations, or by seeking out activities in a separate locality. To generate and access social capital people have to be innovative, they cannot rely on the traditional and supportive structures evident on Dock Lane. The consequence is a less conservative, more dynamic form of community, with less emphasis on strong ties, but instead involving weaker bridging ties to dissimilar groups, and linking ties to power holders. Whilst for many residents, the odds against them (poverty, difficult relationships or bringing up children alone, along with living in a frequently alienating and generally isolating environment) were understandably too overwhelming for the resilience of positive perceptions of community, trust and of cultures of mutuality, the collective mobilization of a group of residents demonstrated nevertheless that Bridge Street was a neighbourhood which showed remarkable resistance in the face of decline. While 'resistance' is generally used to describe action which is explicitly political in its nature, involving, for example, mass movements (see Castells, 1997), here strategies of resistance are manifested in more ordinary, localized, but still political, activity. Philip Abrams (Bulmer, 1986) in his work on community activism, had referred to local involvement as the 'new neighbourhoodism', political in the sense that people were actively making a challenge.

The need for re-development had galvanized local action. The majority of urban regeneration schemes are not initiated by the communities themselves (Smith and Beazley, 2000) and indeed are frequently resisted, but Bridge Street is a-typical. Mobilization was not simply re-active to decisions made elsewhere. Active residents described how, with the support of community development officers, they fought hard for regeneration funding in a campaign which included a march to Parliament for example. Once redevelopment began, local activists continued to exercise individual agency and strove to retain resident control. The encouragement of local participation on the part of regeneration bodies through a residents' steering group can appear, Crow and Allan argue, to be less about fostering empowerment and democratic self-determination and more about assisting state bureaucracies to accomplish their objectives (Crow and Allan, 1994: 162). Participating Bridge Street residents were mindful of the dangers of incorporation. As one put it, they '... wouldn't let the regeneration agency walk all over them'. In some cases this involved deliberatively subversive tactics: 'I'm for the tenants, I'm not for running up the [Regeneration Agency's] backside. ... I make a point of finding out what's going on, and when I get information, I pass it on to the tenants'. Their combined efforts resulted in alterations to some of the housing plans for example, and in interested groups being consulted before new activities, such as childcare schemes, were set up. A growing sense of self efficacy and assertiveness, evident in resistance to and questioning of top down agendas, had been nurtured by community development work on the estate. Community development, for its advocates, aims to enhance participatory democracy by helping people to organize themselves on issues of joint concern and to achieve social change (DCLG, 2006).

Members of the Tenants Management Committee felt that they gained much for their community by working collectively with groups and agencies both within and outside the estate, insisting that without team work they would not have been able to achieve as much as they did. Co-operation empowered residents in their struggle to achieve regeneration aims, but there were additional ways in which their collective endeavour strengthened the community. Firstly, whilst on Dock Lane a strong sense of local attachment was commonplace, on Bridge Street, commitment varied markedly between residents who were heavily involved in local campaigns, activities and projects, and those who were not. It is amongst this small section of the neighbourhood's population that Willmott's 'attachment community', acquires meaning. By taking part, they gained the confidence to resist the estate's negative image and re-construct their identity with it. Both engaged and non-engaged residents acknowledged that the neighbourhood's strength lay in the growth of its formal collective life. Secondly, bridging ties, seen as essential for building coalitions and generating wider social or 'thin' trust (Putnam, 2000), were being forged between people of different ethnic, cultural and interest groups, as well as with active residents on other regeneration estates. A participant explained: 'They used to all keep themselves to themselves, but over the last few years, there been a lot of groundwork done to bring the groups together ... The Summer Festival, for example, had a really good feel about it, because we're all here working in the same community'. On Dock Lane, most people's understandings of community frequently involve association with people like themselves, however defined. For at least some of the participating residents on Bridge Street and on Dock Lane, 'community' takes on more inclusive, solidaristic meanings.

Not everyone wants to join things however, and there are many constraints on involvement even amongst those who do. A particular impediment for some people was the neighbourhood's poor reputation. As a local woman explained: 'Why join anything, or go on courses? People round here think that no-one on this estate ever gets anywhere, so why bother'. Community has to be 'made', to use Wellman's (1979) term, on Bridge Street, a spur for some to action but there were many others for whom a generalized lack of neighbourhood trust acted as a deterrent, colouring their attitudes towards tenants' groups, for example. Individuals who did not trust their neighbours tended to regard the committee members with suspicion too. Participation is in any case likely to remain a minority activity on the estate; even in the New Deal for Community areas, established more recently, where a key objective of initiatives funded by the Labour Government was to encourage civic engagement in highly deprived wards, levels of formal involvement with partnership agencies remained stubbornly low (Batty et al., 2010). On Bridge Street most residents looked to changes in more ordinary aspects of day-to-day life for improvement. Along with aspiring to a decent home and a job, they wanted to live in a friendlier community. Rather than viewing place based communities and the traditional norms and forms of activity we associate with them as an irrelevance in the modern world, East Londoners (across the three estates) continued to express their continuing desire for a localized manifestation of community life and the advantages it entails. For example, for a young single mother on Bridge Street who described herself as feeling extremely isolated and lonely, an imagined community took on a very traditional appearance. She talked about the sort of co-operation and neighbourliness which she wished existed on the estate: 'If we could all get along, it would be a better place to live. It would help our health if we could all help one another, and support our neighbours. It would be nice to be able to ask a neighbour in for a cup of tea, for a chat, or help someone financially or go on a picnic together, rather than come in and lock your door. Or we could baby-sit for each other. They don't do any of this on this floor. Neighbours smile, but that's all. People don't trust each other'. Co-operation amongst residents was not totally lacking on the estate, but everyday forms of reciprocity were hard to develop and sustain here. Yet there were signs of recovery in certain aspects of local life: changes afoot largely resulting from regeneration indicated a chance perhaps that at least a few of her hopes might eventually be realized.

Conclusion: A revitalized community?

Our social networks, and the social capital they embody, are organic entities. A critical element of social capital concerns the embeddedness of the norms in the social structures. When the structure of social relations change, Coleman (1990) argued, the norms change; disruption can be highly damaging to social capital. The East London research did to some extent confirm the fragility of social capital for individuals. Many of the features which had helped to build community life on Dock Lane had disappeared or were declining rapidly. Bridge Street was also changing, in its case, for the better. Housing regeneration, intensified community development and outreach work on the part of service providers, as well as attempts to design out crime, were doing much to change people's outlook. Some tenants in the new housing were already reporting a change in patterns of neighbourliness and relationships of trust between residents, and conventional street design was an important influence. Advocates of 'New Urbanism' believe that it is possible to develop a sense of place and belonging through the built environment and that this is key to revitalizing a sense of community in distressed neighbourhoods (Bothwell et al., 1998). Bridge Street was still in the early phases of regeneration; on Canal View, the third estate considered in 'Poverty, Community and Health', physical regeneration was complete, the old blocks had been demolished, and residents were living in traditionally designed homes of small terraces or set round squares. The contrast between the accounts of their former relatively isolated lives in tower blocks and their new found sociability 'living on the ground' was especially striking. Comparing the difficulties she had raising children in the old towers with life in her new home, a Canal View house dweller reported: 'Now, kids are always within eyesight and earshot, and neighbours look out for each other's children just as they did 30 years ago. We can encourage children to develop social skills which they didn't have when they were in the flats'.

On Bridge Street, behaviour in terms of neighbourly interaction might well begin to alter along with changes to the physical environment, but it seemed less likely that the negative perceptions of the estate as a whole or an absence of community spirit could so readily be transformed in this case. A source of the lack of trust between neighbours identified by the young woman quoted earlier who described the sort of community life she wished she had, lay in the co-operative but exclusive practices of a small group on her floor. She explained: 'When I moved into this flat the neighbours did code knocking on the pipes.

They watch to see if you are "one of us". They were afraid that I might grass [about drug dealing taking place] but they gradually realized that I was OK'. She seemed to have reached a stage where being accepted meant being ignored, rather than treated with suspicion; strong norms can operate to protect group interests of a non-traditional as well as a traditional kind.

Yet the optimism displayed by some residents living in the new homes was palpable nevertheless. One elderly man, who had moved into his new warden assisted flat only a few days earlier, had even begun to leave his front door open, something he would never had done in his old flat where he had lived in permanent fear of break-ins. Other residents, who, though still in their old accommodation, had been allocated new homes, were given a say in some of the design features. For them, feelings of demoralization were beginning to be eroded and replaced in some cases by a renewed hope for the future, by perceptions of enhanced control over their environment and by a raising of individual and collective self esteem in the sense that people reported that they no longer felt that they were being judged as 'second class citizens'. Those tenants already relocated were finding it easier to get to know their fellow residents, and some were learning to trust them. For others, however, entrenched attitudes would be much harder to shift. Yet opportunities to meet others, whether encouraged by estate design or facilitated by other local resources do at least have potential to play a part in breaking down the suspicion and hostility which typified social relations here. An exception to the lack of casual meeting places in the area was a café on the main road outside the estate where regular users, including residents who had previously been very judgemental towards others living on the estate, had learnt that people are far less alarming once you get to know them. The woman quoted next had once believed all of her neighbours to be 'up to no good' but was beginning to change her opinion: 'I've got to know more people since working in the cafe including those I was too scared to speak to before in case they jump down your throat. But once you start talking to them, they are not what you thought they are'.

6
Social Capital in Urban Neighbourhoods: The Potential for Unity and Division

Introduction

A familiar critique of 'community' is that it is a notion based on social closure and a narrow collective outlook; similar misgivings have been raised about the reciprocal bonding ties involved in social capital, while another major dimension of social capital, associational activity, may itself be limited to serving narrowly defined interests. It has also been suggested that a desire for community on the part of policy makers is unlikely to be compatible with other ideals or normative frameworks (see Young, 1990) such as social integration, social cohesion or solidarity. Sociologists have reasoned that some of the factors associated with communities and which have helped to produce the kind of everyday local solidarity characteristic of traditional working class life, may not be supportive to wider solidarity. For Westergaard, for example, the narrow concerns and particularistic ties of neighbourhood and family act to constrain the growth of solidarity and wider identification (Westergaard, 1975).

Amongst issues which differentiate the work of social capital theorists introduced in Chapter 2 are those which include the weight given to various influences on social capital and the differing roles allocated to the structure of social networks. Social capital in Putnam's conceptualization is inseparable from a thriving civil society (Putnam, 2000); for Coleman (1990), social capital inheres in the structure of relations between actors and is found throughout society, while for Jacobs, it stems largely from social interactions which take place in the city streets (Jacobs, 1961). Her approach may be especially relevant for understanding variation in social capital between poor neighbourhoods. While it has been recognized that access to social capital is (like resourceful networks) inequitably distributed across class and other social groups (Hall, 1999; Muntaner and Lynch, 1999; Bourdieu, 1986), and between housing tenures, these general trends provide little explanation for varying contexts of place.

The spirit of Durkheim (and to a lesser degree, Marx) hovers benignly over discourse on social capital. Social integration, solidarity and ideology, plus stability, self-interest and class consciousness, are all recognized as sources (Portes, 1998; Coleman, 1990). An issue concerns the kinds of networks – made up of strong or weak ties (Granovetter, 1973), homogenous or heterogeneous contacts – which are most effective. Durkheim strove to identify the sources of cohesion and solidarity in society. His distinction between the mechanical solidarity which he associated with traditional pre-industrial societies characterized by interdependence, value consensus, conformity and ethnic homogeneity, and the organic solidarity of modern times – a form of social cohesion based upon relationships of exchange and co-operation between *unlike* individuals and groups (Durkheim, 1933/1893; Allcorn and Marsh, 1975) – is reflected in contemporary work on social capital which distinguishes between 'thick' and 'thin' forms of trust (see for example, Newton, 1997). The first is associated with social networks which are 'dense' or close knit, where members of an individual's network know each other, the second with looser, more amorphous ties. Coleman, for example, identified density and network closure as necessary for the trusting relationships in which mutuality is embedded. Not unlike Durkheim, who envisaged a key role for mediating institutions in ameliorating social divisions and fostering organic solidarity, Putnam expects associational membership to produce 'thin' or wider, generalized social trust. Jacobs also focuses on looser ties, but for her, the context is different. She argued that neighbourhoods rich in social capital were made up, not of closed communities, but were centered on the interactions of a wide range of dissimilar people. Social capital itself takes a number of forms, differentiated by, and derived from, types of social ties. Analysts have classified it as either 'bonding' or 'bridging'. Bonding capital (embracing strong ties) involves similar people such as family members or members of an ethnic group and is based on supportive relationships; bridging capital (of weak ties) connects individuals to dissimilar groups and external assets (Putnam, 2000; de Souza Briggs, 1998). Additionally, a distinction has been made between bridging and linking ties. Linking ties connect people hierarchically into decision making processes, and can involve, for example, people with different levels of power and social status (Woolcock, 2001). While bridging capital is likely to have a crucial role to play in integration, linking ties can be advantageous for assisting self advancement or in helping people to secure community resources for example.

Whilst a lack of social cohesion can be a real source of social and political anxiety, we seem nevertheless to have slipped into a way of thinking in which the downsides of urban life, which include a presumed decline in co-operative social relationships, are overemphasized at the expense of some of its positive features. Social pessimism, it has been argued elsewhere, is an impediment to progressive politics (Taylor, 2008). The approach taken in this chapter is to contextualize social capital by looking at influences on its forms and sources across several urban neighbourhoods and to give particular consideration to characteristics of the social networks involved. A key question concerns the potential of the local arena as a source of more inclusive social networks, less conditional social capital and wider solidarity, as opposed to a setting for conflict and division. Dock Lane and Bridge Street residents' experiences are contrasted with those from the third housing estate considered here, Canal View, and illustrated additionally with occasional reference to our recent work in another part of East London on public spaces (Dines et al., 2006; Cattell et al., 2008).

Canal view

Dock Lane and Bridge Street were profiled in earlier chapters. Known 100 years ago as the poorest part of the poorest part of London, the area known as the 'the Sink', where Canal View is now situated, was generally despised. Some older residents refer to the time when their grandparents were 'dumped' in the area: it was 'here or the workhouse'. The wider area remains one of those places generally maligned by the media, but the localized reputation has changed. The original Canal View Estate was built by the Greater London Council in the late 1960s and early 1970s, one part consisting largely of bungalows, and the other of tower blocks. Many of the longer term residents moved to then new estate as a result of local slum clearance. They brought norms and ways of living with them which we associate with the traditional working class communities of the 20th century when branches of the same family would often live in close proximity to one another for example. An older Canal view resident who had lived his entire life in the area described how four of the seven houses in the block where he had lived as a child were occupied by members of his mother's family who, for example, would 'take it in turns to make a big roly-poly pudding each week'.

The estate had been surrounded by light industry, which at the time of the research was mostly defunct and lying derelict, while large local employers of semi-skilled or unskilled labour had re-located or closed. Radical physical regeneration to the 1960s housing stock took place in the late 1990s; in common with Bridge Street, it was residents' collective action involving the persistent efforts of a small group of tenants which led to eventual re-development. Linking ties forged between tenants and housing advice groups, the local council and other agencies contributed to the achievement of regeneration goals: the towers were demolished and replaced with traditionally designed terraced housing and squares. The demand for radical regeneration was not universal however. An equally active and vociferous group campaigned to keep their homes on the estate. They too were successful; the original bungalows were refurbished and remain on the 'low rise' or 'old side'. When researched, older people formed a majority on the old side; families with children on the new, and two residents groups represented their separate interests. On the developed side, the tenants' association takes the form of a Tenant Management Co-operative (TMC) and all residents are expected to be members. Visually, Canal View is a very attractive neighbourhood: residents on both sides take pride in their estate and in their role in regeneration.

Heterogeneous and homogeneous ties and the awareness of difference

Whilst the derivation of individual and group identity is generally complex, the influence of neighbourhood characteristics and their interaction with East Londoners' perceptions of similarity and difference can be seen as important elements in identity construction. Not unexpectedly, some people preferred to mix with those whom they regarded as similar to themselves according to such characteristics as age, family or ethnic group; but perceived homogeneity, for Gans (1961), the propensity to see others as like oneself, could be derived also from shared experience of place, or of what Amin (2006) refers to as regular places of association like schools, clubs or work places. The classical sociologist Tonnies (1955/1887) conceptualized 'community' itself as something arising from shared experience. Being an East Ender was integral to the identity of residents living on both Canal View and Dock Lane and while understandings frequently assumed a normative dimension, for example East Enders are 'friendly people, always ready to help each other'; 'rough and ready,' as well as 'liking a laugh', having lived and worked locally for some time were also amongst criteria deemed important for 'East Ender' status. For older people, pensioners' clubs on all three estates consolidated and sustained these aspects of their sense of self, for others, propinquity, living in a cul de sac where neighbours had known each other for most of their lives, as well as being a source of comfort, could similarly re-enforce a self contained, insular identity: 'You feel more comfortable with people like yourself, the old crowd'. A place like this in Dock Lane, explained some of its retired residents, made it possible for some people to insulate themselves from the demographic changes they saw around them. 'This little square is like the old times' said one, while a man from another part of the estate observed: 'You need a passport to get into that square if you're under 45'.

In contrast to residents whose keen awareness of similarity and difference was inseparable from what 'community' meant to them, there were many others whose preferred form of collective life embraced diversity, involved inter-group mixing and reflected a respect for difference. In these cases, understandings of community were not in conflict with their desire for integration. Community was perceived variously for example, as '... no racism, it's about integration, tolerance and understanding'; '... you get the youngsters involved with the older ones'; or, as one individual typically expressed it: 'It's having a laugh and mucking in together'. The outlook illustrated by the last quotation linked traditional East London working class attitudes to having fun through easy socializing with more contemporaneous ideas on participating in local life as well as, in this case, a personal preference for integration. The origins of individuals' values are divergent and not reducible to any single influences, whether of a structural or cultural nature, but there were residents in all three neighbourhoods nevertheless who located their own tolerant attitudes at least in part in having opportunities to mix with dissimilar others: attending school meetings or chatting to parents at the school gates; working or volunteering in a multi ethnic environment; attending mother and toddler clubs, toy libraries and courses which attracted a mix of people. Even shopping streets, though occasionally a setting for disharmony, can be valued as sites for negotiating difference. Where interactions of this sort did not happen, individuals appeared more likely to perceive others as different, and to treat them with suspicion.

Despite important extraneous influences, such as the growing assertiveness of black young people for example who reported that they were not prepared to tolerate the racism experienced by their parents when younger, it was clear nevertheless that the local arena could influence network characteristics in the direction of both exclusivity and inclusivity. The analysis can be further developed by looking more closely at contextual influences on forms of social capital, in both its 'thin' or 'thick' trust variants, and on some of its key sources: population stability; social inclusion; integration; self interest, and solidarity.

Local characteristics and sources of bonding and bridging capital

In contrast to Bridge Street, where an unstable population contributed to a depleted store of social capital, when the original Canal View estate was built in the 1960s, incoming residents, who were largely people from the surrounding area, arrived with established ties. Existing norms of co-operative self help survived relocation because the social structure was resilient. Positive perceptions of community life, as well as appreciation of certain local resources (primary health care services were praised here for example) consolidated local attachment and influenced residents' decisions to stay. A 15 year old girl whose parents' and grandparents' experience of living in the area predated the building of the original estate expressed typically warm sentiments: 'I know everyone, it's my estate, I love it'. Some tension between the need for stability of the social structure necessary for community sustainability and the fluidity concomitant with integration was nevertheless apparent. Housing allocation policies following large-scale regeneration of the estate assisted in the perpetuation of dense networks and 'thick trust'. Former tower dwellers were able to choose their neighbours in the new housing, a result was to solidify existing patterns of reciprocity – as indeed it did at times in Dock Lane's history – but at the same time made integration of newcomers more difficult. As a recent arrival said of more established residents, as well as of East Enders generally: 'They don't need anyone else'.

The distinction made by social capitalists between bonding and bridging ties, though meaningful, is not in itself wholly capable of capturing the reality of social life in a given locality. A sense of community for East Londoners is about more than the existence of strong, supportive bonding ties, locals make frequent reference for example to the kind of weaker ties associated with a casual street life. There are echoes here to Jane Jacobs' work on social capital in American neighbourhoods in which she conveys a passionate belief that the city streets and their resources, in engendering contact, were key to '... a feeling for the public identity of people, a web of public respect and trust' (Jacobs, 1965: 66). Opportunities for casual interaction in East London afforded through such quite mundane features of the built environment such as street markets, sitting-out areas, children's playgrounds and a canal-side walk, as well as routine activities such as journeys on foot to a school or workplace, emerged as highly relevant to a sense of community, and for consolidating social relationships. Even simply observing (and recognizing) people walking through an estate on their way to take the children to the local primary school from the vantage point of one's front window could, for some people, help foster a sense of belonging. Certain casual meeting places underpinned the co-operation necessary for the maintenance of informal social control: 'Everybody was out in the summer down by the canal [a popular part of the estate for strollers], so that's why we know what child belongs where', said a Canal View woman who informs parents if she notices children getting into trouble or danger on the estate. The significance of facilities like these for social capital however cannot be considered in isolation. Demographic change on a part of the Dock Lane estate for example was understood as affecting patterns of co-operation for maintaining informal social control, and with it the local culture of collective efficacy. A gender imbalance, itself a consequence of both loss of local work and housing allocation policies, the former especially, had made an impact. The only man of working age in his block reported: 'In this block of eight maisonettes I'm the only one who goes to work. The rest are mainly single parents. When there are problems round here – like drunks on the swings at night – they all wait for me to do something about it. When we first lived round here there were lots of men. We didn't have any bother then, because they'd all come out to sort out any trouble'.

Simple causal relationships between opportunities for interaction and harmonious social relations cannot, in any case, be assumed; social engagement is socially constructed as well as socially constrained or facilitated. Residential streets and other public spaces for example can be contested social arenas, sites of division as well as cohesion, of negative as well as positive engagement (see for example, Bridge and Watson, 2002; Keith, 2005). Problems encountered in the East London settings centered on issues around perceived ownership of places, unequal power relations, and conflicting interests as to what takes place in, or who uses, a particular resource. A worrying example in the context of national concern over a decline in children's outdoor play and growing levels of obesity concerned a designated play area for children in the middle of a residential square on Canal View kept locked and unused to avoid disturbance to residents living nearby. In another example – something which had become a cause célèbre at one time – a gate was erected on the old side of the Canal View estate to prevent some people from the developed side passing too close to some of the bungalows on their way to the local shop and thereby causing alarm to those living in them who felt that their privacy was being invaded. The gate was demolished again after majority resident opposition. Those slightly inconvenienced by its existence outnumbered those highly inconvenienced without it; the case heightens awareness of what can sometimes be the democratic limitations of enthusiastic localism. Some residents felt disillusioned by the incident, not simply because the outcome was other than they wished for, but because it brought to the surface the circumstance of a lack of solidarity between the two halves of the estate.

For most people, nevertheless, casual exchanges made when out and about were valued as a positive aspect of local life and deepened their sense of community. Discussions with people across all three East London neighbourhoods as well as those participating in our public spaces research (Cattell et al., 2008) showed clearly that casual social encounters afforded by a range of places – the hustle and bustle of shopping streets and markets; the 'little hellos' on residential streets or at bus stops; the get-togethers in small sociable residential squares; the casual chats on benches in children's play areas or when visiting mothers and toddlers' groups or child minders' clubs; the fleeting exchanges made whilst strolling in a park or longer news gathering discussions when collecting children from school – were often a key element in people's attachment to where they lived and helped sustain their own sense of personal inclusion into community life. Whether such interactions involve difference will, to some extent, depend on the context; for Jacobs (1961) it was casual contact with people very different from oneself which was essential for a thriving street life. There were examples of neighbour-friendly housing areas on the estates where relations between different age or ethnic groups appeared relatively cohesive, but there are limits to the ability of physical features of the immediate environment to facilitate wider integration. Opportunities for intermingling alone may be unlikely to overcome pre-existing tensions, for instance, whether these involve age, ethnic, and interest groupings or territorial issues, and may even deepen them. The events which led to the removal of the Canal View gate, for example, left lingering bitterness for many years afterwards.

Jacobs argued that the streets themselves could only be a key source of integration and 'exuberant diversity' when the tangible facilities a street life requires are present. A supportive example is provided by the experience of people living on a square adjacent to the Canal View estate. Here social difference was delineated along class and tenure lines: homeowners lived alongside housing association tenants, and resentment grew from an alleged initial lack of transparency on the part of developers over the mixed tenure nature of the dwellings. This was a friendly micro neighbourhood, where some families made supportive friendships with ease, but residents nevertheless identified little intermixing between social tenants and home owners, while a communal green area in the middle of the square had been a site of friction between travelers' children – whose families were living in surrounding flats and houses – and other residents. In the latter case, it took determined and concerted efforts on the part of social entrepreneurs living on the square to find ways of mediating different interests and begin to encourage mutual understanding between those involved, but in the former, potential assistance in the form of a simpler remedy was at hand. Opportunities provided by a well used under fives play bus which regularly visited the square were beginning to break down lack of trust between some social tenants and home owners and helping a few people to establish loose bridging ties with other users, or to at least treat each other with respect. It has been argued that the dominance of social housing lies at the heart of 'concentrated poverty' and that people with higher incomes must be attracted into deprived areas (Power and Mumford, 1999; Low, 2000), something which Local Authorities in London have encouraged in recent years. The mixed tenure development in the Canal View area showed little early success however in terms of integrating homeowners with social renters, or indeed in developing homeowner stability. By enhancing the social use of the square however, facilities like a play bus show at least some potential for more integrative social relations.

A thriving street life was certainly something which may have been easier to attain when certain resources were more plentiful. Older East Londoners remember colourful, lively neighbourhoods in the past, places which were fun to live in. An elderly Canal View man, referring to the gradual decline of shops, workshops and small trades taking place over the years he had been living in the area, indicated how resources like these underpinned a robust sense of attachment, and facilitated the kinds of social exchanges which are an important expression of East Enders' collective identity: 'I love the East End, I love the hustle and bustle of it, though there's not so much bustle here now. You can always get on with someone from the East End, and have a laugh'. The kind of banter which he describes was taking place in a context of relative homogeneity; past East End neighbourhoods were on the whole inhabited by people of the same occupational class and ethnicity. Nonetheless, other things being equal, there is little reason to suppose that a more generous provision of the kind of resources and facilities which attract people across social groupings could not play a similar role in helping shape social consciousness of a more inclusive kind in today's more diverse neighbourhoods. It would be unrealistic to infer mechanistic relationships between sites of association – however well resourced – and open networks or integration, but the light-hearted exchanges which sometimes take place in public places carry especial potential.

Busy social arenas, though less ubiquitous in parts of East London today, include markets; people's accounts of their use of them are often especially animated. Strangers, as well as familiar others have a role to play in community life if the opportunities to stop and chat are there. A Dock Lane resident for example talked about the ease with which she is able to talk to and share a joke with others: 'Even people lining up at the bakers, although they don't know you, will tell you wonderful stories'. Casual interaction like this alone is unlikely to override negative social attitudes to difference, but public places such as a multicultural market which became a focus of research in the public spaces study show potential for fostering inter-ethnic understanding by providing opportunities for people to meet which might not happen in a more organized setting. For some people, the market served as an unthreatening environment for negotiating bridges between different groups of traders as well as shoppers. As a regular user put it: 'Next to the Bengalis selling biscuits is a Jewish guy selling curtains. They would never have met a Jewish bloke [...] those Bengali guys, it's most unlikely that they'd find themselves in a colleague situation where they can ask questions, they can joke with him ... I can't see another space where that could possibly happen. You could set up a society to bring Jews and Muslims together: he wouldn't turn up and they wouldn't turn up, because these sorts of outfits attract special people' (Dines et al., 2006: 23).

Some East London residents identified the potential of leisure facilities like cafes, sports and social clubs for bringing together diverse groups. But if these were to help create Jacobs 'exuberant diversity', they would need to attract, not simply people with a shared identity like the long term older residents using pensioners clubs for example, but a wider a range of groups. People involved in the Canal View TMC for example had been campaigning for a new building to use as a community facility that would welcome all. Amongst its most vociferous advocates were those who saw the potential of community buildings for integration. As an active man insisted: 'We want it open to every colour, creed and age group, where everyone could go behind the bar and make a cup of tea'. He, along with other committee members, had received and felt they had benefited from 'equal opportunities' training arranged by the TMC; other advocates of the community hall were individuals who had been active in more formal aspects of local life in one form or another, through membership of tenants' groups, political parties or trade unions, for example. It might be fruitful therefore to consider at this point the extent to which formal participation in this part of London was able to create conditions for the genesis of 'thin trust' as Putnam suggested.

Participation and localities, solidarity and 'thin trust'

Local variations in formal participation underline social capital's context specificity as well as emphasizing the distinctiveness of urban housing estates. Unusually high levels of resident involvement in tenants' groups on Canal View reflected a history of collective action around regeneration, satisfaction with its end results, and a desire on the part of many residents to maintain the high standards in the physical environment their efforts had achieved. On the developed half of the estate, additional inducements included recognition of the effectiveness of co-operative tenant management, along with sustained and seemingly successful stratagems adopted by TMC staff to nurture a participatory culture. The development of an environment in which people felt free to drop in to the Co-op office based on the estate for a chat as part of their normal routine for example, contributed to the feeling of grassroots ownership which came across strongly at this time. Whereas on Bridge Street it became clear that low levels of pre-existing day-to-day trust could discourage involvement, Canal View's generally friendly and co-operative environment ensured that people not able to attend meetings were kept informed by participating neighbours.

One of the most striking features of associational life on Canal View however, on both the developed and older side, was that the distinction between formal (or civic) and informal (or social) participation had become blurred. When East Londoners in general talk about their experiences of getting involved in their local community, their stories frequently refer to activities such as helping with refreshments and organizing jumbles, bingo sessions, or socials, just as much, or more than, formal activities like turning up for meetings or sitting on committees. Canal View residents of all ages spoke warmly of the TMC social committee, suggesting that it was pivotal to the success of the local participatory culture. Social activities and day trips were regularly organized, as well as ad hoc events and front garden competitions. Informal participation like this can also lead to more formal involvement, a resident explained that people go on outings for example, get to know committee members, and in some cases then feel more confident to try volunteering themselves. The TMC Annual General Meeting (which I attended) was a lively occasion which successfully combined both kinds of engagement. A marquee was set up for the meeting itself while various play activities outside kept children entertained. A very enjoyable street party followed in the evening: 'It was brilliant' said residents the following day: 'We had a disco, we had a barbecue, and there was a bouncy castle and things for the children. I mean most people came, some of us were out there until three o'clock in the morning!' Having fun together binds people together and to the area they live in, and collectively organized activities on Canal View were able to support this aspect of local identity. Yet their potential contribution to local life in this case lay in more than bolstering any narrow, homogeneous notions of community: social activities were considered to be effective by some participants in helping to make connections between dissimilar individuals in terms of age, ethnicity, or length of residence. There was potential here for the development of new forms of community consciousness whilst continuing to embrace and build on valued elements of the old.

The potential of more formal participation for fostering bridging ties or developing more organic forms of solidarity showed some variance between the estates. Tenants' groups on Dock Lane for example were perceived by some black residents as the domain of older white people, men especially, when researched. On Bridge Street, structures which enabled a diverse range of voluntary and self help groups to come together in regeneration and other community activities were generally recognized as fora for building bridges and effecting more tolerant attitudes. A participating resident explained: 'They [tenants', child care, elderly organizations and Qu'ran reading groups, as well as Somali Women and West Indian associations] used to all keep themselves to themselves, but [now] ... we're all here working in the same community'. In the Canal View case however, a not insignificant aspect of social capital in the form of local formal involvement at this time was exclusionary, and characterized by attitudes of intolerance. TMC activities on the new, developed side, by targeting new arrivals, were helping to integrate newcomers with established residents but taking the estate as a whole, the legacy of regeneration has been paradoxically to both strengthen certain communities within the neighbourhood and to solidify existing divisions. A bitter (pre-regeneration) dispute between those people living in the original bungalows who wanted to keep their homes and those in the towers blocks who wanted the estate rebuilt, had left a legacy of power struggles and rivalry between opposing camps. Former activists on each side consolidated intra-group social capital involving both reciprocal aid and active participation, but continued to distrust the opposing camp. On the developed side, a gregarious man who was always ready to assist his neighbours explained: 'I will mix with all ages, shapes and sizes, but I can't relate to the old side, there's been too much agro in the past'. A potentially positive step was the setting up of an estate development committee embracing both sides to discuss issues of joint concern, but it would take some time and effort to develop a common purpose. A typical comment, this time from a resident on the old side of the estate was: 'They may have short memories, but we have long ones'.

The human capacity for organic solidarity – identification and recognition of common interests with, and co-operation between different groups – has not been extinguished in East London. The Bridge Street example is illustrative of the very real benefits to be derived from assistance from long term community development work within a neighbourhood. In other cases, sometimes solidarity just needs an accelerator. A very different example, and one involving grassroots radical action, comes from our public spaces research where the threat to a valued amenity resulted in the setting up of a multi-ethnic campaign group to resist plans for the radical development of a market site (Dines et al., 2006; Cattell et al., 2008). Putnam has argued that social capital is harder to build in the presence of diversity (Hallberg and Lund, 2005); this example, located in one of the most diverse boroughs in Britain, re-enforces one of this chapter's dominant themes, that is, awareness of the contemporaneous and historical context is needed when assessing the sources of solidarity and wider trust. The potential of a locally based participatory culture for bringing different groups together will be weakened nonetheless if social capital in Britain as a whole is in a state of terminal decline. East Londoners' experiences considered here appear to fly in the face of apocalyptic notions of a decline of community and collapse of social capital, at least in those settings where conditions remained or were becoming favourable. Age and generation issues were more complex however. Generational change can to some extent be understood as a symptom of changing local conditions and evaporating resources, but when we consider the life experiences of older and younger people they are differentiated by more than the changing local context. Ideas which couple a decline in social solidarity and trust for example with increasing consumerism and individualism in society are addressed in the next chapter.

Conclusion

Canal View was rather unusual, a place with both a high degree of reciprocity *and* participation, but although this was a neighbourhood very rich in social capital, it was not altogether socially cohesive. Despite the good natured mutuality which defined community life here as a whole, the case was not illustrative of communitarian notions of community as unified and without discord. There has been a tendency in the literature on social capital in relation to health inequalities for example, to treat social capital and social cohesion as conterminous: this was not the case on Canal View. Participation in one aspect of local life (though certainly not all) bolstered the interests of distinct groups. The looser ties associated with participation in regeneration campaigns, as well as bringing people together, can, in some contexts, re-enforce social divisions.

An area rich in social capital for individuals may, or may not, attain inter-group integration, while cohesion and division can co-exist within the same setting, or may assume different forms. Hostilities on Canal View were not a reflection of poor social relations between different ethnic or cultural groups or between neighbours, indeed the estate seemed relatively well integrated in this respect. The co-operative nature of tenant organization appeared to have had some success for example as a medium for developing an anti-racist ethos on the estate. But a co-incidence of social distinctiveness and entrenched attitudes with a geographic polarization was significant here. The specific form of social division evident in the Canal View neighbourhood, though derived from its regeneration history, became nevertheless solidified by the way the population was distributed. Antagonistic relations between former pro and anti-regenerationists coincided with a spatial divide; protagonists lived on opposite sides of the estate. Not only did people in the two groups have little desire to socialize with the other side, they had little reason or opportunity to mix. For Jacobs, successful neighbourhoods were those without clear boundaries, they overlapped and inter-weaved (Jacobs, 1961: 120). Canal View at this time could not be described in these terms, although relatively small in size compared to both Dock Lane and Bridge Street, it was nevertheless understood by many residents at this point in its history as almost two separate estates. Investment in facilities accessible by both sides might nevertheless be expected to carry potential for shifting intransigent attitudes and building bridges. Sociability alone may not lead to co-operation, as Peren et al. (2004) have argued in another context, but is nevertheless clearly a start.

Casual meeting places have potential, if only occasionally for solidarity, then more frequently for tolerance, or as Jacobs suggested, make it possible to be on excellent sidewalk terms with people very different from oneself. Whilst by no means a universal panacea, facilities which encourage a casual street life can be considered as potentially productive for people in working class areas like East London where light hearted exchanges have been such a visible aspect of everyday life and culture. Integration requires more than this nonetheless. Firstly, taking the case of Bridge Street, dissimilar participants in tenants' groups and campaigns were united and motivated by a common regeneration aim and a shared vision of the estate's future, while structural links with different groups facilitated by community development workers helped foster attitudes of tolerance and facilitate wider co-operation. Secondly, whilst perceptions of 'other' typically take on a social or cultural form, social cohesion is not advanced by an inegalitarian distribution of resources, whether at the local, regional, or national level. A Dock Lane man for example speaking of the tendency for scapegoating in such circumstances, insisted that 'When there is plenty of work, and an area is thriving, they don't pick on ethnic groups'.

7
Well-being and Happiness: Balancing Community with Independence

Introduction

Research evidence garnered from the mid-19th century onwards, and which gathered momentum during the latter part of the 20th century, led to increasing recognition on the part of researchers and eventually policy makers that the distribution of such factors as income, housing and employment, along with educational opportunities, are critical influences on a range of physical and mental health and illness indicators. It is these material circumstances which largely structure inequalities in health not only between nations, but also across social and cultural groups within the same countries (Whitehead, 1993; Acheson, 1998; CSDH, 2008). Despite their critical significance for our health chances, material factors do not appear to be able to provide the whole picture however. It is not clear, for example, why average life expectancy in Britain is less than the averages for some other developed countries, such as Sweden, Canada, Italy and Australia, or why disparities in health chances between rich and poor within some countries, Britain included; appear on some measures to be increasing (Wilkinson and Pickett, 2010; CSDH, 2008).

While research into health inequalities has traditionally used quantitative survey methods and adopted hard measures of health, illness and disease such as life expectancy, limiting long term illness or infant and adult mortality rates for example, a separate strand of work has recently prompted a shift towards more subjective approaches to health, in particular, to positive health as well-being, happiness and quality of life. Definitions of 'well-being' and 'happiness' are diverse but most typically embrace features associated with the quality of social relationships. As Chapter 2 notes, variants on the themes of well-being and happiness in current discourse can be seen to echo certain aspects of 19th century social thought, William Morris's emphasis on fellowship and happiness for example, and Karl Marx's understanding of the antithesis of well-being as separation from our social being. On the policy front, the search for solutions to boost well-being and happiness has become a subject of cross party political interest in recent years (Bunting, 2007; Reeves, 2007; Bacon et al., 2010), culminating in a 'Happiness Index' launched in 2011. First mooted by the (then) Prime Minister's Strategy Unit in 2002 (Donovan and Halpern, 2002), the ONS have developed the index to measure our social, psychological and environmental well-being. The happiness agenda is largely an approach to health which can also be traced to the World Health Organization's earlier promotion of 'well-being' as 'positive health' (WHO, 1948); understood as a dimension of a 'social model' of health which locates individual experience within social contexts and is concerned especially with people's interpretation of them (Gatrell et al., 2000). Given that epidemiological evidence has demonstrated relationships between aspects of well-being and harder measures of physical and mental 'health' (Chida and Steptoe, 2008) there may be justifiable reasons to suppose that changes in levels of well-being and happiness or indeed variation in their distribution could make a contribution to the shape and persistence of health inequalities.

A problem with a sole focus on the influence of material conditions on health and well-being lies in a particular set of circumstances: despite increasing wealth, rises in GDP and more stable employment levels in western societies, we are generally not happier. Instead, we appear to be becoming increasingly more miserable and depressed (Lane, 2000; Layard, 2005; Friedli, 2009). Ehrenreich (2007) traces a growth in unhappiness over several centuries, and back to the development of Calvinist individualism. She points to the isolation which Weber identified with Protestantism (Gerth and Mills, 1970), but more especially to the loss of our ability to enjoy ourselves collectively, through celebrations in public spaces for example. More usually however, the sources of our distress are considered to be of more recent origin, and lie in the confluence of a dominant neo-liberal political ideology with free market economic values, and in a late capitalist system which social theorists and political commentators identify with prevailing values of individualism, materialism and a rabid consumerist culture (Galbraith, 1958; Sennett, 2006; Bauman, 1998). The negative impacts of growing individualism, what James (2007) has described as 'affluenza' or 'selfish capitalism' are not confined to the psychological health of individuals but are seen to affect also the social well-being of their communities. A shift from collectivistic to more individualistic societies is recognized by prominent social commentators, including the Archbishop of Canterbury, Rowan Williams (2008), for example, as having damaged co-operative principles and practices, while surveys demonstrate that as a nation we are concerned about ways in which our society has become more individualistic, greedy and selfish, seemingly at a cost to our sense of community (Mowlam and Creegan, 2008; Watts, 2008). Nevertheless, the social harms inflicted by neo-liberal regimes may, it has also been argued, lie more in the effects of policy choices, in particular those designed to favour the interests of finance capital (Cooper, 2008; Jordan, 2006) and less in universal value change. We should in any case take care perhaps not to allow awareness of the norms' deleterious effects to overshadow consideration of any possible positive advantages. Durkheim (1952), for example, considered the key to a society's health lay, not in the dominant values of *either* individualism *or* collectivism, in self interest *or* the common good, but in the relationship between them (Taylor and Ashworth, 1987).

Common-sense understandings of well-being and happiness

Given the significance and weight given to global economic, political and social change in these discourses on sources of unhappiness, I may be mistaken in privileging the role of neighbourhoods in enhancing our well-being and quality of life, and asking too much of local communities, of people's social ties and a locally sourced social capital in their ability to offset negative effects of cultural change. These misgivings did not appear to be wholly born out in the East London studies however. When residents talked about their understanding and experience of health and well-being, recalled happy or unhappy times in their lives, or elaborated on what 'community' meant to them, their comprehensions of these separate issues, when compared, indicated a great deal of conceptual common ground. Happiness and health for example were often seen as inseparable, and it was the social conceptualizations of well-being, embracing social interaction, social relationships and neighbourhood based social capital, which dominated many of their narratives, leitmotifs which in turn were central to perceptions of a positive community. As well as the value placed on mutuality and local involvement when reflecting on its significance for well-being, people touched on a third dimension to their understandings of community: simply enjoying life in the company of others. Mingling with or simply observing others in vibrant public places for instance, whilst amongst the ordinary experiences recounted to illustrate perceptions of community, were at the same time understood as cheering or therapeutic. The local community had by no means become peripheral to East Londoners everyday lives nor, they believed, to their health and wellbeing.

It was also clear nevertheless that people's awareness of important influences on their own sense of well-being and happiness encompass a wider range of features than those associated with social relations or the characteristics of the immediate locality which support them. Some of these were discussed in earlier chapters, and included for example the esteem derived from being in work and contributing to society, or the direct effects of material factors like poverty and physical features of the local environment. Some people, in acknowledging the importance of keeping the mind and body active for alleviating everyday stresses, while at times preferring to do so in the company of others, also recognized, not unexpectedly, the therapeutic effects of more individualistic pursuits, such as gardening, sewing and reading, or just relaxing in a quiet outdoor green place. What is especially interesting however is that while the growth of individualism in modern societies is generally discredited as damaging to well-being by social scientists, the concepts of 'community' and 'individualism' were not always used by East Londoners in a way that suggested they believed them to be conflictual. Despite the value placed on feeling part of a caring community there was also some recognition that excessive inclusion for example, or over-reliance on local ties, were not always personally desirable. Even especially enthusiastically expressed attitudes to community life could sometimes be qualified with a desire for privacy: 'Community spirit? It's about having a good time ... and people taking care of each other, but without being nosey'.

A degree of independence was deemed a necessary pre-condition for good health and happiness by respondents, as were attributes such as freedom of choice, freedom of action and self efficacy. 'Being able to do what you want to do' was a phrase used repeatedly here. For many of the young people and those with families we met on Canal View, for example, an overarching goal was to have a 'nice life' and to have the sort of job which would enable them to afford it (Cattell and Herring, 2002a, 2002b). The pursuit of 'the good life' as material consumption may well be detrimental to the development of more meaningful pursuits and to psychological health (Giddens, 1991) but it's a generalization which can sit uncomfortably with the experience and aspirations of people living in poor areas. A desire to live the kind of life accepted as normal by today's standards was part of the motivation for studying to improve job prospects for example. As one young mother explained: 'Well in three years time I want to have qualified, and earn decent money to support me and the children in the way that I want them to live ... I don't want to have worry about bills ... can I afford to buy myself a car? ... a mortgage? ... take the kids on holiday?' It would be difficult to see the attainment of new skills, along with some increase in freedom from money worries, as anything other than legitimate needs and goals, the achievement of which would most likely enhance her future well-being and happiness, and that of her children, rather than put them at greater risk. The recent financial crisis and economic recession bring it home to us that a blanket critique of the effects of 'individualism' on well-being in which consumerism and aspiration are conflated, and which does not distinguish between the needs of the poor and the avaricious behaviour of the rich, can be in danger of side-lining the significance of multiple benefits of certain material factors on well-being, and the ways in which some people remain excluded from those benefits. What is important, and as relevant now as it was when Tawney (1931) railed against the injustices of inequalities of wealth, privilege, and opportunity, is that components of the 'nice life' and opportunities available to achieve them, are distributed more equitably.

It was nevertheless commonplace amongst East Londoners to believe that society in general but the younger generation in particular were more individualistic, more focused on the self and the pursuit of personal happiness and advancement than were previous generations. An East Londoner who had recently returned after many years living abroad, was struck by changes which he attributed to the continuing effects and legacy of 'Thatcherism': 'Attitudes have changed ... it has reached the stage of bare faced selfishness'. Opinion evaluating social change was mixed however; whilst for some people these were trends manifesting themselves in increasing materialism, a selfish individualism and a disinclination to co-operate, transformations were not always viewed negatively. Respondents, especially those interviewed on Canal View towards the end of New Labour's first term, were quick to point out for example that working class people and women with families today have access to a broader range of educational and work opportunities compared to earlier generations, at least, that is, when work is plentiful. Although it is perhaps questionable how realistic some of them were, many of the young women and young mothers we spoke to on Canal View had career ambitions, some had been able to take steps to realize their goals via the expansion of free nursery places and subsidized child care introduced by the last Government. At the same time, tax credits had made employment for this group more financially worthwhile. Their employment related goals stood in contrast to the experience of older and middle aged women whose options had been more limited. Some had worked as skilled machinists in the once thriving East London rag trade, others had turned their hand to whatever could be fitted in with the demands of their homes and families, such as home working or unskilled work in local factories. This kind of work rarely provides a ladder out of poverty; several of the older women lamented the fact that their own educational and employment opportunities had been much restricted and were glad that today's generation not only had greater choice but were actively electing to take up other options. In the present policy climate of cut-backs, women with young families from working class backgrounds may once again find the pursuit of a career to be a more difficult undertaking.

Significantly, the personal ambitions of the younger women did not displace their strongly felt community attachment. Those undergoing further education and training and setting their sights on a better future included single mothers whose mutually supportive local relationships, as I show later, were much valued for protecting their well-being. As earlier chapters have indicated, residents do frequently locate their general sense of well-being in 'community' related factors, in interaction with others for 'feeling alive'; in a sense of belonging; in social capital involving reciprocal aid or local participation, and in casual banter with passers by and neighbours.

Social and therapeutic advantages of the setting

There were a number of advantages to be gained from living on the Canal View estate. Firstly, for example, local primary health care services were in the main highly thought of, not least because many of the staff had worked in the area for many years and were well known and trusted by local people. Trust relies on a degree of stability in social structures (Coleman, 1990), and here the trust inhering in relationships between health professionals and residents could be directly beneficial to health in the sense that help was sought and advice generally followed. A valued member of the health care team was the local Health Visitor who perceived her role in a broad, community oriented public health sense. Secondly, unlike the un-regenerated Dock Lane, or Bridge Street where physical regeneration was ongoing, the physical transformation of the

Canal View estate had been completed. Tenants who had moved into new housing were glad to leave the stresses of overcrowded flats in various states of disrepair behind them; felt safer in better designed and lit streets: 'You can look down the terrace and see everyone go in and out: it makes you feel safe', and were able to gain pleasure from the improved visual quality of their environment, all things which more commonly form part of the taken for granted daily experience of the better off. New green spaces were important too. While places such as those mentioned by people taking part in our public spaces study such as a secluded area in a park, a peaceful spot near a pond, or a pleasant cemetery were recognized as having therapeutic qualities (Dines et al., 2006; Cattell et al., 2008), even small green oases within a housing estate like Canal View can take on special significance for the mental health of people living in flats. A resident who had moved from a (now demolished) tower block where she had felt 'hemmed in' to a low rise flat with a small planted border nearby explained: 'I was gradually going round the bend [in the Tower]. Now if I have got any troubles, I can go out and walk around and just look at the plants: it makes you feel calm'.

But regeneration effects can also be more complex, and interact with other local features to impact on well-being in a number of different ways. A young man for example who had grown up on a 'problem' estate believed that moving to Canal View had helped him feel more optimistic and happy. It made him realize that: 'Things can be better. Living where people are pissing in the lifts and stuff like that, living in that sort of environment drags you down sometimes, it's like everything is a drag. And when you come back to an area that's nice, it sort of lifts your spirits really'. He was talking about his impressions of a number of things, the reputation of the area, the behaviour of local people, their friendliness and helpfulness, as well as the condition and visual quality of the buildings and streets. The physical environment and its effects cannot always be readily separated from those of the social environment. It was clear throughout the East London studies that people appreciate public areas for their social value for example, and that their shared use was among key factors contributing to the maintenance of a sense of well-being.

The key differentiating feature between Canal View and the other housing estates considered here, Dock Lane, with its tight knit supportive networks of family and neighbours typical of a former occupational community, and Bridge Street, distinguished by weaker ties derived from the local participation so essential in an area with a more fluid population, was that it was well placed to combine the social and therapeutic advantages of both community models. Chapter 6 outlined reasons why Canal View was quite unusual, a place with both a high degree of reciprocity *and* participation. Not only were residents typically enjoying supportive relations between friends and neighbours, but taking part in local civic life seemed almost the norm for people living on the estate rather than the exception. These features, and the circumstance that the tenants' group on the developed side operated as a co-operative, make it a useful case for looking more closely not only at social capital's positive impacts, but at its limitations in terms of benefits to well-being as well as at particular groups excluded.

Well-being, supportive friendships and life stage

The continued need for supportive local friends and the importance of the contribution they made to health and well-being was confirmed by people across different age groups. There are concerns however, that *actual* friendships, especially amongst youngsters, are declining in Britain (Nuffield, 2009), prompting the need to reflect on conditions favourable to them. On Canal View a relatively low turnover of families at this time meant that young people for example could maintain the mutually and emotionally supportive friendships they had established when younger. Some focused on the buffering effects of support from friends at times of stress for example: '... because I've known most of my friends like since I was like four years old ... Any problems I've got I'll speak to them'. Others mentioned more practical and regular co-operation with friends: helping each other with homework, or lending and borrowing items like CDs, clothes, and small amounts of money and pooling resources like music equipment.

Reciprocal arrangements between local friends and neighbours were especially important for single mothers with small children. Poor, single mothers face a higher risk of mental ill health; they may have greater exposure to negative life events and possess lower self esteem than married mothers; at the same time they have been found to have lower levels of social support than those living in households containing a couple (Ceballo and McLoyd, 2002; Brown and Harris, 1978; ONS, 2002). Some of the women on Canal View had left destructive relationships and were rebuilding damaged self esteem, and most were on low incomes. As well as much needed emotional support, together they provided each other with all kinds of instrumental assistance; friends often dropped off and picked up children from school and baby-sat for each other; neighbours shared the supervision of children playing outside. The degree of altruism evident in everyday examples amongst this group was striking. For example: 'She had lost her social security book. I did not have any money because I had already gone and spent my money on shopping so I said bring the children over and I will feed them for you, until your money comes through'. Most commonly, mothers indicated that these relationships were based on principles of exchange. In another case, for example, Amy described how she and her close local friends could turn to each other. One of them had just lent her some money: 'She's a diamond, Anna ... That's how she is, and I would do the same for her. Rebecca's the same. I mean when I was decorating she was in with the gloss brush and to me that is friendship' (Cattell and Herring, 2002a: 77).

Reciprocal support, whilst mutually advantageous to the mothers, could be expected to produce benefits for their children's emotional well-being and psychological adjustment. A review of the literature on parenting styles for example (Ceballo and McLoyd, 2002), found that that mothers with higher levels of instrumental and emotional support behaved in a more positively nurturing way towards their children than those more isolated. Not all the young Canal View parents were long term residents but social relationships appeared relatively easy to make in this setting, partly because the housing design and estate layout facilitated mixing, but also perhaps because people at this phase of the life course were to some extent relatively well catered for, whether in terms of housing suitable for the needs of families, available facilities and services like mother and toddler clubs and a play bus, or access to a good health visitor. The latter for example helped several to resolve financial problems and offered support when relationships ended as well as giving advice on child care. Yet there was something else happening here: compared to Bridge Street for example, where a generalized demoralization connected to living in a distressing environment could inhibit individual agency, people's satisfaction with the Canal View neighbourhood seemingly enhanced their willingness to engage with and help each other.

Older people provided each other with a great deal of support, in times of illness for example, but also for coping with everyday tasks. The strength of the local community culture on this estate – exemplified by the ubiquitous comment: 'If I am in any bother, I can knock on any door and get help' – was such that it constituted a 'neighbourhood store' (Coleman, 1990) of social capital accessible from outside individuals' own friendship ties. While day-to-day reciprocal aid can be critical for maintaining quality of life in difficult circumstances, there were necessarily limits to the help older people could give each other, but because the culture of co-operation was so deeply embedded in this particular community frail older people could tap into it to gain help from those younger and more physically able. One woman reported for example that she relied on the window cleaner and passers by to change light bulbs, hang curtains for her and do other odd jobs. In this neigbourhood, what Jacobs refers to as 'the unconscious assumption of support' (Jacobs, 1961: 65) was a resource even accessible in death: 'People don't lie long, you know when they drop dead indoors', said a respondent, 'Because the lady over the road, on Saturday night she knocked on her next door neighbour's [someone she did not know well] and said 'I have got a pain in my chest', so of course the woman had called the ambulance, and stayed with her. She died in the night, but you know she wasn't on her own. This is how it is here' (Cattell and Herring, 2002a: 77).

Certain local resources can help solidify and perpetuate a co-operative neighbourhood culture, and on Canal View this was something especially noticeable in the case of older people. The pensioners' hall, where regular meetings and activities were held throughout the week provided a social setting whereby both long term residents and newcomers could absorb and contribute to local social and therapeutic norms. Interestingly, the club also operated as a kind of social and health conscious neighbourhood watch. As a regular explained, her attendance reduced any anxiety she might have about her own health: 'I go over twice a week ... and we get a chance to have a little chat together and if you hadn't seen anyone for a couple of weeks you could enquire and everybody knows if someone is not well and hasn't been about. So we all know what is going on. I find that very helpful'. The everyday activities of the club, which reflected and reinforced another aspect of local culture: having fun, often through co-operative activity, helped motivate regular attendance. They also had direct therapeutic value in themselves. A recently widowed woman for example had joined initially simply to combat loneliness, but then found that she had begun to enjoy life once more: 'I really have enjoyed it, and as I say it is the best thing that could have happened to me'. Perhaps she had been able to do what William Morris had been convinced (but on which he did not elaborate) was a key ingredient to a happy life, that is, she had turned her troubles into pleasure, through action (Morris, 1979: 194–5).

Whilst valuing the community life they had, residents made it clear nevertheless that access to a rich reciprocal culture did not diminish their desire for a degree of independence. Older people insisted that to maintain the privacy and autonomy they saw as vital for their well-being and to cope successfully with day to day tasks and challenges, would require more input from public services, social services especially. The desirability of formal help from public agencies to 'look out for' vulnerable people was something which was frequently mentioned, residents referred for example to estate wardens who used to provide assistance but had been withdrawn. The voluntary activity of a local elderly woman who had collected prescriptions for people on the estate and delivered them to their doors (known affectionately as 'Lil the Pill') was much appreciated by her housebound contemporaries, and her death left an obvious gap. The point may be obvious, but is nevertheless worth re-stating in the present policy climate: plentiful social capital within a neighbourhood cannot by any means supplant the need for help from public sources to encourage people to lead full and active lives. Taking the aspirant young women in this study as an example, while they very much valued the co-operative friendships they had with local women, because they wanted more than a 'little local job' also realized that they had to draw on wider networks and resources as well. They were fortunate in having access to a local health visitor who had become a valued mentor, encouraging them to return to education or training and providing initial contacts.

Formal and informal participation and happiness

William Morris's ideas on the relationship between co-operation and health and happiness were introduced in Chapter 2. In the ideal society he envisaged, by participating in small communities people would be encouraged to exercise their talents both for their own sakes and for the good of their communities (Morris, 1884). Benefits accruing to both were evident on all three East London estates. Individuals involved in tenants' groups and other forms of voluntary activity gained in self esteem and a sense of achievement, and from opportunities to acquire new skills and make new contacts. The communities themselves were strengthened by the improved physical and social environment residents helped secure through collective action and in increased local commitment. As one Canal View woman put it as she tended a small communal garden near her flat: 'So, it's the more you're involved in your community, the better care you take of it'. Some limitations to the benefits of involvement in terms of the empowerment expected in policy circles to derive from community control over decision making and the implications for personal happiness were nevertheless apparent. Participation when co-opted by Governments and regeneration bodies becomes less radical and emancipatory an entity than it was for Morris, and may impede rather than usher in political aims, whether these are for a 'good society' or the 'big society'. For some Canal View residents for example, involvement in a new phase of regeneration, though initially rewarding, had become a source of stress and frustration, especially when they felt that they were expected to rubber stamp decisions made elsewhere. More powerful partners continued to set the agenda. Though overall the merits of involvement of different kinds tended to outweigh the disbenefits, a situation of poor relations between participating residents and regeneration agencies meant that, at this point in time, this participatory community fell short of the ideal envisaged by Morris, where self government would go hand in hand with happiness.

Equivocation on the benefits to well-being and happiness were less evident where people recounted their experience of grassroots activities or more informal kinds of participation. A member of a credit union in Bridge Street for example reported that: 'Once people are involved, they come in here for a chat, make friends, become more confident and assertive. We've had a few people who joined feeling a bit low, when they come in for a chat it picks them up a bit. People are financially happier too, they can ring up and say "I've got a crisis, I need this money urgently". We don't want to know what it's for'. The Bridge Street Credit Union owed its success in part from the help and encouragement it received from local community development workers. It is significant that sections of the health promotion literature recognize common ground between community development and their own practices, highlighting for example, the emphasis on empowerment issues in both (Wakefield and Poland, 2005).

Social exclusion: Young and middle aged people

Canal View residents were fortunate in having relatively wide access to social capital, but there still remained people excluded from satisfying social relations, and not from choice. Often these were individuals who were also excluded in a wider sense. It is the multifaceted nature of social exclusion faced by people in disadvantaged circumstances which damages their well-being and elevates their risk of unhappiness and poor health. The experience of two groups at critical times of transition: young people and unemployed middle aged people, can be used to illustrate the effects of overlapping disadvantages on health and well-being, as well as demonstrate individual trajectories to exclusion.

Some of us, wherever we live, across deprived or wealthier areas, make rational choices which do not place the local arena at the centre of our lives. Amongst the teenagers on Canal View for example were those who had broadened their horizons and were taking up leisure, educational and, for the older ones in his age group, work opportunities elsewhere, but others led very local lives. Severely restricted finances meant that they were especially dependent on local facilities, but, and in common with many parts of Britain, these were totally inadequate for their needs: 'There's nothing for youngsters' was a frequent lament. The impoverishment of social provision for them on Canal View stood in contrast to that for retired people especially who had a purpose built community hall for their sole use at this time. It was felt that the older persons' long term and ongoing local participation in tenants' groups and other activities, and the relatively powerful position in which this placed them, helped ensure that their demands were met. They were certainly well-versed in campaigning skills: a local councillor acknowledged a readiness on the part of the local authority for example to prioritize their requests. The example lends support to concerns raised in Chapter 2 that local civic participation and interventions which aim to encourage it may not produce an equal distribution of resources and may actually perpetuate social inequalities rather than ameliorate them (Walker, 2002; Wakefield and Poland, 2005). Discrepancies in social provision between generations acquire an even sharper edge when comparisons are made between the experiences of today's East London youngsters with those of older residents when young. Youth clubs for example had at one time been able to help bestow young people with a positive sense of place identity. As an elderly Canal View man reported: 'Our club was the biggest in London, we were very proud to belong to it ... we supplied a lot of the London clubs with footballers'. The youth club at the time of the research was in contrast perceived as run down and under staffed. Canal View residents as a whole voiced a deep sense of unfairness in regard to the resource imbalance on the estate at this time; some of the young people themselves would have welcomed local access to creative pursuits, such as music making, as well as sports facilities. Creativity, through the arts and drama, as Wilby (2008) argues, can develop the talents of excluded groups and generate a climate of social inclusion.

Generational variation in local involvement can to some extent be understood as a symptom of changing local conditions and evaporating resources. Older residents appeared more likely to be involved in organizations than younger residents because they had been exposed to more opportunities for involvement in their formative years. Youth and sports clubs, experiencing everyday workplace solidarity, involvement in work social clubs or unions were activities which they believed were amongst factors shaping their commitment and motivating current involvement. While residents across the three East London estates complained that younger age groups showed little interest in organized community life, it was nevertheless clear that a recent history of a lack of investment in appropriate facilities was a contributory factor. Younger people were missing out on many of those features of an area that facilitate the exchanges which generate social capital and play a role in developing its normative sources, solidarity included. Some of those excluded from appropriate leisure activities were at the same time at risk of economic exclusion: opportunities for skilled apprenticeships were inadequate and semi-skilled opportunities, as in former manufacturing areas across Britain, had largely evaporated. East London youngsters at this time included some doubly disadvantaged in relation to health chances. They would be unlikely to realize two of the principle understandings of well-being and happiness espoused by residents: satisfying community engagement and self efficacy in the sense of achieving a better life. Despite some successes of the New Deal employment programmes established under the Labour Government, the numbers of British young people not in education, employment or training have continued to grow for some years, and there is concern that they will face elevated health risks throughout their lives (www.everychildmatters.gov.uk.ete.neet). The current economic climate together with substantial cuts being to public services (a major employer across East London) is expected to result in their predicament worsening still. They face futures where exclusion from secure employment and a decent income is a reality and where the social and therapeutic benefits to be gained from the collectivity of the workplace, unions and clubs might well be denied them. At the same time, it is now a matter of real concern that the gains made in youth provision as a result of investment made by the previous government in the last few years are likely to be eroded and youth clubs closed.

Social networks, especially important for helping to protect the health of disadvantaged people, are organic entities; their evolvement over time reflects transitions across individual lives as well as transformations of communities. Lack of work and the severed ties and reduction in income it entails had contributed to the isolation, unhappiness, and in some cases, depression of some East Londoners. This appeared to be a particular issue for middle aged residents, some of whom had difficulty re-building their networks. The problem could be exacerbated by an aspect of culture connected to what has been identified elsewhere as a tendency for the friendship ties of working class people, men especially, to be restricted to particular contexts, such as work, sport, or the pub (Allan, 1979). Nick, for example, a Canal View resident, explained that once he had stopped working he had quickly lost contact with his former work mates as their lives were no longer the same. Unemployment can act to restrict the range of contexts in which new friendships can form, and the importance of remaining milieu like the local neighbourhood acquires heightened significance. For those East Londoners without a fund of compensatory locally based networks on which to draw, loss of work could be an especially harsh social experience. Rose for example used to have extensive local ties, but over time her friends, neighbours and family had either moved away or died. She and her husband had become increasingly socially isolated, a process which had been exacerbated by recent unemployment. At the same time, their severely reduced income placed restrictions on the maintenance of their existing social ties outside the immediate locality. Unemployment, poverty and the monotony of their day-to-day lives left them feeling vulnerable and depressed. The present climate of job cuts, in which people in their fifties are generally expected to face a particular severe risk of unemployment, could be expected to produce a widening of health problems amongst this age group. The disadvantages they face are not simply connected to the phase of the life stage however but are reflective of their class position. For middle-aged people like these in East London, vulnerabilities of age group, as in the case of the young people described above, can not be considered in isolation from the liabilities of class. Nationally, middle-aged working class people face a higher risk of long term illness and premature death for example than their middle class counterparts (Acheson, 1998).

Rose and her husband, and others like them, needed assistance to find work, but, and as they acknowledged themselves, they also required help to enter more fully into the lives of their communities via access to facilities appropriate to their interests and income. Work elsewhere has suggested that the effects of unemployment, including poor psychological health, are heavily mediated by the social location of the individuals experiencing it (Gaillie et al., 1994), something which was certainly apparent in the East London studies. People who had also lost contact with former work mates but who, in contrast to this couple, had been able to replenish their social networks with new ties within the neighbourhood were in a more favourable position and beginning to enjoy life once more. Mark, for example, who though in middle years had a young family, had built on his wife's contacts with supportive neighbours to create a network of local friends who he could call upon: 'The last couple of years I've had a few bad health problems and they have been very helpful and supportive to the missus, running her to the hospital to see me and taking her shopping, looking after the kids, I couldn't have done without them'. He talked about the value he placed on the regularity of his life and the reliability of his companions, in a sense he was replacing the daily structure afforded through work with new routines. He saw his friends most days through: '... bumping into them: we've all got the same sort of habits and the same sort of lifestyles, all get up at the same sort of time, we'll pop outside with a cup of tea and see who's knocking about'. Chance encounters happened relatively frequently and easily in the streets and squares of the friendly Canal View estate, during the summer at least. Mark, along with others on the estate no longer working, dreaded the winters however when he felt more isolated and would have welcomed an informal indoor space where he could meet his friends and pursue his hobbies.

There will always remain individuals whose unhappiness and distance from local life will have much more to do with their personal circumstances and their experiences across the life course than they will with the characteristics of the places they live in. Indeed research has demonstrated that health inequalities are not confined to the effects of people's present situation, but are generated across the life course. The focus of this work is generally on material influences or behavioural and psychological risks (Graham, 2000; Davey-Smith, 2003). Several tragic life events, together with ongoing physical health problems had left Freda for example socially isolated and feeling depressed. Her overwhelming sense of loneliness and despair was striking; she had forgotten what sort of things made her happy and described being unhappy as something that 'gnaws away at you inside'. Her recollection that she had been reluctant to move on to the estate in the first place provides an illustration of the lack of control which social tenants have over life's decisions relative to homeowners (a circumstance which may well worsen with current policy changes on housing benefit), with all the negative implications for well-being which this implies. Life had taught Freda some harsh lessons; the few friends she had in the past had reportedly: 'all done the dirty' on her, for example. Her consequent distrust of others put severe limitations on the social capital she could access. Despite this, she was able to benefit nevertheless from the rich neighbourhood store of mutuality on Canal View. Her main social contact was with altruistic neighbours who invited her over each day for coffee, would fetch her paper and her shopping and generally were on hand to help. She would have been very much worse off if she had been living in a place devoid of a strong local co-operative culture.

Examples like this highlight the importance for health of local characteristics which contribute to the development of norms and expectations of help, but also point up the need for organized befriending schemes for example in areas where informal support is less readily forthcoming. An unemployed middle aged man living on the socially isolating Bridge Street for example believed that if he had been living in a more favourable and sociable environment his heart problems and depression would have been less serious, and added, with reference to a difficult time when his wife had been visiting her family in Pakistan: 'I can positively say, if I'd had someone to lean on, someone to talk to, to console me, it [my bad health] would not have gone this far ... basically, I was totally alone'.

Conclusion: Balanced lives

A thriving community life is a prominent aspect of the many meanings of well-being and happiness understood by respondents. Social capital – in its various forms – is an important dimension and a resource which accumulates and dissipates in tandem with personal, social, environmental and economic change. Yet it does not stand alone: people derive happiness and a sense of well-being from diverse sources. The continuing need on the part of individuals for supportive local relationships or for the benefits to be gained from co-operative formal or informal involvement does not supplant a desire for self efficacy, a degree of privacy, or personal advancement. Nor does a rich and valued community culture of social capital render any less necessary the help from public services needed for people to attain attributes deemed necessary for well-being. The better off in society, through access to a wider range of experiences and resources, have always had greater chances of health and happiness; a socially just society would ensure that these opportunities are more evenly distributed. Those at most risk of leading unhappy lives in the East London studies were individuals who were doubly disadvantaged, excluded from both a satisfying community life and at risk of economic exclusion. The part played by happiness and a general sense of well-being in the development of social inequalities in physical or mental health based on conventional measures becomes more transparent once we acknowledge the multifarious influences on well-being.

The greater the variety of resources in an area, the greater the possibility that diverse needs related to well-being can be met. Recent research has suggested that happiness is contagious: a study by Fowler and Christakis (2008) demonstrated that an individual's happiness is connected to the happiness of others with whom they are connected. The enjoyment to be gained here on the part of East Londoners from casual banter or from simply observing social vibrancy suggests that happiness can also be derived however from interaction with people unknown to them as well as members of a social network. Misery can in any case also be infectious; physical proximity is unlikely to be enough to raise the spirits if one's neighbours are unhappy, while, as Crisp and Robinson (2010: 57) also note, neighbours can diminish the experience of living in a deprived neighbourhood as well as advance it. Along with decent jobs and incomes, conditions helping generate happiness and contentment will, at the neighbourhood level, include good housing and quality public services, they will also involve opportunities for meeting others and pleasurable collective leisure activities. These don't have to be high profile, celebratory events: the cumulative effects of quotidian, regular occurrences on well-being and happiness should not be underestimated. Involvement in voluntary activity, despite certain important limitations, can be, as Chapter 8 will show, highly beneficial to individual well-being. A neighbourhood based social capital whether in the form of relatively high levels of participation or a thriving local culture of reciprocity is itself advanced by appropriate local resources; continued attention to improving opportunities to support both collective activity and individual needs and aspirations in deprived areas remains essential for people to achieve an equitable balance between independence and interdependence, and which may be essential if we are to be serious about the further reduction of health inequalities. A problem with the 'Happiness agenda' is that it gives scant attention to issues of equality and the distribution of resources.

8
Social Network Characteristics and Health and Well-being

Introduction

Earlier chapters provided an illustration the diversity of patterns of social ties to be found within a community; in this chapter I further explore variation in relationships between different social network characteristics and pathways and processes linked to health and well-being using a network typology grounded in the lives of the people studied. Informal and formal social ties and social activities are generally associated with better health chances but it is not generally clear which kinds of networks, differentiated by strong or weak ties, homogeneous or heterogeneous contacts, are most effective in protecting health or promoting well-being. A particular issue considered here concerns ways in which different network formations are able to maintain well-being and boost resilience to hardship and adversity. The typology developed (and outlined in Chapter 3) refers principally to the degree of similarity or dissimilarity of component ties, estimated with reference to the range of membership groups which make up the network. It also refers to interviewees' positive or negative reference groups (Bott, 1957; Merton, 1957), adopted as a way of looking at differences in attitudes towards difference and to mixing with and co-operating with others. Bott for example, had suggested a link between the degree of density of a person's network, and their social consciousness: '... the more loose knit their networks, the greater the necessity for them to use constructed reference groups, abstract categories of person, as the referents of their norms and ideology' (Bott, 1957: 223). The models used reflect structural characteristics of the network and the cultures in which they are embedded; the link they facilitate between diverse, complex and changing influences on people's lives with different processes, coping resources, values and behaviours

Box 8.1 The East London Network Typology: Structural Characteristics

The Socially Excluded Network is typified by a small number of membership groups, themselves limited in size. Examples of residents with these networks include newcomers, unemployed men, women in difficult relationships, isolated older people, single parents whose families do not live locally, carers, a refugee, and a woman who immigrated on marriage.

The Parochial Network consists of a small number of membership groups but in some cases there are extensive contacts within them. The network is generally comprised of a local extended family, plus a smaller number of local friends or neighbours. The structure is dense (most individuals within the network know one another) and the ties homogeneous.

The Traditional Network includes a larger number of membership groups relative to the Parochial group. It is made up of family, neighbours, ex workmates, old school, youth/social/sports clubs friends. The structure is dense, tight knit. Examples are mainly long term residents, predominantly older people, and a smaller number of younger residents who have worked locally and been involved in trade unions or social clubs.

The Pluralistic Network is an open network consisting of a relatively large number of membership groups. Generally the network is loose knit: friends and family are less likely to know each other than in the other models. Principal examples refer to people active in voluntary organisations, and who frequently were not born and raised locally.

The Solidaristic Network refers to a network pattern which consists of wide range of membership groups, is made up of both similar and dissimilar people and has a network structure with both dense and loose elements. These networks share some characteristics of both the Traditional and the Pluralistic models: strong local ties plus looser, weaker contacts derived from involvement in organisations and community initiatives. Individuals whose networks correspond to this model also typically have a wider range of positive reference groups than those whose network characteristics are consistent with the other four models.

make the identification of network types a useful heuristic tool. The principle focus is on individual's lives. Meanings that chronic stressors like poverty hold for people, and understandings of mechanisms which buffer their effects on well-being are also considered within the network model framework.

The social network typology

The subjects of this chapter are people living on the Dock Lane and Bridge Street estates. Residents' networks in each neighbourhood generally corresponded to five models: Socially Excluded; Parochial; Traditional; Pluralistic, and Solidarstic. Box 8.1 briefly indicates their structural elements; cultural components are described below.

The *Traditional* network is that most closely associated with a traditional working class community and culture centered around mutuality and local attachment, but also a degree of closure. The *Parochial* network is so named because it consists of people seen as similar to oneself. Local ties, particularly family ties, remain strong for people with Parochial networks, but these residents do not have some of the additional experiences shared by those in the Traditional group. In a sense the culture is more parochial; insularity is illustrated by comments such as: 'I'm not one for friends; my family are my friends'. Elements of the *Socially Excluded* network could be considered as evidence of a decline of community norms, but the picture is complex and the model incorporates a wide range of people who, temporarily or long term, have truncated social networks. Both the *Pluralistic* and *Solidaristic* models reflect wide networks and participation in organizations, but the latter are also closely integrated into the local community and tend to share some of its traditional attributes. In addition, these residents can be differentiated from others in the study with regard to aspects of social consciousness: they typically recognize some shared interests with dissimilar groups and are more likely to express solidarisitic attitudes.

Traditional patterns of social networks reflect the traditional characteristics on Dock Lane described earlier and, along with the Parochial group, are typical of the estate. Reciprocity is a dominant norm, 'looking after your own' a common expectation. Traditional network models are found on both estates, but in Bridge Street, which has not been a work based community and where attachment to place is weakened, they exist in a slightly paler form. There were families on Bridge Street for example, whose networks, values and behaviours embodied elements of the traditional model but who nevertheless, given the opportunity, would readily leave the area. On both estates social and economic change, out migration, and residents' perceptions of changing attitudes towards co-operative activity, suggest that residents in the Traditional category are a diminishing group, more typical of the older generation than those of working age.

For some Bridge Street residents, the locality is not a dominant aspect of their lives. Residents involved in tenants' groups and voluntary organizations are an exception: as on Dock Lane their networks can be loosely grouped as Pluralistic or Solidaristic. For many of the remainder, social ties are either restricted, or dispersed in some way. On both estates factors contributing to a situation where individuals' networks currently or in the past corresponded to the Socially Excluded model included personal circumstances and biographies, but on Bridge Street a lack of local trust also deterred residents from making social contacts. I will suggest later in this chapter that the coping mechanisms people adopt in response to poverty and life's difficulties can vary according to the kind of social network they have around them. There were similarities on the two estates between how residents were able to cope, but there were also differences. Innovatory coping mechanisms evident on Bridge Street included disassociating oneself from the estate by, for example, avoiding walking through it, discouraging ones children from playing outside, or establishing friendship ties in a separate locality. Some of these things were done at no small personal cost. Lucy for example retreated from the neighbourhood and distanced herself from it by focusing her attention on and keeping up appearances in the home, a tactic which she acknowledged resulted in debt and on-going anxiety.

The socially excluded network and health and well-being

A feature of the network models was that certain attributes and attitudes we recognize as health protecting or damaging were related to network type. People with the more restricted networks, for example, were more likely to express feelings associated with negative health outcomes. Many people find that their networks are restricted at certain points in their lives. They may spend much of their time at home through age, infirmity or disability; they may be new to an area with young children, or may be experiencing hostility from neighbours. Unemployment, especially long term unemployment, can also act to truncate an individual's social ties. As a transient situation, being new to an area usually has the least serious implications for well-being, and the isolation associated with it easiest to overcome, at least where local conditions are favourable for getting to know people. It was those residents not simply unable temporarily to participate in the life of their communities, but socially excluded in a wider or deeper sense that were more likely to express feelings of pessimism, powerlessness, or low self esteem, or experience aspects of stress related illness.

Some women with Socially Excluded networks linked a domineering or violent partner directly with their poor emotional health. Maggie, for example is a gregarious person living on Dock Lane, but had not always been so: 'When I was living with this violent man ... it was emotional, mental and physical stress, I was made to feel the lowest of the low ... I felt suicidal at the time, but the kids kept me going'. Feelings of powerlessness are a dominant theme of narratives like this. Heather's health, she explained: '... used to be all right 'till I married. He tried to kill me, I've left him, but it's difficult to feel free of him; he still tries to control me, and I'm still a bag of nerves'. Both women were in situations were there were few sources of support available to them. The association of negative aspects of close relationships with an increased risk of mental illness both at the time of the experience and in the future is well established (see for example, Fuhrer et al., 1999), but when social networks are restricted as in these cases, the quality of existing relationships becomes especially critical for well-being. The women's stories do in any case suggest a reciprocal relationship between a difficult partner and few contacts, as Maggie explained: 'I wasn't allowed to have friends or family round ... The situation wouldn't have been so bad to cope with if I hadn't been so isolated'. Jackie told a similar story, she had lived with a violent husband for many years: 'I wasn't allowed out; I wasn't allowed to speak to neighbours.'

Well-being improves along with developing lives and new contacts. Maggie, for example, secured a part time job and was volunteering at a local school; Jackie is divorced and involved with a tenants' group. Their trajectories call into question 'broken Britain' perspectives which equate growth in loan parenthood or divorce as evidence of a break down in family or community life: as single women, they were able to become much more integrated into the community. For other people however, problems are so deep rooted that they can be difficult to overturn. Jenny, a lone mother herself, described the plight of many of her contemporaries living on the Bridge Street estate for example. Whilst acknowledging that they had multiple problems she herself believed their main source of stress stemmed from emotional dependence on unsuitable partners:

> 'Men don't want to give up their freedom or their money; they may resent the child, but may still want to keep the woman on if another relationship doesn't work out. So [the young women] may have another baby, and hope he will stay this time. But young men these days don't want to take on responsibility. They see single parents as easy because we have a need to be loved. Then the man goes, or just comes back for sex, and the woman gets depressed. The mothers get blamed [by society as a whole] but they are just looking for love. The Government think we have just one child after another, but we really want it to work. Single parents have told me that they have had partners living with them who have brought another girlfriend back with them to the flat ... The self esteem of these women is so low that they want a man even on these terms; they are depressed, but hide it well'.

A very different kind of relationship, a caring role, can also have detrimental effects on both the carer's sense of well-being and on their social connections. John, for example, left work to care for his wife who has MS, and sees his life as dictated by his wife's requirements. His emotional life varies he says, with how well his wife treats him; he is bitter about the situation he finds himself in and can only see his situation getting worse. He does not keep in touch with his old workmates, because 'All they talk about is work, and I miss it so much'. Nasreen, also a carer, is 22 and lives with her mother. Despite having lived in the area for 17 years, Nasreen has few social contacts either on or off the Bridge Street estate, has no other relatives in this country and has never worked. She had hoped to go to University but her mother's poor health and dependence on her prevented Nasreen from taking up that option. Her mother distrusts strangers and is reluctant to accept help from others. Nasreen describes herself as deeply unhappy. For those whose circumstances mean that their networks are already likely to be restricted through family circumstances or unemployment, the impact of the area where they live is especially critical. Like Nasreen, Mejabin and her husband Rashid lead lives of utmost solitude. Apart from Mejabin's family in Pakistan, almost their only social contacts are each other and their small children. Restricted social ties operate in parallel with severely circumscribed lives. Mejabin spoke animatedly about her former life working as a teacher in Pakistan when she had a nice home with her family and lived a full life. Now she talked about her poor sense of well-being alongside the narrow confines of her current existence: 'I don't look after myself, I don't eat enough food, or get enough rest and my little boys are too attached to me. I just cook and clean; I'd like more variety in life'.

While in the last example, it is a life lived within very narrow parameters which is most striking, the health effects of isolation need to be considered also within the context of poverty and unemployment overshadowing everyday lives. Rashid was made redundant three years before I met him. His cardiac problems and anxiety are improving with treatment but he believes that a job, by promoting his inclusion, would boost his health enormously: 'Trying to come to terms with unemployment is difficult. When I worked [in a white collar job] I was part of normal life, part of society, in the mainstream of things, I was doing something for my family. It's very important for morale'. East Londoners' stories across network models indicate ways in which poverty or unemployment directly impaired their sense of personal agency and self efficacy. For Elsa for example, a young single parent on Bridge Street, being poor puts severe constraints on how she conducts her life: 'The system is in control of my life, I wait for Tuesdays, then shop, then put so much for rent, electricity etc. Any little mistake you make, and you can be in trouble. If my little girl doesn't like the food I give her then she goes hungry'. Residents like these, while acutely aware that poverty was having a direct and negative influence on their health and well-being, also recognized nevertheless that 'isolation', could exacerbate its effects. Elsa had recently split up from her partner and has few other contacts; her story illustrates how poverty, personal circumstances and negative life events could interlink to adversely affect the well-being and health related behaviour of her children as well as herself: 'When I split up, I didn't eat properly, my hair started falling out and I lost weight with the worry ... My daughter is a fussy eater: maybe it's because she's unhappy, wondering what's going on, or maybe it's because I'm not eating'.

Amongst men in the study were several who located feelings of fatalism and hopelessness in their experience of unemployment. Kevin, a Dock Lane man with a number of health problems, saw little hope of a future in which work was a part. His account of his earlier life illustrates what is often the long term nature of social exclusion as well as his individual trajectory: 'I can't read or write, but I did labouring years ago. I've been on courses but nothing ever happens, it's always the man next to you what gets the job, the man with qualifications. I bunked school, and my family didn't care. Dad chucked me out when I was eleven after Mum walked out on us. I lived on the streets for three months. Dad never reported me missing, he didn't care'. Personal disadvantage suffered across the life course has been compounded in his case by the restriction of job opportunities in the area. At the same time, he has had little opportunity to form social contacts. Some of the usual sources – childhood, school, work, or leisure activities – were truncated or non-existent. He is not a joiner of clubs, and a dramatic decline of working class pubs in his area further restricts opportunities for men like Kevin to socialize. Pressures can build up in various ways, affecting relationships with neighbours for example: 'I got into trouble from fighting with the bloke downstairs'.

Fatalism, relating to one's own life and health and the way society works in general, and political cynicism were linked in some cases. For example: 'It's a waste of time voting, they are all the same, they are there for themselves'. But poverty did not invariably go hand-in-hand with political cynicism. A man who took an interest in current affairs and expressed a number of ideas on how services could be improved, nevertheless felt powerless himself to play a part in achieving change. He described his feelings of demoralization along with the stigma which he associated with receiving benefits. The effects of his situation were, in themselves, he believed, direct obstacles to his becoming involved in local organizations: 'I don't have the power to straighten out my own life so how can I do other things [like voluntary work]. I feel helpless ... I will vote Labour though, for public services and the common person ... I want to lead a normal life, I want to work again and look after my family, but it's not under my control. When you can't do it the depression and the illness creeps in'.

Taken together, examples like these might seem to suggest that what carries most significance for pathways associated with an individual's health and well-being is not their lack of social connections, but poverty and unemployment, or the experience of a difficult relationship. Stories of close relationships, for example, were constantly interwoven with common sense understandings of health. For example: 'If they are giving you a bad time, then that's depressing. If you've got somebody good in your life, you've got everything to live for' or, 'A bad man can make life hell'. The implications however of each of these various difficulties – for feelings of self esteem, control, hope and so on – are generally more serious and have more potentially damaging effects on health and well-being where social networks are restricted. In Rashid's case for example, social exclusion, in a broad sense, was a result of his material but also social deprivation, he had few contacts outside his nuclear family and lived in a tower block with a high resident turnover and a neighbourhood depleted of everyday social capital.

The health related attributes of people with socially excluded networks can be briefly contrasted with those of residents who were able to live fuller lives. Involvement in local activities, for example, produces obvious benefits, such as: 'I'm getting out and about, I feel happier and I've lost excess weight', but participation was also readily acknowledged as having a number of additional health promoting qualities. The more highly active residents interviewed were more likely to feel in control of their lives, display high self esteem and express hope for the future than those not collectively engaged. Pre-existing good health, or feeling happy, confident and in control could well predispose participation nevertheless, while conversely, as we saw earlier, feelings of powerlessness and demoralization can inhibit action. Yet there were residents on both estates who talked about ways in which becoming involved had changed them. In some cases it had helped mend damaged lives. A young Bridge Street man believed that taking part in community projects was helping him to surmount the psychological scars left by an unhappy and abusive childhood: 'Giving is helping me to find my sense of self worth, it is helping me to move beyond my past'. For him, love is both derived and given through community activity.

Services and initiatives are a potential lifeline for some people and a means by which they can develop their friendship and support networks. In Nasreen's case for example, isolation could not be reversed overnight, but a women's project on Bridge Street was helping her to turn her life around and gradually re-build her self esteem. Though initially still very unsure of herself, working for one day a week in the project's office had given her something to look forward to and she was feeling less depressed. Families experiencing difficulties can access intensive and long term help from the Newpin centre located near Dock Lane. Some of the young mothers attending are suffering from depression; some are very lonely, or may have children with development issues. As well as developing healthy attachments between parents and children, the centre aims to build mothers' emotional well-being and encourages them to take control of their circumstances. Heather, for example, explained how Newpin was helping her: 'There are other people to talk to, I listen to their problems, and, if I have a problem, I expect them to listen to me. It helps my depression ... I used to be a shy person, but I've come out quite a lot since coming here'. Similarly, this facility is making a real difference to Deanna, a single parent with a small son living in a tiny flat where she feels under pressure from neighbours to keep him quiet. Centre workers are helping her to cope with her problems (including a partner on drugs) and to develop socially: 'I feel a different person now; I know more people and feel more confident'. They also assisted her through bereavement by supplying the kind of emotional support her existing personal ties were unable to give. For those at a different point in the life stage, very elderly people who may be experiencing more restricted social lives than when younger, regular social activities or lunch clubs such as those organized by religious groups, charities and the Local Authority, along with community transport schemes which provide help in getting there, were very much valued. A woman in her nineties explained: 'I'm happy when I'm sitting here. I like to just listen to the others talking. If you have a health problem you can tell the others about it'.

Network models and coping with poverty and life's difficulties

These observations on the relationship between network model and psycho-social mechanisms involved in well-being are not unrelated to the size of the network, especially at the extremes. However, when we look at the benefits bestowed by different networks and the forms of social capital associated with them, the picture appears more complex. Some of the Dock Lane residents with a Parochial network for example had numerically extensive social ties. This kind of network can be very good at providing practical support, or conferring identity, but may be limited in other ways. A further way of understanding relationships and processes involved suggested by the narratives is connected to the coping resources and mechanisms inherent in different network types.

Stress is generally experienced as harmful to health and well-being, and can take the form of acute stressors or 'life events' such as bereavement or divorce, chronic strains like poverty, and every day hassles (Thoits, 1995). Antonovsky (1987) highlights the importance of identifying 'health giving' or 'salutogenic' factors that can help people withstand or respond positively to difficulties in their lives. East Londoners' narratives illustrate how their social networks help them to cope with poverty and life's difficulties in different as well as similar ways. Unless they are specifically receiving help from service providers and workers in community projects, people with more restricted ties understandably find it difficult to cope, and their access to social capital may be fragile. One of Kevin's few close and supportive contacts for example was his father-in-law, whose death precipitated an episode of depression for Kevin. For some people, their day-to-day problems may be so overwhelming and their coping resources so depleted that they almost give up trying. In other cases, those involved in difficult relationships on both estates don't have access to a particular form of social capital identified by Coleman: trust embodied in the relationship between partners. In yet others, residents' social contacts may be too low in resources themselves to be able to provide support; in such cases, the more numerically restricted the networks the more serious therefore are the negative implications for well-being. Mulki for example is a widow and refugee living with her three children on Bridge Street; she has not seen her family in Somalia for many years. One of her few contacts in her neighbourhood is a fellow countrywoman. Mindful of the danger of overloading her, Mulki is reluctant to approach her friend for help however, because she too is on her own and has poor health as well as six children to bring up.

For some people, even those happily partnered, life has always been an uphill struggle. Geraldine, a Dock Lane resident in her forties (with a Parochial network) expressed it as '... never having had a chance to enjoy life'. Geraldine and her husband are unemployed, to manage she buys from catalogues, but it's coping at a cost: 'It's terribly hard to manage, I've always been hard up. I buy things for me second-hand; if I need anything for the house I have to get into debt. It's the only way to get things, out of the catalogue. It's a struggle to pay back but I rob Peter to pay Paul'. She often cries herself to sleep 'worrying how to cope, who to borrow off now'. In response to problems like debt, bereavement and relationship problems, some residents, Geraldine included, reported that they turn to smoking to cope. Giving up has been recognized as particularly difficult when your self esteem is low, when you feel powerless and pessimistic (Marsh and MacKay, 1994).

The Parochial social network and coping

Frequently, the networks of the Parochial group, through expectations of mutual aid and norms of bounded reciprocity, can work very effectively. Michelle for example, a 34 year old black East Ender, lives with her husband and four children on Dock Lane. Her main contacts are her very large local extended family: her brothers, sisters and parents as well as her in-laws all live within five minutes walk. They supply most of her and each other's needs, be it emotional, financial, or help with the children. The social capital and other coping resources accessed by people with homogeneous networks like this is clearly beneficial, but isn't always enough to meet needs. Amongst the loan parents participating in the study on Dock Lane, many of whom gained a great deal of support from their families living nearby, were several for example who were unaware of where they could get advice on benefit entitlement or obtain information about minor health problems. Their networks, involving largely 'people like us', did not facilitate access.

The loss of the strongest link in a dense social network can have a particularly adverse effect upon well-being; it can also damage the network's internal cohesion. Until her death a year before the study, Anne's mother was a great source of practical and emotional support and now Anne is lost without her: 'Mum would give me money for the children's things; she'd get me food as well when I was hard up. She was a good mother and a good friend. I've had a whole year of stress, and kidney and stomach trouble ... Mum was strong. When she died the family fell apart'. Network density can have additional drawbacks. Whilst research has demonstrated the role played by emotional support in buffering the effects of negative life events on physical and mental health (Brown and Harris, 1978; Stansfeld, 1999), for the Parochial group, the tight knit structure of their networks, illustrated by comments such as 'The family know my friends, everyone I know they know', means that network members may provide little relief in crises. People mentioned for example that other family members were too involved and distressed themselves to be supportive to each other when their parents died; such dense networks may even act to re-enforce the impact of negative events. In contrast, a widow whose networks corresponded to the Solidaristic model described how her looser contacts had helped her overcome bereavement: 'The family were a bit too close, we were all hurt ... but work was my safety valve, a life line at that time. They treat you normally, you can have a laugh and a joke with them'.

A reflection, at least in part, of a lack of opportunities for worthwhile employment or training, it transpired that early motherhood was a characteristic of most of the women interviewed with Parochial networks. A Dock Lane youth worker suggested an additional reason: 'for a lot of the young girls round here, their ambition is to have a baby, as a way of escaping from home'. In some cases (though not all) motherhood does not appear to enhance their lives, and ironically, they can still be very dependent on the families they were trying to break free from. Kathie's childhood wasn't happy, and she continues to have a difficult and at times volatile relationship with her mother. Yet she spends much of her time at her mother's home opposite her own and visits every day. She tried living away from the Dock Lane estate for a year, but found it difficult to cope on her own and continues to suffer from panic attacks and depression. Several interviewed in this group as a whole felt that having children young had curtailed their social activities as well as impairing their ability to cope. Sometimes Kim goes to bed and does not want to get up: 'I've been a mum since I was 16, sometimes I just want to be myself'. Their experiences help to explain the findings of studies which demonstrate that women who had children in their teens have an increased risk of mental illness in later life (see Henretta et al., 2008). Geraldine, a woman in her forties and mentioned earlier, had her first baby at 18. She spoke of what this meant to her in terms of the restrictions it had placed on her life: 'Life has always been hard, and I've always suffered from depression. I had my family young, so didn't see much of life, I couldn't go out clubbing it and pubbing it, I never went out and about'. The biographies of these women can be contrasted with those of residents with Traditional network patterns considered next who, when recalling their youth often drew on their recollections of the workplace to describe happy times. The timing of periods of work and having children could be a contributory factor here: research elsewhere has indicated that men and women who followed the sequence of work, then marriage, then parenting, for example, were less likely to be depressed than those who acquired these roles in other sequences (Jackson, 2004). Whilst the differences in experience and opportunities available to women across the two network models are not reducible to any single factor, employment history was nevertheless a notable feature. Chapter 4 suggested that good social relations at work helped strengthen resistance to adversity, while the supportive friendships made in the factories or docks were generally long-lasting.

Traditional social networks and coping

Those with a Traditional network type cope with their everyday lives through mutual aid. This is particularly clear in old age, when friends shop and cook for each other and family members help during illness. Food was often used as an example in stories describing the culture of co-operation amongst friends, while the exchange of food features in shared social activities, including coach outings organized by locals themselves. Audrey, a widow, has kept in touch with many of the friends she and her late husband knew when they were working in the local factories. She offered a nice definition of friendship: 'When I make a bread pudding I make one for John too. People think we're an item, but we're not, its just friendship'. Food, whilst inseparable from the co-operative norms and expectations of this group, was also frequently referred to in connection with maintaining individual good health. 'I always try to cook proper dinners', for example. Seemingly common place examples like this are worth alluding to because they contrast sharply with the narratives of some people whose networks fell into the Socially Excluded or Parochial categories: younger people in those groups especially held a somewhat ambivalent relationship to food.

The members of an individual's Traditional network have a great deal in common, they will probably have grown up in the locality, worked together in the same workplaces, gone to and continued to attend the same clubs, and may have married locals. A good level of support can usually be relied upon when needed. Pam for example is a widow in her seventies with a tight knit network of family and local friends. For help in times of illness or in emergencies, she goes to her daughter-in-law's mother who lives nearby (her son married a local girl), or to a local friend. For emotional support she has an old work friend (now living in an adjacent borough), and for particular problems like housing issues can ask a local councillor, who is also a friend. Friends were very kind when her husband died, perhaps too kind at times: 'They never left me... it was good of them, but sometimes I could have wished them to buggery, I wanted to be on my own'. Ellen, in her late sixties, was a school cleaner for 23 years, and her husband worked in the docks. She appreciates the support she receives from her family, her daughter looked after her when she came out of hospital for example, and they pay for her to have treats and outings. Families, though a prime source of support, can be a mixed blessing for the elderly. Audrey (73) is also a widow. Although her children no longer live locally, she is glad that they phone her everyday and that she is able to see them at weekends. At times nevertheless she felt that their advice was not always appropriate. She moved into new accommodation just before her husband died: 'That's why I don't like it, there are no memories here. My family slung everything out; they said I should start anew'. She is able to re-live her happy memories with old friends however at the local pensioners' club, and added: 'If I couldn't get out I'd be very unhappy'. This group have the advantage of being highly active socially. Pam and Audrey 'help out for the local Labour Party', 'It's part of the culture', explained Mavis, another older resident, 'we're all Labour round here'. Pam, Audrey and Ellen are also involved in organizing pensioners' clubs; Audrey underlined the reciprocal basis of her own activities: 'I just enjoy being with people and doing something, and making sure that other people get something to do. When I worked as a home help I saw so many who never went out or did anything, and I worried that I would be like that'.

It is not that friends are more supportive or beneficial to well-being than family ties, the help of both is valued; either at times can also be less so. People in the traditional group were better able to cope successfully partly because their lives reflected a history of coping with poverty co-operatively, but also because, when compared to people with networks narrower in scope, they had a wider range of membership groups to balance their lives. The contacts they made at work, in youth clubs or at the Docklands settlement, the social skills learnt, the self esteem they derived, the support they received – but also gave – continued throughout life, and sustained them in good times and in bad. They continue to visit each other on the estate, or meet to talk over old times in the pensioners' club, or go shopping for the more infirm. Their experiences and build up of resources like social capital over time help them to cope with everyday life and health problems.

Whilst mutual aid was central to how these traditional East Londoners managed their lives, great stress was laid on the norm of coping in adversity, 'getting on with it', taking what life throws at you and 'not making a fuss'. To admit to not feeling in control would be anathema to many. Remaining independent for example was referenced proudly by very elderly residents as an indication of their continuing ability to cope. A strong desire to avoid debt is also part of this shared culture; a valued coping strategy is to manage on your income. Younger people with Traditional networks subscribe to a similar set of values. Thirty three year old Lisa for example lives with her husband (a factory worker) and child in Dock Lane. She met some of her many contacts when she worked in a local supermarket where she was also a member of the union; others she got to know at a social club once located nearby. Lisa, like others in this group, disapproves of people who will get into debt and then have to worry over how to re-pay it. A difficulty arises however when individuals who place emphasis on the value of coping financially then get into arrears through no fault of their own. An unscrupulous loan company had landed one of the older women in the study with a debt which she has repaid many times. The stress was making her ill: 'When my husband died 10 yrs ago, I got some clothes from a catalogue ... I paid it, yet they went on demanding more and more money. I'm still paying them'. Because she feels too ashamed to tell people about it she is reluctant to seek help.

A cultural stress on coping and being strong willed is also reflected in attitudes to preventing ill health. Lisa for example, is certain that: 'Life affects health if you let it get on top of you'. Similarly, Marie refused to let local conditions on Bridge Street get her down: 'Living here ... has not affected my health. You can say yes, it is depressing and get depressed, or you can make the best of it'. Both young women explained their attitudes alongside reference to the influence of their mothers and Grandmothers, who were 'copers', both also subscribed to a strong work ethic. 'Getting on with it' and 'not making a fuss' were also sentiments typical of attitudes to managing existing health problems, amongst older residents especially. Not admitting to worrying about health is considered a virtue: 'My [bad] health has never prevented me from doing anything' said Pam. 'I don't make a habit of going to the doctors: you can get to be a hypochondriac. I don't think its right to waste the doctor's time if you can get the tablets to do it yourself'. Nevertheless, despite the desire to remain in control over health issues, attitudes can mask a strong streak of fatalism, especially where smoking is concerned.

Pluralistic social networks and coping

People with wide, Pluralistic networks cope actively: they are well informed and able to access a range of resources. Just as they believe that they have some control over their environment, and can take an active part in achieving change in the neighbourhood, they recognize that they have a role to play in protecting their health. They are aware of health promotion advice for example and generally act on it, and readily make demands on the health services. A broad range of membership groups and wider access to sources of information appear to co-exist with a positive outlook on life. Amongst the men and women with Parochial and Socially Excluded networks considered earlier expressions of political disaffection were common, and a personal lack of hope could co-exist with minimal expectations of societal change. In contrast people whose networks correspond to the Pluralistic model believe progress is possible and see a role for themselves in the process.

Bessie for example lives with her husband in one of the tower blocks on Dock Lane, and before retirement worked outside the vicinity. She chairs the tenants' association for her block and sits on various housing committees. Belinda, a single parent in her thirties, had moved to the estate from the North of England following divorce; she is highly active in a range of local tenant, regeneration, and community organizations. Women like these gain a great deal from participating and relate feeling in control of their lives to being actively involved in trying to change things for the better. Through their looser ties, they are able to access the 'information potential' form (Coleman, 1990) of social capital most effectively. Thirty year old Tessa, for example, used her contacts made through the voluntary organization where she works to find out about additional health care for her elderly mother. Tessa herself has had a number of health problems in the past, not unconnected to a problematic childhood and youth. Her health has improved since she's been working and making new friends. Gaining in confidence and self esteem is also part of the explanation: 'I've changed a lot in the last five years, its having to deal with people. I've learnt all the social skills I didn't learn at school'.

Residents in this group can, however, miss out on the kind of emotional or practical support associated with dense, closer ties, or with day-to-day neighbourly interaction. Like Bessie and Belinda, Tessa is not able to use her family as a source of support, though not in her case because of physical distance. She lives with ailing parents; trying to cope with the demands they place on her has been a long term source of anxiety for Tessa. In Bessie's case, she does not feel she could call on neighbours in her block as a source of help, explaining that 'they haven't been here long enough'. Like Bessie, Belinda also suffers from solitariness sometimes, more keenly when she considers her own situation within the local context: 'Round here its very family orientated, they all have cousins and so on locally'. Whilst she has become acquainted with a large number of local people through her formal community involvement, she knows no-one well enough to ask for support. At the same time however, she recognizes that she is someone who finds it difficult to ask for help for herself: 'I don't rely on anyone, so no-one can let me down. However, when I've had a bad week, when I've had a lot of pressure connected with meetings, and the children have been playing up, it's then that I feel isolated. I wish someone would knock on the door and say I'll have your kids for an hour. I miss having my family around to do that'. The Pluralistic group are committed to their neighbourhood, but their own sense of personal identity with the community appeared weaker than that of many others on Dock Lane; they see their fellow residents with a less rosy and sometimes critical eye. Belinda for example is hesitant about seeking help and becoming too closely absorbed in a place where, she reports, swearing and aggressive behaviour is commonplace.

Solidaristic social networks and coping

Residents whose networks correspond to the Solidaristic model cope interactively. Like the Pluralistic group, they have the advantages which being active in organizations can bring but, like those with Traditional and Parochial networks, can also access the support of close personal or neighbourhood ties. Membership groups are diverse: Lena's for example include her family, her extended family in the West Indies, neighbours, church people and fellow members of a self help group located near Bridge Street. While social networks embracing both similar and dissimilar people facilitate easier management of day-to-day life and everyday hassles, residents with Solidaristic networks are also better equipped to withstand a certain amount of stress associated with events such as break-ins and bereavement, not by 'getting on with it' but because they have built up social capital of both the thick and thin trust forms. June for example, a young mother on Dock Lane, can ask anyone – neighbours, local friends and family – for help if she is ill or needs assistance with the children: '... the first person to put their head round the door', while contacts made through the tenants' association keep her well informed and have widened her friendship ties. Her description of what she gains from involvement echoes that of many others in the study; her activities have both a buffering effect on stress and provide direct benefits to her sense of well-being: 'It makes you more aware of people's problems, and your own problems do not seem so big ... It gives you a good feeling as well, a sense of achievement that you have helped'. Local involvement, as previous chapters have demonstrated, is not consistently experienced as positive, but in such situations people with Solidaristic networks were better placed to ride difficulties as they had close supportive ties to fall back on.

The cultural characteristics of Solidaristic networks, like those of the Pluralistic, are less likely to include the parochial element common to other network models and more likely to share a vision of hope for the future. Whilst this can relate to a better life for themselves or their families, hope is also frequently expressed in terms of a better society, a more equal society for example, or a more harmonious one. Individuals are frequently involved in a wide range of organizations. Examples on Dock Lane include Chris (53) for example, a factory worker and school governor, training as a voluntary worker; Erin (34), who takes part in church activities and in her tenants' association, and Henry (78), a man involved in sports, youth and social clubs since his youth, and now active in a restoration project and the local Conservative club. Val (50) combines a close knit and long established local extended family with a diverse range of contacts met through her association with numerous organizations and initiatives such as residents' groups, a restoration project, after school clubs and other projects for children. As the chair or prime mover in a number of these, Val works hard to improve the lives and living conditions of people in the area. In common with their counterparts on Bridge Street, all of these residents talk enthusiastically about involvement opening up their social networks socially, culturally, and geographically. The rich qualities of Solidaristic networks are health promoting, people gain support from friends and family, and have access to additional forms of help and information through their looser contacts (Henry for example had just consulted the Citizens Advice Bureau for advice on a legal matter), as well as having outlets for their energies.

The active creation of social ties

The mixed membership groups of active individuals with Solidaristic networks on the Bridge Street estate, like those on Dock Lane, confer a range of health protecting and enhancing benefits. Ameira works part time and is involved in several local initiatives; she runs an after school Qur'an reading group for example. She can rely on family help with childcare; her many local friends and contacts can provide financial and emotional support or practical advice. Despite having experienced several burglaries and other neighbourhood problems, such as gangs causing trouble for her, Ameira appears happy, confident and fulfilled. She is nevertheless a-typical of people on Bridge Street in the sense that she has lived in the district all her life. In neighbourhoods like this, where long term residence is the exception rather than the rule, the active creation of social ties through participation or other means is especially important for the well-being of its residents. Denny and Jill are more representative of Bridge Street dwellers, they do not have families nearby and their close local contacts had to be actively sought out and maintained. Both had lived on the estate for about 12 years when we met, and were in their thirties: Jill is a white single parent actively engaged in tenants' and community groups; Denny is a black British mother living with her children and unemployed partner. Denny runs a credit union, does voluntary advocacy work, is taking a first aid course on the estate, and has enrolled on a college access course. Significantly, she has found that stressful problems arising from one form of involvement can be buffered by support gained through another: 'Church has given me the strength to carry on with the credit union in spite of problems, in spite of people distrusting me'. Setting up a credit union in a place where levels of trust are low, as Coleman (1990) recognized, is no easy task, but her efforts, together with help from community development workers and the regeneration agency, led to the association slowly gaining membership and support.

Residents like these also value the personal benefits they derive from the process of participation itself, not least its educative function. As Jill explained, 'I like to come away from meetings feeling that I've learnt something'. Jill emphasizes that through involvement she has acquired the confidence to seek out information to help her manage difficult aspects of her life: 'Social security controls a lot of peoples lives on the quiet. Yet I know what I'm entitled to'. Mollie, a wheelchair user living just outside the Bridge Street estate, is similarly well informed. She belongs to several disability groups, and serves on a number of committees, work which has linked her to a wide range of people, including Members of Parliament. She feels fearless in bargaining for health care and the services she needs, and associates feeling empowered with the knowledge and confidence she has gained. It is entirely possible, and probable, that Mollie possessed many of these attributes before she became involved, but she is nevertheless convinced that she has developed along with her increasing activities and become better able to cope with her disability.

Getting involved in formal and informal community ventures can have especial significance for the well-being and quality of life of vulnerable individuals. A resident whose long term and wide involvement on Bridge Street had given her a particular insight suggested that active involvement can give those with unhappy backgrounds a reason for living. People for whom such comments might be appropriate include Celia, an asylum seeker in her late thirties with a highly traumatized past. Her husband and child are dead; she suffered abuse on the estate at the hands of fellow countrymen from opposing political factions and, when I met her, continued to fear for her life. Celia is on the management committee of a local initiative for women; helps deliver meals to homeless people, and has 'adopted' an old lady via age concern who she takes to church. Her involvement, she believes, has given her the strength to face the future. What is conspicuous about her case is not simply that a Solidaristic network can be actively created with help from service providers and voluntary groups as well as through Celia's own efforts, or that it carries real therapeutic benefits, but that some of the loose ties she began to make have rapidly become closer. Her experience highlights the fluidity of our social connections: distinctions between categories of 'bonding', 'bridging' or 'linking' ties soften and blur when real life cases are confronted. When she arrived in Bridge Street from another but less well-resourced local estate Celia received assistance from a number of local organizations including the Women's Project, a local Church and Victim Support as well as an Educational Visitor, who were also able to put her in touch with appropriate national and international bodies. Workers and volunteers from the Women's Project helped her to move flats, and she very much valued the emotional support she was continuing to receive from them: 'They have made me feel loved'.

Celia's case stands out from the ordinary, but more quotidian examples are equally significant for illustrating the potential of weak ties to grow in strength. Doreen for example has been on the estate for more than 20 years, and is probably the most heavily involved resident activist and volunteer on the Bridge Street estate. Like Celia, she spoke of ways in which loose ties gained from regular and intense involvement can over time become closer and stronger. She can turn to her immediate family for support, but also to the members of the regeneration steering group: 'It's really like an extended family in many ways, and like families, you do get disagreements, but we sort it out'. The family analogy was also used by participating residents in self help groups to convey a sense of the closeness of the relationships they have made. Lena's involvement in a disability resource centre for example, not only helps her to cope with her health problems, but does much to confirm a positive self image and confer a sense of identity, attributes we normally associate with 'bonding' ties: 'It's like a family, everyone helps one another. We are all people with a disability; it gives you a sense of it being alright'.

When Durkheim (1952) urged us to seek the key to well-being in an equilibrium of moral forces, he was referring to society as a whole. One might suppose, nevertheless, that the individual's social networks which would be most health promoting would reflect, or be capable of conferring, a balance between the principles of altruism and egoism he identified. People with mixed networks would act both in the interest of others and themselves. A pathway for achieving a beneficial balance became evident in the cases described above where ties made through working for the common good in turn become sources of personal support. In other cases, people emphasized the reciprocal nature of their involvement: they derived therapeutic benefit from activities targeted at helping others. Such equivalence is not always readily attainable however. While for Durkheim, 'intervening institutions' would act to redress increasing societal trends towards egoism and anomie by encouraging altruism, a minority of active East London residents believed that at times they did too much for others. They felt overloaded by the demands placed on them, spoke of feeling out of control, and reported that their health suffered. For Val for example, voluntary activities had become a full-time and demanding but unpaid job. Another case is that of Agnes, a nun whose order is committed to the poor. She works to encourage self help projects on Dock Lane and on initiatives to assist refugees. Agnes is usually in excellent health, but has suffered from exhaustion when continually putting the needs of others before her own, and links the suppression of her own needs, such as her wish to visit her family in Ireland, with feeling out of control at times.

Religious orders which value sacrifice and self denial and engender excesses of altruism on the part of their members may make for extreme cases, but volunteering more generally can have an exploitative, negative side, as in Val's case. Where reciprocity was an associational norm however, the trade-off with self interest could be more easily achieved. Participation in self help groups, such as an association for West African women and their children which encouraged co-operation via a wide range of activities and acts as a source of mutual support, seemed to be particularly beneficial to the quality of life of its members. With so many commitments, it could be expected that Vilma for example, who is divorced and has four children, would be suffering from overload: 'On a typical day I wake at five, do a cleaning job for two hours, come home, take the little one to school, then I go to work at the Benefits office'. Her health and sense of well-being are however, excellent. She feels that she gains as much as she gives from her relationship with the Association. She derives satisfaction from helping others in difficulties, enjoys the many social activities organized, and has received practical help herself in the form of a financial loan at a time when she had difficulty in feeding her children.

Reference groups, social consciousness and perceptions of inequality

Previous chapters have detailed some of the ways in which local features can influence the nature and structure of residents' social networks; at this point I want to draw attention to the role played in network formation by individuals' values and attitudes towards similarity and difference. The perspective has relevance for well-being in the sense that, as this chapter has shown, different benefits or disbenefits can accrue from networks made up of similar or dissimilar others, but also because identity issues could have significance for our understanding of relationships between people's perceptions of inequality and their health and well-being. If such perceptions are detrimental to health, as Wilkinson (1996) argues, then perceived homogeneity (Gans, 1961) might well be crucial. Robert Merton for example, suggested that individuals see themselves as deprived or privileged by comparing their own situation with that of other groups, reference groups (Merton, 1957).

A feature which distinguishes respondents interviewed with Solidaristic networks from many of those whose ties correspond to different models was their readiness to identify interests in common with a diverse range of groups. For some, this was a form of social consciousness coupled with a class orientation of society. Conversely, those with a narrower range of positive reference groups tend to see themselves in competition with people who they perceive as different from themselves, but who on many counts are little different. Residents were critical of people getting higher social security benefits than themselves, the person in the post office queue getting a better pension, someone with a bigger council house, or who had managed to get a job. These are poor people too, but are seen to be less deserving. Sometimes ethnicity is an issue, or age, or being a newcomer. Those with a broader range of positive reference groups however do not see the lines of division as quite so close. Frequently motivated by political or religious beliefs or by particular life experiences they tend to see inequalities between rich and poor as the important ones, and those between social classes.

Vilma for example reported: 'I have black and white friends, Jamaican and African friends, and workmates ... I mix with anybody, I believe in being friendly and loving one another'. She divided Britain into two main groups: '... the Tories and the rest'. Similarly, Agnes, when describing her own identity with local people avoided drawing cultural or social distinctions within the neighbourhood itself: 'I see the poor and unemployed here, both ethnic groups and native East Enders. They are wonderful people, I love them; they are a people apart, a culture of their own'. She added: 'The more ethnic groups you have in a society, the richer it will be'. People like these on both estates are as committed to their community as the residents with Parochial and Traditional networks, but here, the community is wider, much less exclusive, much more inclusive. Erin for example empathizes with families who neighbours find troublesome and who might more broadly be viewed as 'undeserving', living the kind of family life sometimes invoked by politicians as evidence of a 'broken Britain'. Discovering a religious faith along with increasing community involvement had prompted a change in her attitudes:

> 'I started to see things differently. You care about people more, other than friends and family. Round here its "you look after your own, don't let others take liberties". Now I look further a-field, I don't judge people. We had a rowdy family here in the flats but I realized they must have had problems, and may need help'.

In most cases the direction of the relationship between local involvement and wide positive reference groups is not readily obvious. Solidarity emerges in residents' narratives as an interactive process involving values and action, and operating within a context of heterogeneous social networks. Participation, where it opens up the breadth of social ties, can for some people encourage altered attitudes. Doreen's experience of housing regeneration activities for example, suggests that positive reference groups grow along with expanding membership groups; that identifying shared interests and developing tolerant attitudes happens in tandem: 'Obviously there are groups that you tend to be a little bit wary of, but when you get to know and understand their cultures, that tends to go, when you find that they are working for the community as a whole'. Nevertheless, a propensity to see others like oneself is in some cases likely to have preceded involvement. When asked to elaborate on their personal value systems, as well as drawing on political or religious convictions, people refer to both wider life experiences when compared to that of others and to shared experience of specific disadvantage. In the first case, having mixed race in the family was mentioned for example, as was varied employment experience, making them: 'not as blinkered as some people from round here'. In the second case, people looked back to particularly difficult times in their lives. Jill, for example, explained how she learnt about extreme poverty and inequality:

> 'Britain isn't fair, so many have untold amount of money, so many are poor. I did a week as a homeless person once ... I got so fed up at the time, so depressed; people treated me like scum, as a lesser person. Some made advances towards me for prostitution ... My health suffered of course; I was starving, and caught bronchitis ... That's why I want to help people'.

Jill's experience may have been fairly exceptional in the context of this study, but her sentiments were not. An especially prominent shared feature of these diverse narratives concerned a repeated reference to the role played by perceptions of inequality and hatred of the injustice people saw around them in shaping their outlook and motivating action. For example: 'I've seen such wealth, and such poverty, such inequality. The children round here are so poor ... I can do something to help'; 'Everyone should be treated the same, everyone treated equally, young or old, rich or poor, black or white'. Some drew on childhood experience to illustrate the source of their convictions: 'Anger has driven me' explained a woman recalling the hardship experienced by families when dockworkers were laid off. These residents want to see a fairer, more equal society. They express strong opinions on class distinctions, monetary greed, and the vilification of the unemployed; whilst perceptions of Britain as unjust is by no means something that differentiates them from others in the study, their interpretation of unfairness and inequality, together with a strong sense of collective agency, do. Their aspirations for a better society include a Britain, for example 'working in harmony', and embracing 'more understanding of each others cultures'. A particular focus of their hopes is on what they see as a growing divide between rich and poor. A typical comment was, for example: 'I'd like to see the poor being able to live a better life and have an average standard of living ... The rich do alright, they don't know how the poor live'.

Conclusion

Social networks mediate and moderate the harsh circumstances of people's lives and their experience of health and well-being; the social processes involved differ across network models. Patterns of networks, made up of dense or weak, homogeneous or heterogeneous ties involving 'thick' or 'thin' forms of trust and associated norms were shown to have distinct implications for psycho social pathways involved in health effects; they were also linked to different coping resources and responses to adversity. The flexible and mixed network structure characteristic of the Solidarity group placed them in a particularly advantageous position. These residents created and maintained strong and weak ties – bonding, bridging, and linking – which were able to complement one another.

The network models, to no small extent, reflect the social richness or impoverishment of lives lived. People with Traditional networks for example, had good times to look back on; the clubs they frequented in their childhood and youth were fondly remembered, as were the wider availability of jobs and plentiful contact with workmates outside work. Despite problems, they continued to refer to aspects of their lives which they were currently enjoying. Amongst people whose networks were more restricted there were those who had little to say about times when life had been good. Poverty and unemployment; having children when very young; difficult relationships with partners, together made for lives characterized by struggle. Nevertheless, lives change with new opportunities and resources. With the help of service providers and workers in community projects, or through engagement in self help groups or local organizations, some people had been able to move on from isolated and unhappy phases of their lives and were able to contrast their well-being favourably with their earlier experience.

The approach adopted here aids understanding of the processes involved in the protective influence of social ties on well-being. Network types, whilst in part shaped by resources and opportunities available, also reflect individual and collective values and attitudes; these in turn can be a reflection of the social ties accessed. Social consciousness for example is involved in a dual relationship with structural characteristics of an individual's social networks. Although the direction of relationships can sometimes be inferred from the narrative data, relationships appeared essentially dynamic. The critique of social capital for its circularity (Portes, 1998) is persuasive, but what is important nevertheless, is that these relationships are recognized as sometimes recursive. Health giving hope, the East London research indicates for example, can be a source as well as a function of social capital.

When people's understandings of poverty and inequality were considered, it became apparent that deprivation can be both a cause of hopelessness and a spur to social action. Much depends on how the structure of inequality is perceived and on the nature of the response. An internalized response, for example, feelings of passivity, acceptance, shame and hopelessness, are clearly harmful to a sense of well-being; holding a vision of something better however along with co-operative and collective action, can frequently be highly beneficial. The indication that those with a narrow range of positive reference groups see themselves in competition with similarly poor people, resonates with Runciman's (1966) work on relative deprivation, in which he suggested that people's perceptions of deprivation and understandings of class consciousness vary according to the social comparisons they make. It also reflects contemporary modes of class analysis which discuss ways in which, rather than drawing hierarchal contrasts, people draw comparisons with others in a similar situation to themselves (Savage, 2000: 159; Bottero, 2004). Conversely, however, the East London research has also shown that where strong perceptions of inequality between rich and poor do exist, residents may be motivated to take co-operative action which carries the potential for benefiting health and well-being directly, and also indirectly through the expansion and broadening of their social ties.

9

Conclusions: Poverty, Community and Health in the 'Good Society'

Varying local communities

Where we live and what it can offer contributes to the uneven distribution of health chances; by the same token, investment at the local level can alleviate wider structural inequality and its effects. Certain groups of people – those on low incomes, at certain stages of the life phase or at vulnerable times of their lives – tend to be more reliant than others on the local arena and its resources. Where local conditions are favourable, life chances can be enhanced; where inadequate, vulnerabilities are compounded. The part played by a general sense of well-being in the development of social inequalities in physical or mental health based on conventional measures, and in disparities between poor areas themselves, becomes more transparent once we acknowledge the multifarious influences on well-being and happiness and the particular significance of resources in poor areas needed to support different aspects of people's lives.

A particular focus of this book has been on the role played by co-operative local social ties in maintaining health and well-being. When people talked about their understanding and experience of health, recalled happy or unhappy times in their lives, or elaborated on what 'community' meant to them, their comprehensions of these separate issues, when compared, indicated a great deal of conceptual common ground. The local community had by no means become peripheral to East Londoners everyday lives nor, they believed, to their happiness and well-being. It was demonstrated that specific neighbourhood characteristics, in helping to mould the connections between people, influence community life and the nature of social capital within a locality. One of the housing estates considered, Dock Lane, was an area of 'thick trust', to some extent a 'traditional' community despite the adverse effects of economic change; the

Bridge Street area was one of 'thin trust', of looser connections derived from participation in regeneration activities and resistance to what had been rapidly worsening local conditions. Canal View, the third example, was unusual, a place with both a high degree of reciprocity and participation, a locale with potential to combine the social and therapeutic advantages of both community models.

Strong community loyalties and a shared sense of history were instrumental in the resilience of a positive community spirit on Dock Lane. The norm of reciprocity and the strong, dense and supportive 'bonding', but at times also exclusive and excluding ties involved typified the setting. Components of community life here were able to nurture health and well-being by providing access to mutually supportive relationships but also by enabling individuals to maintain 'ontological security' (Giddens, 1990) through meeting needs for a sense of local identity, belonging, and safety, and for a degree of constancy in the physical and social environment. The substance and sense of community on Dock Lane, though less strong than it once was, had been sustained into the present. The estate had been remarkably resilient in the face of neglect, but a strong local culture like this will weaken unless the norms continue to be capable of transmission to newer residents and younger people. The population was still relatively stable when researched, and the design of much of the housing remained neighbour-friendly, but additional local resources and facilities which had furnished opportunities for social engagement had, as in many locales in Britain, been allowed to dwindle.

The economic, social and commercial history of East London is reflected in ways in which social capital accumulates or dissipates across the lives of individuals and their communities. The Dock Lane case highlights some of the generational changes in community life experienced in former industrial and manufacturing areas. Middle aged and older people had more opportunities to lead sociable and happy local lives when young than many young people in poor areas today. They experienced plentiful local jobs, there were clubs and trade unions to get involved in, and they were able to access a much more generous provision of local commercial and leisure facilities and had more meeting places of various kinds. They also expected to be able to remain in the neighbourhood if they chose to do so. The continuing agency of this age group and in some cases their influence on younger residents contributed, in no small part, to the community's resilience; for the next generation, its future looked less certain.

On Dock Lane positive perception of local people were a major source of commitment and residential stability, but on Bridge Street neighbourhood relationships more typically involved distrust and suspicion, with family dispersal and strain rather than a local supportive extended family, anomie as opposed to a strong local culture, and alienation instead of attachment to and pride in the community and its history. Community initiatives were helping to encourage people to develop their social networks, but for most individuals everyday forms of mutuality were harder to develop and sustain in an area where, for example, the residential population was highly unstable. The collective mobilization of a group of residents demonstrated nevertheless that Bridge Street was an estate which showed remarkable resistance in the face of its neglected infrastructure and impoverished community life. The consequence was a less conservative, more dynamic form of community, with less reliance on strong ties, but instead involving weaker bridging ties to dissimilar groups, and linking ties to those with more power and authority. By taking part in collective activities, individual residents not only experienced directly beneficial effects to their sense of well-being and happiness but, and unlike non-participants, gained the confidence to resist the estate's negative, demoralizing, and consequently health damaging, image.

The Bridge Street case underlines the fallaciousness of arguments which place blame for community decline simply on the behaviour of poor and vulnerable people themselves: local conditions had been unable to support aspects of a thriving community life. It provides little evidence to support notions of a contagion or miasma effect evident in discourse on 'concentrated poverty', on the development of values and behaviour associated with 'underclass' or indeed with declining social capital. Rather than the concentration of the poor appearing to be the problem, it was an alienating and poorly resourced physical environment interacting with the stigmatized reputation of the area and its people which contributed to isolating residents from each other, restricted the flow of information, and acted as a block to the development of trust or a local day to day co-operative culture. Conversely, different local resources and conditions which included for example, the intensive efforts of community development officers working closely with service providers and regeneration agencies, had helped bring different groups of people together to actively construct a more emancipatory, solidaristic and inclusive form of community life.

Canal View was an area unusually rich in social capital. Satisfaction with the visual quality of the area and with certain local facilities and public services like primary health care (and national satisfaction with the Health Service had increased markedly during Labour's term of office (Toynbee and Walker, 2010), together with appropriate housing allocation policies had encouraged population stability, a prime source of social capital. Traditional housing design and attractive outdoor areas facilitating social interaction were amongst factors which, as on many parts of Dock Lane, encouraged neighbourly help and co-operative child care and assisted in maintaining a degree of informal social control and perceptions of neighbourhood safety. Residents of all ages placed a high value on the reciprocal relationships they had formed between local friends and neighbours, but the strength of the culture of mutuality on the estate was such that it constituted what Coleman (1990) had referred to as a neighbourhood store of social capital, accessible over and above an individual's personal ties by those in particular need.

Although rates of volunteering are generally not high in Britain, and lower in working class areas than in middle class neighbourhoods, on Canal View, a long term history of local volunteering, the co-operative structure of tenant management and associated perceptions of grass-roots ownership, along with a desire to maintain the gains to the physical environment made through collective action, all encouraged relatively wide formal involvement. It was a blurring of distinctions between formal (or civic) and informal (or social) participation which was especially notable here however: involvement in some informal settings can be enjoyable and motivate people to try additional forms of volunteering.

Social capital's limitations

In the ideal society William Morris (1884) envisaged, by participating in small communities people would be encouraged to exercise their talents both for their own health and happiness and for the good of their communities. In East London, individuals involved in community organizations gained in self esteem, self efficacy and a sense of achievement; from opportunities to acquire new skills and make new contacts, and from a renewed sense of optimism. Some limitations to involvement were nevertheless noted in relation to both individual and collective rewards. Firstly, participation when co-opted by Governments, regeneration bodies and other official agencies becomes in some contexts less radical and emancipatory an entity than it was for Morris, for whom self government went hand-in-hand with happiness. For some Canal View residents for example, involvement had become, not a source of empowerment (an important facet of our well-being) but of stress when they felt that they were expected to give legitimacy to decisions made elsewhere. While for participating individuals across the estates the merits of involvement overall tend to outweigh the disadvantages, there were nevertheless additional drawbacks for highly active residents, some of whom felt overburdened, exploited and resentful. Equivocation on the benefits to well-being and happiness were less evident however when people recounted their experience of grassroots activities, self help groups or more informal kinds of participation.

Secondly, while residents' involvement in tenants' groups, campaigns, projects and other voluntary activities produces real gains for the community in terms of an improved environment or in strengthened local commitment, in instances where participation is largely directed towards narrowly defined interests, there is always a danger of some groups gaining disproportionately, that one group's empowerment becomes another's loss, and that the participation of some becomes a source of resentment amongst others. A third, and related issue, is that even in social capital-rich places there remain people excluded from satisfying social relations. On Dock Lane for example a strong local culture of reciprocity was experienced as excluding by some newcomers. In other cases, and across physical contexts, individuals without access to social capital are often people excluded in a wider sense also. The experience of young people without expectations of worthwhile employment and recently unemployed middle aged people who had been unable to replenish lost workplace ties, was used to underline the effects of overlapping disadvantages on well-being.

Whilst older residents in each area complained that younger age groups showed little interest in organized community life, believing them to be more materialistic and focused on personal advancement than were previous generations, behavioural change can to some extent be understood as a symptom of changing local conditions and evaporating resources. A serious under-funding of localized provision for teenagers could help explain national statistics which indicate that young people aged 16 to 29 are less likely than other age groups to feel civically engaged (ONS, 2002). Older residents also appeared more likely to be involved in organizations than younger residents because their present activity was often rooted in their experiences of work and the local facilities of the past. For some people, workplaces emerged as locales for motivating lifelong commitment. Writing nearly 100 years ago, G. D. H. Cole (1919) believed participation in the workplace to be a precondition for involvement elsewhere; these East London residents learnt to participate, not through industrial democracy as Cole had expected, but in unions or factory social clubs, as well as in the youth clubs they had once frequented. They were simply continuing with a part of their lives which had always been important to them. By contrast, for today's young people, the immediate prospect looks bleak and joyless: the advances made in youth provision in deprived areas over the last few years, such as those associated with

Labour's My Place programme (Toynbee, 2011), are already falling victim to cuts. Youngsters excluded from appropriate leisure activities are at the same time at risk of economic exclusion: in 2010 the unemployment rate among those aged 16–24 stood at 20 per cent (Parekh et al., 2010). The axing of youth employment schemes could be expected to result in their situation becoming even more desperate, while the National Council for Voluntary Youth Services are alarmed that too little attention is being given to the cumulative effects of cuts for young people (Williams, 2011).

A fourth limitation to the significance for well-being of a locally sourced social capital is that there will always remain individuals whose unhappiness and distance from local life will have much more to do with their personal circumstances and their experiences across the life course than they will with the characteristics of the places they live in. Nevertheless, vulnerable people living in an area devoid of a rich neighbourhood store of mutuality were in a worse position than people living in an area where features of community life were capable of ameliorating the effects of disadvantage on health. Taken as a whole, rather than judging place-based communities and the traditional norms and forms of activity we associate with them as an irrelevance in the modern world, those taking part in the East London studies continued to voice their appreciation of the advantages entailed in localized manifestations of community. Overall understandings require some further qualification, nonetheless. In the first place, while residents' perceptions of what community means to them touch on a complexity of issues, they also differ markedly between those who value it as a social and cultural entity involving interaction between and co-operation with similar others, and those for whom inclusiveness and diversity are requisite and welcome components. In the second place, community based social capital is privileged as a key dimension of individuals' well-being and health, but understandings need nevertheless to be considered alongside additional and more material issues touched on in this context.

Community as a source of solidarity

In addressing questions on the potential of the local arena as a source of more inclusive social networks and wider solidarity as opposed to a setting for conflict and division, particular consideration was given to the degree of heterogeneity of residents' social networks and the factors which help shape it. It was suggested that the distinction made by social capitalists between bonding and bridging ties, though meaningful, is not in itself wholly capable of capturing the reality of social life in a given locality. When talking about factors which deepened their sense of community for example people make frequent reference not only to strong bonding ties, but to weaker ties associated with a casual street life. At times public places could be sites of negative engagement and distress, but for most people, opportunities for casual encounters afforded through quite mundane features of the built environment, especially in places where they feel comfortable to linger, helped sustain a sense of personal inclusion.

A more generous provision of facilities which attract people across social groupings, especially where they provide opportunities for light-hearted exchanges, have potential to help shape social consciousness of a more inclusive kind in today's diverse neighbourhoods. Opportunities for intermingling alone however will be unlikely to overcome pre-existing tensions, rivalries between different sections of the population, or strongly held discriminatory attitudes, at least in the short term. It would be unrealistic to infer mechanistic relationships between sites of association – however well resourced – and open networks or integration. Our values are not reducible to any single influences, yet there were residents in all three neighbourhoods who located their own tolerant attitudes at least in part in having opportunities to mix with dissimilar others: attending school meetings or chatting to parents at the school gates; working or volunteering in a multi-ethnic environment; attending mother and toddler clubs, toy libraries, play buses and family centres; enrolling in courses, or joining in social activities organized through tenants' groups and social clubs. Tolerance or mutual regard may not in themselves readily lead to social integration or blossom into organic solidarity, but will at least be amongst important prerequisites. For example, having fun together, recognized as a key dimension of East End community spirit, while experienced as directly enjoyable, also binds people together and to the area they live in. In some, deliberately inclusive, contexts, collectively organized social activities, in helping to make connections between dissimilar individuals in terms of age, ethnicity, or length of residence, show promise for the development of new forms of community consciousness whilst continuing to embrace and build on valued elements of the old.

The significance of formal participation for developing organic forms of solidarity showed some variance according to context. Chapter 2 began by briefly locating social capital in a longer tradition of social thought. Cole for example, considered formalized links between associations and co-operatives as essential for 'associational socialism' (Hirst, 1990; Cole, 1920), a pragmatic approach which contrasts with Westergaard's idealist proposition that vision is necessary to extend solidarity's boundaries (Westergaard, 1975). The Bridge Street case lends some support to both, and indicates recursive relationships. Dissimilar participants were united and motivated by a common regeneration aim and a shared vision of the estate's future, while structures which enabled a diverse range of voluntary and self help groups to come together in regeneration and other community activities (though not on the scale envisaged by Cole), were generally recognized as budding fora for building bridges and developing solidaristic attitudes. Cohesion and division can co-exist within the same setting however, or may assume different forms: in the Canal View case, the legacy of regeneration had been paradoxically to both strengthen social relationships within the neighbourhood and to solidify divisions between opposing interest groups. The case highlights a circumstance in which participation can sharpen distrust where narrower group interest rather than shared vision is a powerful motivator for action. Governments tend to assume that processes of participation are invariably harmonious, but excessive localism carries real dangers as well as rewards: it is capable of producing, not necessarily a 'big society', but a more divided, fragmented and unfair one instead.

Hostilities on Canal View were not a reflection of poor social relations between different ethnic or cultural groups but between former pro and anti-regeneration campaigners. A co-incidence of entrenched attitudes with a geographic polarization was significant here, and is something which has parallels with those parts of Britain where for example ethnic or class segregation takes a more distinctly spatial form than is generally the case in London. Protagonists lived on opposite sides of the estate; each had their own tenants' groups and separate community activities, circumstances which offered few opportunities for inter-mingling and shifting intransigent attitudes. While in contrast, grassroots campaigns like those set up in response to the threat of loss from re-development of a multi-ethnic East London market or a valued church, both of which tapped into valued aspects of local history and culture, do have greater evident potential for transforming social consciousness, co-operation for the common good though formal participation does not always happen without assistance. The Bridge Street experience underlines a key role for community development workers and service providers working co-operatively in helping to develop more organic forms of solidarity at the local level.

Preceding chapters, in exploring social capital's key sources: population stability; social inclusion; integration; self interest, ideology and solidarity, noted some evident tension between the need for stability of the social structure for the social inclusion of individuals and a sense of community on the one hand, and the fluidity concomitant with neighbourhood integration on the other. It is not necessarily the case however that the normative frameworks of community, and integration and cohesion, are universally oppositional. Rather, the bonding, bridging, and linking ties, the channels through which different dimensions of social capital emerge can more helpfully be seen as complementary rather than conflictual. For communities to be inclusive and integrative, but also sustainable, a range of local resources are needed to both encourage contact and meet varied needs. The advantages to community life of greater social engagement are many. To take a few examples, by getting to know long term residents a proud local culture can be more rapidly absorbed by newcomers whose own motivation to belong is then strengthened. Conversely, in settings with a stigmatized reputation, meeting places, especially of an informal kind where people can spend time laughing and joking with others, help break down the distrust and suspicion between residents which can typify social relations in such places. The benefits are not restricted to improved social relations: environments which bring people together are also appreciated for the contribution they make to the maintenance of a sense of well-being. The shared and collective use of public places while providing opportunities for consolidating supportive ties can also have more directly therapeutic qualities: smiling at or sharing a laugh with passers by; exploring shared memories with members of a social club; engaging in gossip and exchanging information while visiting a market, waiting at the school gates or queuing at the Bakers or just simply feeling part of the social vibrancy in a busy place, can all be cheering, just as can 'sticking up for' workmates on the factory floor.

A frequently noted feature of the traditional communities of the past in contemporary discourse (and one sometimes used to invalidate the relevance of concepts of community for today), concerns their population homogeneity. Features such as the much wider range of local resources and opportunities for involvement compared to today and which contributed to their strength (see Frankenberg, 1966; Dennis et al., 1956), are given much less prominence. References to a facet of social organization occurring regularly in East Londoners' narratives concerned the local labour market: plentiful local work in the past clearly differentiated generational experience. People lacking experience of a work based history of collective action will be less likely to be subject to influences associated with fostering a collectivist ethos. Whilst the thick trust and conditional solidarity of past working class communities developed under conditions where their populations were generally made up of white manual workers and their families; some of today's heterogeneous and now increasingly work poor neighbourhoods are in danger of being deprived, not only of an important potential source of integration, but excluded from opportunities to develop alternative values to individualism as well.

Well-being, community and individualism

The approach to 'well-being' and 'happiness' embracing communal and collective dimensions of life adopted here largely originates in the ideas of William Morris for whom fraternity and co-operation were indispensable requirements for happiness, and of Karl Marx who understood its antithesis as separation from each other and dislocation from our true selves. The growth of individualism in modern societies is generally discredited by social scientists as socially and psychologically destructive, but the concepts of 'community' and 'individualism' were not always used by East Londoners in a way that suggested they believed them to be oppositional. People talk about deriving happiness and a sense of well-being from diverse sources: a continuing need for mutually supportive local relationships or appreciation of the benefits to be gained from involvement do not supplant a desire for independence for example, for self efficacy, or a degree of privacy, nor especially for personal advancement or a better standard of living. Nor does a rich and valued co-operative culture obviate the necessity for assistance from essential public services for people to attain those additional attributes they deem necessary for their well-being, whether in the form of career advice and training opportunities for example, help in accessing benefits and for coping with relationship and family problems, or in the case of elderly or infirm residents, support in helping them to maintain autonomy and cope successfully with day-to-day tasks. As Bowling argued recently, understanding the drivers of well-being across age groups is of high policy importance (Bowling, 2010). Social capital involving reciprocal aid, participation and trusting relationships is in any case itself advanced by appropriate resources, services, and opportunities. Community is not something that can be considered in isolation from the local infrastructure. The design and quality of the built environment can encourage social interaction for example, while some services and initiatives, in providing help, advice and support are a potential lifeline for some people and a means by which they can move on from isolated and unhappy phases of their lives and develop their friendship ties. Over the next few years we face unprecedented cuts in the funding of local authorities and other public bodies. But continued, rather than reduced, investment at the local level to support collective activity on the one hand, and individual needs and aspirations on the other remains essential if people are to achieve an equitable balance between interdependence and independence, between the common interest and self interest which Durkheim recognized as key to our health and well-being. Those at most risk of leading unhappy and unhealthy lives in the East London studies were individuals who were doubly disadvantaged, excluded from satisfying community relationships and unable to do what they wanted to do in life.

No silver bullet can single handedly deliver happiness for all, but the greater the variety of resources and amenities within a vicinity, the greater the possibility that diverse needs related to well-being discussed throughout this book will be met. These are the same conditions required to help balance a desire for community with that for social integration: adequate resources will always be necessary to help make communities inclusive, integrative and sustainable. It is not being suggested however that the strength of the effects of local characteristics is such that extraneous influences (whether structural or cultural), or individual experience over the lifespan, are minimized. Nor is there an implicit assertion that area based initiatives should take precedence over national, universalistic interventions to reduce poverty and inequality. A low income has direct and serious effects on health and well-being; recent research illustrates the importance of getting right the national policies designed to reduce poverty. A rise in child tax credit and child benefit were responsible for a fall in 2010 in the number of children living in poverty in workless families to its lowest level since 1984, for instance (Parekh et al., 2010). Taking current government policy into account, the Institute of Fiscal Studies now predict a worrying increase in child and working age poverty between 2010–2013 (Brewer and Joyce, 2010). Nevertheless, within neighbourhoods, local resources and amenities have a substantial role to play in encouraging people to lead the kind of full and varied lives which, as William Morris also insisted, are vital for our well-being.

Social network models

Whilst mindful of the multiplicity of factors that can directly affect the health of people living in poor areas, the principle conclusions reached in this book are that (i) social networks are significant mediators and key moderators between the harsh circumstances of people's lives and their lived experience of health and well-being, and that (ii) the processes involved in these relationships can vary with different network formations. Network models differentiated by internal features such as strength, density and homogeneity showed variation in the health giving factors they bestowed. Whilst the 'networks of experience' identified in Chapter 8: *Socially Excluded; Parochial; Traditional; Pluralistic, and Solidaristic,* capture structural constraints and opportunities, they also embody aspects of human agency – cultures, values, meanings and responses to adversity. In this way social networks can be seen to perform a significant but dual role in processes involved in health inequalities. They provide a link between macro and micro factors, what C. Wright Mills (2000) described as the relation of personal troubles of milieu to public issues of social structure, but at the same time, can be part of the process of coping with or resisting structural inequality.

The distinct structural and cultural dimensions of different network patterns said much about variation in the general sense of well-being of people with low incomes, and about the ways in which they were able to negotiate stressful events and ongoing problems. For example, certain attributes and attitudes we recognize as health protecting or damaging – such as hope, fatalism, pessimism, self esteem and perceptions of control, as well as companionship and social support available – were related to network model. The effects of problems known to increase risk of poor health, such as difficult close relationships, problematic neighbours or the experience of bereavement, as well as those more directly related to lower social class – poor housing, unemployment and poverty – are exacerbated for people whose social networks are numerically restricted, or, if more extensive, narrow in scope in terms of the heterogeneity of their make up. While more extensive social ties are generally recognized as related to better health chances, when the benefits bestowed by different network patterns, and the forms of social capital associated with them were considered, the relationship was shown to be more complicated. The numerically extensive social ties (made up of family members and neighbours) of people with 'Parochial' networks for example were usually very effective in providing practical support, or conferring identity, but could nevertheless be limited in other ways, in providing coping resources for a wider array of needs for example. At the same time, the tight knit internal structure of the Parochial network meant that members could provide little relief in times of family crises. People with 'Traditional' social networks were better able to cope successfully partly because their lives reflected a history of coping with poverty co-operatively, but also because, when compared to those with networks narrower in scope, they had a wider range of membership groups to balance their lives. The contacts they made at work or in social clubs, along with the social skills learnt, the self esteem derived, and the support they received – but also gave – continued throughout life, and sustained them.

People with wide, 'Pluralistic' networks cope actively: through the looser ties made via involvement in local organizations, they are well informed and able to access a range of resources. Just as they believe that they have some control over their environment, and can take an active part in achieving change in the neighbourhood, they recognize that they have a role to play in protecting their health. A broad range of membership groups and wider access to sources of information co-exist with a positive outlook on life. The mixed membership groups of active individuals with 'Solidaristic' networks confer a range of health protecting and therapeutic benefits. Like the Pluralistic group, residents whose networks correspond to this model have the advantages to well-being which being active in organizations can bring, but like those with Traditional and Parochial networks, can also access the support of close personal or neighbourhood ties. Taking the typology as a whole, the more varied the make up of a network, the greater the range of resources accessible, and the greater the potential benefits for health. The flexible, fluid and mixed network structure characteristic of the Solidarity group placed them in a particularly advantageous position; these residents actively created and maintained strong and weak ties – bonding, bridging, and linking – which were able to augment one another for example. An additional and distinguishing feature of the Solidaristic group concerned their wide range of positive reference groups.

It could be argued that the processes within network models described here and based on constituent membership groups are simply a reflection of the class structure, and that, by focusing on an array of coping and other resources, the typology is capturing some of the ways in which class based health inequalities are created and structured. Almost all of those taking part in the studies however were from semi skilled and unskilled backgrounds, many were unemployed, and all were managing on low incomes. That is not to say that distributional issues were insignificant – they were – or that what is being described and inferred does not refer to nuances in a hierarchal system of social classes: a certain level of pre-existing personal and collective resources make it easier to build social capital, for example. It can much more difficult to find the motivation to mix or become involved locally if other aspects of one's life – such as poor housing or personal problems as well as low income – dominate everyday existence. Slight differences evident in material and personal advantages however cannot totally explain the overall patterns in social networks and their relationship to well-being found here, nor can they explain differences between estates. The models do nevertheless capture transformations in working class experience: they are concerned with communities of place, time and structure as well as the members of those communities on whose experiences and perceptions they are founded. The distinction between the Parochial and Traditional network types for instance, reflects changes in opportunities for forming and maintaining social connections, such as decline of local work, trade unions and social clubs. Additionally, an apparent paucity of residents on one estate (Bridge Street) whose networks corresponded to the Parochial group is an indication of contemporaneous neighbourhood effects, and highlights the vulnerability of social capital to the negative effects of certain distinctive local characteristics, a high population turnover included.

For the individuals concerned, the social network models are on one level an expression of two class related factors: social consciousness and the richness and impoverishment of lives lived. A feature which distinguishes people with a Solidaristic network is a propensity to perceive more people as similar to themselves in some way and a readiness to identify interests in common with a diverse range of groups. Often these were attitudes coupled with a class orientation of society. Work on health inequalities is generally concerned with objective measures of social class and linked features such as the distribution of material resources. The narrative data utilized here enabled consideration also of more subjective dimensions and understandings of class embracing perceptions of inequality and poverty, class consciousness, and social identity.

Wilkinson and Picket (2010) have highlighted the effects of inequality across multiple aspects of our lives. Their comprehensive treatment of international evidence in 'The Spirit Level' makes an irrefutable case for strong links between greater societal equality and better physical and mental health. 'Poverty, Community and Health' has suggested additional or alternative explanations concerning the processes involved to those they propose however. In the Wilkinson model, the relationship between inequality and health operates through psychological mechanisms such as shame, disrespect, social anxiety and perceptions of inferiority induced by interacting with people of higher social status (Wilkinson, 1999, 2001). Such mechanisms are significant for some individuals and in some contexts, but the emphasis on status, which appears to rely chiefly on a deferential conservative model of class relations (see Lockwood, 1966), is an approach which the narrative data used here suggests has less applicability as a generizable interpretation of what happens amongst populations in poor areas. It was interesting that perceptions of being a 'second class citizen' were overturned in some cases by the offer of a decent home on Bridge Street and by residential involvement in consultation processes. It was the distribution of resources together with perceptions of a degree of control over decision making which were amongst the important factors at play here. Chapter 8 indicated that perceptions of inequality can in any case have positive as well as negative health effects; deprivation can be both a source of hopelessness and a spur to social action. The ways in which people perceive inequality to be structured – the forms of social division pinpointed, the range of people identified with – is relevant to these outcomes, as is the nature of the response to inequality and deprivation. There are likely to be a multitude of possible responses, including a range of individualistic, creative and eccentric reactions necessary to any vibrant and tolerant society, but two in particular can be mentioned here. A reaction involving, for example, feelings of passivity, defeatism, and hopelessness, is clearly harmful to a sense of well-being, but an externalized response, a vision of something better, along with co-operative and collective action, can frequently be highly beneficial to the individual concerned, as it is to the community they live in.

Those with a narrower range of positive reference groups tend to see themselves in competition with people who they perceive as different from themselves, poor people too, but seen as less deserving. Being at the sharp end of a situation where resources are scarce can be an important influence on ways in which people rationalize and express their ideas on unfair aspects of society. When there aren't enough homes suitable for families, for example, or incomes are totally inadequate for needs, or where the local labour market is contracting, positive reference groups in some cases become narrowed and negative ones expand. Those whose personal value systems encourage a willingness to mix with a broad range of people see the lines of division differently however. They tend to consider inequalities between rich and poor as the important ones, and between social classes. It is where strong perceptions of inequality between rich and poor exist that people are frequently motivated to take co-operative action to achieve change.

The second, and perhaps most essential feature of the social network typology is that models are a manifestation of the richness or impoverishment of lives lived, a reflection of the variegation or invariability of experience. For example, for those whose patterns of ties correspond to the Socially Excluded model, most of whom were unemployed, it was lives lived within very narrow parameters which was most striking, and sparse sources of pleasure. Work elsewhere has shown that many teenage mothers find motherhood a positive experience (Duncan, 2007), but several of the women in the Parochial group for example felt that having children young, and before they had been able to spend time employed, had severely curtailed their social activities as well as impairing their ability to cope and affecting their emotional health. When their biographies were contrasted with those of women and men with Traditional network patterns, the latter, when recalling their youth, often drew on their recollections of the workplace to describe happy times. Good social relations at work helped strengthen resistance to adversity while supportive friendships made in the docks and factories were generally long lasting.

East Londoners with Pluralistic and Solidaristic networks had plentiful outlets for their energies and interests, and talked enthusiastically for example about participation opening up their social networks socially, culturally, and geographically. On the whole they identified a wider range of social, economic, environmental and political circumstances which they believed could affect our health than others in the study, some believed 'staying in a rut' to be especially damaging. They had – and took – opportunities to ensure that they did not stay in one. William Morris might have empathized with these examples: it is the very variety of life, he believed, which is pivotal to our happiness and well-being. For Morris, variety of life was as much an aim of the ideal society as equality of condition (Morris, 1974). His ideas on the state as dispensable are less convincing nevertheless: Morris's utopianism gave us little sense of how his ideal egalitarian, co-operative communities would be achieved. The better off in society, through access to a wider range of experiences and resources, have always had better chances of health and happiness; a government truly committed to social justice would make it a priority to ensure that these opportunities are much more evenly distributed.

Some implications of current policy agendas for poverty, community and health

By enabling local authorities to take action that will contribute to the social, environmental or economic well-being of people living or working in their area beyond their normal statutory duties, the 'power of well-being', introduced in the Local Government Act 2001, would have made a useful starting point for developing policy designed to maximize opportunities for sustaining and improving individuals' health and well-being. It marked a shift away from the problems people face towards what can promote positive outcomes (ODPM, 2005a; LSE and the Young Foundation, 2006). In the Current policy climate however, cash strapped councils faced with losses in the area based grant allocated to deprived areas and having to make draconian cuts to services, are not in a strong position to adopt this kind of approach. In a context of continuing health inequalities in Britain, it is also regrettable that the coalition government have decided not to take forward those provisions in the Equalities Act (Government Equalities Office, 2010) which placed a duty on councils and other public bodies to consider the impact of their policies on the poor. Despite Government rhetoric on fairness, it's a political stance that does not equate fairness with equality. The relevant section of the legislation, if retained, would have had solid potential for protecting the health and well-being of poorest groups, especially if utilized perhaps alongside related policy developments and ideas in this area. A report on the measurement of economic performance and social progress (Stiglitz et al., 2009) called on world leaders to move away from purely economic measures of national well-being; in Britain, the Prime Minister, David Cameron, has launched the Happiness Index. Developed by the Office for National Statistics, from April 2011 questions based on the index are being added to the General Household Survey to measure aspects of our quality of life and well-being (Grice, 2010; McVeigh, 2011). While the focus of the research is to be welcomed, in the context of the subject matter of this book, of complex interrelationships between poverty, community and health, its utility will depend upon whether questions adequately reflect the multiplicity of influences on and people's diverse understandings of happiness and give careful consideration to social, material and individualistic needs. Its efficacy will also hinge on how the results will be acted upon if the index is not simply to become a smokescreen for any disproportionately detrimental effects that Coalition policies may have on the poorest people and poorest places in this country.

The frontiers of the state are being enthusiastically rolled back post 2010 under a cloak of economic necessity and deficit reduction. Many of the current policy initiatives and announcements of changes coming into force before 2015 have alarmingly negative implications for people on low incomes, for the resources and services available in the places they live in, and for the sustainability and vibrancy of their communities. With growth in unemployment resulting from public sector redundancies, for example; a cap on housing benefits in the private rental sector; increases on VAT; the freezing of child benefit and proposed changes to disability allowance and tax credits, levels of poverty are widely expected to increase and the circumstances of the vulnerable to grow considerably harsher. Analysis by the Institute for Fiscal Studies (2010) for example indicates that changes would take the greatest toll on individuals and families with the lowest incomes. At the same time, research indicates that councils facing the most draconian funding cuts are largely those in the poorest areas (Sigoma, 2010), while current NHS reforms, it has been suggested, could themselves widen existing inequalities in health provision (Davis, 2011). Taken together, policy changes appear to make a growth in social inequalities in health almost inevitable. Taylor-Gooby and Stoker's assessment of the Coalition's programme leads them to argue that it involves '... rolling back the state to a level of intervention below that of the United States – something which is unprecedented', and that it will bring both rewards and penalties that '... are potentially greater than under any previous government in this country' (Taylor-Gooby and Stoker, 2011: 14).

In 1945 the widespread notion that we are 'all in this together' encouraged the British people to support policy change in the direction of greater equality. In the 2010s, the same rallying call is being used, not to enhance solidarity, but this time to the opposite effect, to influence attitudes in a way that renders acceptable the effects of austerity measures on the poorest. We are once again being urged to despise the 'feckless' and 'undeserving'. Despite a climate of severe austerity, in the late 1940s, it was the poorest in society who made the biggest gains from the Attlee Administration's radical policy agenda; today the situation is reversed: the poorest, and women, appear to be taking the hardest hits. The implications of this degree of apparent callousness on behalf of the coalition government for widening health inequalities are clear. We could be remorselessly approaching a situation which, if Frederick Engels (1845) were analysing it today, he might well describe as 'social murder', a phrase he used in the 1840s to accuse the government of the day of indifference to the well documented sufferings, bad health and premature mortality of the most deprived.

Thriving networks in strong, co-operative communities ameliorate the effects of disadvantage; any disproportionate diminishment of community life in poor neighbourhoods therefore could be expected to further slow improvement in narrowing health inequalities. Social capital is in no small part contingent on the distribution of resources, facilities and services, some of which are now facing severe restrictions. Local authorities are having to consider making reductions in front line services like day centres and home-care, not to mention community essentials such as youth, sports and luncheon clubs and children's play areas (Hasan, 2010; Gentleman, 2011). An equally critical issue stems from the organic nature of community cultures: any disruption to the stability of the resident population threatens the neighbourhood store of social capital. Some aspects of new housing policy may have positive outcomes in this context, in particular the greater local discretion being given to local authorities to set rules on who is included on housing waiting lists, but others will almost certainly be more harmful. A cap on housing benefits for private sector tenants and the threatened overturn of the right to security of tenure in social housing are likely, if implemented widely, to seriously undermine community sustainability. The present Conservative-led government demonstrates little awareness of the importance of stable communities to the quality of life of people in working class areas, and shows scant recognition of the policies needed to support them. The harms done will not be restricted to the effects on community life and reciprocal cultures: feelings of insecurity and loss of control over life's decisions can also more directly erode health and well-being.

Policies falling under the umbrella of the 'big society' however would seem to have more positive potential, at least on the surface. The Prime Minister, David Cameron, wants to see a society where British people are brought together '... to improve life for themselves, their families and their communities' (Cameron, 2010: 32). The government aim to place more power in the hands of local people and encourage a strong culture of volunteerism and philanthropy (Maude, 2010). The Localism Bill, for example, gives community groups the right to take over local facilities and services (www.communities.gov.uk). Despite some important limitations concerning issues of equity, empowerment and community conflict discussed in earlier chapters, involvement in local organizations and activities strengthens community life where conditions are appropriate and support is available, and frequently benefits the well-being of participating individuals. But the 'big society' is, for its advocates, an expression of an anti-statist political tradition (Norman, 2010); the Prime Minister wishes to free people from 'the stifling clutch of state control' (Cameron, 2010: 32). It is fallacious nonetheless to expect the voluntarism and localism of an imagined 'big society' to be able in any way to lesson the requirement for effective public provision at the local level, or for a more equitable distribution of opportunities for involvement. In the charity and voluntary sector for example, the very community organizations that could be expected to help usher in the new Britain are finding their grants chopped (NCVO, 2010). The big society, if it happens at all – and there is little indication of widespread public demand for people to say, run their own services for example – will have a much greater chance of taking off in places with well resourced, strong communities than in those increasingly impoverished and undermined. Without extra investment in disadvantaged areas, the 'big society' can only be a potentially regressive policy agenda.

The 'good society' and buoyant, synergetic communities

Contemporary thought on the 'good society' shares some common ground with the 'big society', the latter has annexed an appreciation of mutualism and co-operatives for example more usually associated with a socialist tradition (Miliband, 2010), but there are also fundamental differences. The good society refers to a set of ideas which seek a radical alterative to the ideology of neo-liberalism; it seeks a new politics of the common good (Sandel, 2010) based on social justice, solidarity and a reinvigorated social democracy. Maurice Glasman, for example, places the good society within the Labour political tradition: 'Distinctive Labour values are rooted in relationships, in practices that strengthen an ethical life. Practices like reciprocity, which gives substantive form to freedom and equality in an active relationship of give and take; or mutuality, where we share the benefits and burdens of association. And then, if trust is established, solidarity, where we actively share our fate with other people' (Glasman, 2010: 31). Issues around individual well-being and happiness are now being alluded to by politicians and political analysts alongside reference to the good society. For Jon Cruddas, for example, the good society: '... signals a movement dedicated to social justice and intellectual freedom [but also to] the desire for self-realization' (Cruddas, 2010: 16), while the creation of the good society argue Lawson and Harris, '... starts where people are stressed, stretched, anxious, insecure, tired and alienated' (Lawson and Harris, 2010: 33). The sociologist Zygmund Bauman has voiced appreciation of Ed Miliband's awareness that '... the quality of society and the cohesion of community need to be measured not by totals and averages, but by the well-being of the weakest (Ramesh, 2010: 1).

While we may have little sense of what a 'good society' would look like, it needs a vision, as Rutherford suggests, that engages with our everyday lives (Rutherford, 2010). Additionally, it is difficult to see the dismantled state of the 'big society' as a feature of a more egalitarian and solidaristic good society. Such a society, I propose, whilst it must embrace a vision of thriving, participative and nurturing communities, will also rely on nurtured and well resourced place based communities as essential components. Together with sustained political commitment to fiscal, welfare and economic policies aimed at the reduction of poverty and unemployment, it is important that the political project of creating the good society acknowledges the part to be played by an inclusive community life in moving towards the eventual eradication of social inequalities in health. The social networks of people living in buoyant, vibrant communities will include strong ties providing reciprocal aid and a sense of community, but would also embrace freer, outward looking ties. The latter will be both a reflection of and a function of the propensity to seek and recognize shared interests with those outside the immediate primary or interest group. Members of these networks might share and develop sets of countervailing values which, ideally, would run counter to the extremes of both individualism and collectivism, and contribute to a society where people are better able to achieve an equitable balance between independence and interdependence, between values centered on common interest and self interest and which, as Durkheim believed, hold the key to a society's health and well-being.

The local community can be a potential arena for the growth of solidarity and hope, but it cannot achieve paradigm change alone, and excessive localism, as indicated earlier, carries its own hazards. Democratic and essentially outward linking structures are essential for flourishing 'synergetic communities'. G.D.H. Cole's associational ideas have relevance here: while the utopianism of Morris gave us a vision of what could be, Cole's approach was more pragmatic. He believed that an essential precondition for effective political participation was participation and genuine power sharing in all aspects of social and economic life. He was sensitive to the dangers of excessive collectivism however, in Cole's schema there would be no compulsion (Hirst, 1990). We need to give continued and more considered attention to the desirability of creating new structures to support co-operatives and community organizations, democratize participation to ensure representativeness, but also to formalize connections with wider decision making bodies. David Miliband's 'Movement for Change' which involves the training of community organizers across

Britain could, incidentally, be a potentially positive development in this respect. Both the structure of the co-operative community networks, and the values which both nurture and grow from them are likely to have a positive impact on the well-being of individuals and their communities. In addition, these outward looking structures, in empowering, carry the potential of making the eventual realization of redistributive goals a less distant prospect.

It would be mistaken to expect too much of localism alone in fostering synergetic communities, and concerns have been raised by the head of the Civil Service, Sir Gus O'Donnell, about potentially negative impacts of the localism bill on parliamentary democracy and ministerial accountability (Curtis, 2011). The argument is no longer about big government versus small government, but about appropriate balances between local activity and a strong state and well resourced public sector, or, as Cruddas and Nahles (2009) argue, a balance between a strong centre and effective power at the local level. All of this will involve forging new relationships between civil society and the state. Cole provided a detailed outline of how a participatory society might be organized: his small communities and their various co-operatives and associations would have democratic, structural links with the wider social, political and economic society (Cole, 1920; Hirst, 1990). In policy terms, working towards new structures could be a constructive starting point for helping address issues around how we can combine universal standards and a national framework for the reduction of poverty and social inequalities in the distribution of resources, opportunities and health chances, with fine-grained local initiatives and forms of democratic input which recognize and adapt to the different needs of diverse areas.

Encouraging participation in conditions of endemic inequality nonetheless remains a difficult enterprise. Under such circumstances, Judt (2010) cogently argued, other desirable goals become hard to achieve, while too great a gap between rich and poor, undermines solidarity (Sandel, 2010). When Richard Tawney (1931) argued that what matters to the health of society is the objective towards which its face is set, he was urging us, and particularly our governments, to choose equality. In doing so we would be half way to choosing solidarity as well. Yet the power of capital still rides roughshod over utopian ideas and progressive politics. Governments, but also movements, must find ways of curbing the greed of those Hutton (2010) calls the 'undeserving rich'; moves in the right direction include the emphasis – if belated – now being placed by politicians including David Miliband and Jon Cruddas (2010) on the need to seek a change in relationships between the state and the market, while grassroots action targeted at, for example, corporate tax avoidance, or campaigning on the part of coalitions of community organizations like London Citizens for a living wage appear to be leading the way in terms of influencing public consciousness. As well as recognizing the need to strengthen the democratic institutions of self-government, London Citizen's Maurice Glasman calls for: '... an organized resistance to the logic of finance capitalism' (Glasman, 2010: 37), and 'democratic resistance to the domination of capital through the pursuit of the common good' Glasman (2011: 24)). Ralph Miliband had no difficulty in identifying what the essential ingredients of a good society were: 'There are many people ... who are moved by the vision of a new social order in which democracy, egalitarianism and co-operation – the essential values of socialism – would be the prevailing values of social organization. It is in the growth in their numbers and in the success of their struggles that lies the best hope for humankind (Miliband, 1994b: 194–5).

Bibliography

Abbott, S. (2010) 'Social Capital and Health: The Role of Participation', *Social Theory and Health*, 8 (1): 51–65.

Acheson, Sir D. (1998) *Independent Inquiry into Inequalities in Health*, London: HMSO.

Afridi, A. (2011) *Social Networks: Their Role in Addressing Poverty*, York: Joseph Rowntree Foundation.

Airey, L. (2003) '"Nae as nice a scheme as it used to be": Lay Accounts of Neighbourhood Incivilities and Well-being', *Health & Place*, 9 (2): 129–37.

Allan, G. (1996) *Kinship and Friendship in Modern Britain*, Oxford: Oxford University Press.

Allcorn, H. and Marsh, C. M. (1975) 'Communities of What', in M. Bulmer (ed.) *Working Class Images of Society*, London: Routledge, pp. 206–18.

Almedom, A. S. (2005) 'Social Capital and Mental Health: An Interdisciplinary Review of Primary Evidence', *Social Science and Medicine*, 61 (5): 943–64.

Amin, A. (2006) 'The Good City', *Urban Studies*, 43 (5/6): 1009–23.

Antonovsky, A. (1987) *Unraveling the Mystery of Health: How People Manage Stress and Stay Well*, San Francisco: Jossey-Bass.

Atkinson, D. (1994) *Radical Urban Solutions: Urban Renaissance for City Schools and Communities*, London; New York: Cassell.

Atkinson, R. and Kintrea, K. (2004) '"Opportunities and Despair, It's All in There" Practitioner Experiences and Explanations of Area Effects and Life Chances', *Sociology*, 38 (3): 437–55.

Bacon, N., Brophy, M., Mguni, N., Mulgan, G. and Shnadro, A. (2010) *The State of Happiness: Can Public Policy Shape People's Well-being and Resilience?* London: The Young Foundation.

Baldwin, P. (1990) *The Politics of Social Solidarity*, Cambridge: Cambridge University Press.

Bamfield, L. and Horton, T. (2009) *Understanding Attitudes to Tackling Economic Inequality*, York: Joseph Rowntree Foundation.

Batty, E., Beatty, C., Foden, M., Lawless, P., Pearson, S. and Wilson, I. (2010) *Involving Local People in Regeneration: Evidence from the New Deal for Communities Programme*, Sheffield: Centre for Regional Economic and Social Research, Sheffield Hallam University/London: DCLG.

Bauman, Z. (1998) *Work, Consumerism and the New Poor*, Buckingham: Open University Press.

Bauman, Z. (2001) *Community: Seeking Safety in an Insecure World*, Cambridge: Polity.

Becker, H. S. (1966) *Introduction to 'The Jack Roller' by C. Shaw*, Chicago: University of Chicago Press, pp. v–xvii.

Beckworth, D. (2009) 'Inequalities in Health and Community-oriented Social Work: Lessons from Cuba?' *International Journal Social Work*, 52 (4): 499–511.

Bell, C. and Newby, H. (1971) *Community Studies*, London: Allen & Unwin.

Bell, D. (1993) *Communitarianism and its Critics*, Oxford: Oxford University Press.

Beresford, P., Green, D., Lister, R. and Woodard, K. (1999) *Poverty First Hand: Poor People Speak for Themselves*, London: CPAG.

Berkman, L. and Breslaw, L. (1983) *Health and Ways of Living: The Alameda County Study*, Oxford: Oxford University Press.

Berkman, L. and Glass, T. (2000) 'Social Integration, Social Networks, Social Support, and Health', in L. F. Berkman and I. Kawachi (eds) *Social Epidemiology*, New York: Oxford University Press, pp. 137–73.

Berthoud, R. (2003) *Multiple Disadvantage in Employment: A Quantitative Analysis*, York: York Publishing Services.

Berthoud, R., Blekesaune, M. and Hancock, R. (2009) 'Ageing, Income and Living Standards: Evidence from the British Household Panel Survey', *Ageing and Society*, 29 (7): 1105–22.

Black, Sir D. (Chair) (1980/1982) *Inequalities in Health: The Black Report*, Harmondsworth: Penguin.

Blair, T. (1996) *New Britain*, London: Fourth Estate.

Blauner, R. (1964) *Alienation and Freedom*, Chicago: University of Chicago Press.

Blaxter, M. (1990) *Health and Lifestyles*, London: Tavistock/Routledge.

Blaxter, M. (2004) *Health*, Cambridge: Polity.

Blaxter, M. and Poland, F. (2002) 'Moving Beyond the Survey in Exploring Social Capital', in C. Swann and. A. Morgan (eds) *Social Capital for Health: Insights from Qualitative Research*, London: Health Development Agency, pp. 87–107.

Booth, C. J. (1889–1891) *Life and Labour of the People in London*, London: Macmillan.

Boseley, S. (2008) 'Sure Start Success in Helping Children of Poor Families Hailed', *Guardian*, 7 November: 12.

Bothwell, S. E., Gindroz, R. and Lang, R. (1998) 'Restoring Community through Traditional Neighbourhood Design', *Housing Policy Debate*, 9 (1): 89–114.

Bott, E. (1957) *Family and Social Network*, London: Tavistock.

Bottero, W. (2004) 'Class Identities and the Identity of Class', *Sociology*, 38 (5): 985–1003.

Bourdieu, P. (1986) 'The Forms of Capital', in J. G. Richardson (ed.) *Handbook of Theory and Research for the Sociology of Education*, New York: Greenwood Press, pp. 241–58.

Bowling, A. (1991) *Measuring Health: A Review of Quality of Life Measurement Scales*, Buckingham: Open University Press.

Bowling, A. (2010) 'Do Older and Younger People Differ in Their Reported Well-being? A National Survey of Adults in Britain', *Family Practice*, 28 (2): 145–55.

Bradshaw, J. (2000) 'The Relationship between Poverty and Social Exclusion in Britain', *Conference of the International Association for Research in Income and Wealth, Cracow*, 27 August–2 September.

Brannen, J. and Nilsen, A. (2006) 'From Fatherhood to Fathering: Transmission and Change among British Fathers in Four Generation Families', *Sociology*, 40 (2): 335–52.

Brewer, M. and Joyce, R. (2010) *Child and Working Age Poverty Set to Rise in Next Three Years*, Press release, London: IFS.

Bridge, G. and Watson, S. (2002) 'Lest Power be Forgotten: Networks, Division and Difference in the City', *The Sociological Review*, 50 (4): 505–18.

Brown, G .W. and Harris, T. (1978) *Social Origins of Depression*, London: Tavistock.

Brownhill, S. and Darke, J. (1998) *"Rich Mix": Inclusive Strategies for Urban Regeneration*, Bristol: Policy Press.

Bulmer, M. (1975) 'Sociological Models of the Mining Community', *Sociological Review*, 23: 61–92.

Bulmer, M. (1984) 'Concepts in the Analysis of Qualitative Data', in M. Bulmer (ed.) *Sociological Research Methods: An Introduction*, 2nd ed., Basingstoke: Macmillan, pp. 241–62.

Bulmer, M. (1986) *Neighbours: The Work of Philip Abrams*, Cambridge: Cambridge University Press.

Bunting, M. (2007) 'Britain is at Last Waking Up to the Politics of Well-being', *Guardian*, 20 February: 31.

Byrne, D. (1999) *Social Exclusion*, Buckingham: Open University Press.

Calvo-Armengol, A. and Jackson, M. O. (2004) 'The Effects of Social Networks on Employment and Inequality', *The American Economic Review*, 94 (3): 426–54.

Cameron, D. (2010) 'This is a Radical Revolt against the Statist Approach of Big Government', *Observer*, 18 April: 32.

Campbell, B. (1993) *Goliath: Britain's Dangerous Places*, London: Methuen.

Candy. B., Cattell, V., Clark, C. and Stansfeld, S. (2007) 'The Health Impact of Policy Interventions Tackling the Social Determinants of Common Mental Disorder: A Systematic Review', *Journal of Public Mental Health*, 6 (2): 28–39.

Carpiano, R. M. (2007) 'Neighbourhood Social Capital and Adult Health: An Empirical Test of a Bourdieu based Model, *Health and Place*, 13 (3): 639–55.

Castells, M. (1997) *The Power of Identity*, Oxford: Blackwell.

Cattell, V. (1995) *Community, Equality and Health: Positive Communities for Positive Health and Well-being*? London: Middlesex University, Occasional Paper, School of Sociology and Social Policy.

Cattell, V. (1997) *London's Other River: People, Employment and Poverty in the Lea Valley*. London: Middlesex University, Social Policy Research Centre.

Cattell, V. (1998) *Poverty, Community and Health: Social Networks as Mediators between Poverty and Well-being*. Unpublished PhD thesis, London: University of Middlesex.

Cattell, V. (2001) 'Poor People, Poor Places, and Poor Health: The Mediating Role of Social Networks and Social Capital', *Social Science and Medicine*, 52 (10): 1501–16.

Cattell, V. (2003) 'Social Networks as Mediators Between the Harsh Circumstances of People's Lives and Their Lived Experience of Health and Wellbeing', in C. Phillipson, G. Allan and D. Morgan (eds) *Social Networks and Social Exclusion: Sociological and Policy Perspectives*, London: Ashgate, pp. 142–61.

Cattell, V. (2004) 'Having a Laugh and Mucking in Together: Using Social Capital to Explore Dynamics between Structure and Agency in the Context of Declining and Regenerated Neighbourhoods', *Sociology*, 38 (5): 945–63.

Cattell, V., Dines, N., Gesler, W. and Curtis, S. (2008) 'Mingling, Observing and Lingering: Everyday Public Spaces and Their Implications for Well-being and Social Relations', *Health and Place*, 14 (3): 544–61.

Cattell, V. and Evans, M. (1999) *Neighbourhood Images in East London: Social Capital and Social Networks on Two East London Estates*, York: Joseph Rowntree Foundation.

Cattell, V. and Herring, R. (2002a) 'Social Capital, Generations and Health in East London', in C. Swann and A. Morgan (eds) *Social Capital for Health:*

Insights from Qualitative Research, London: Health Development Agency/NICE, pp. 61–85.

Cattell, V. and Herring, R. (2002b) 'Social Capital and Well-being: Generations in an East London Neighbourhood', *Journal of Mental Health Promotion*, 1 (3): 8–19.

Ceballo, R. and McLoyd, V. C. (2002) 'Social Support and Parenting in Poor, Dangerous Neighbourhoods', *Child Development*, 73 (4): 1310–21.

Chida, Y. and Steptoe, A. (2008) 'Positive Psychological Well-being and Mortality: A Quantitative Review of Prospective Observational Studies', *Psychosomatic Medicine*, 70 (7): 741–56.

Clarke, C., Myron, R., Stansfeld, S. and Candy, B. (2007) 'A Systematic Review of the Effect of the Built and Physical Environment on Mental Health', *Journal of Public Mental Health*, 6 (2): 14–27.

Coates, K. and Silburn, R. (1970) *Poverty: The Forgotten Englishman*, Harmondsworth: Penguin.

Coburn, D. (2000) 'Income Inequality, Social Cohesion and the Health Status of Populations: The Role of Neo-Liberalism', *Social Science and Medicine*, 51 (1): 135–46.

Cohen, A. P. (1982) *Belonging: Identity and Social Organization in British Rural Cultures*, Manchester: Manchester University Press.

Cohen, A. P. (1985) *The Symbolic Construction of Community*, Chichester: Ellis Horwood.

Cohen, R., Coxall, J., Graig, G. and Sadiq-Sangster, A. (1992) *Hardship Britain: Being Poor in the 1990s*, London: Child Poverty Action Group.

Cohen, S. and Syme, S. L. (eds) (1985) *Social Support and Health*, Orlando: Academic Press.

Cole, G. D. H. (1919) *Self Government in Industry*, London: Bell.

Cole, G. D. H. (1920) *Guild Socialism Re-stated*, London: Leonard Parsons.

Coleman, J. S. (1990) *Foundations of Social Theory*, Cambridge, Mass: Harvard University Press.

Confederation of British Industry (2007) *Just What the Doctor Ordered: Better GP Services*, London: CBI.

Conradson, D. (2005) 'Landscape, Care and the Relational Self: Therapeutic Encounters in Rural England', *Health and Place*, 11 (4): 337–48.

Cooke, G. and Lawton, K. (2008) *A Study of the Low Paid and the 'Working Poor'*, London: Institute of Public Policy Research.

Cooper, C. (2008) *Community, Conflict and the State: Rethinking Notions of 'Safety', 'Cohesion' and 'Wellbeing'*, Basingstoke: Palgrave Macmillan.

Cornwell, J. (1984) *Hard Earned Lives: Accounts of Health and Illness from East London*, London: Tavistock.

Crisp, R. and Robinson, D. (2010) *Family, Friends and Neigbours: Social Relations and Support in Six Low Income Neighbourhoods*, Sheffield: Centre for Regional Economic and Social Research.

Croft, S. and Beresford, P. (1992) 'The Politics of Participation', *Critical Social Policy*, 35: 20–44.

Crow, G. (2000) 'Developing Sociological Arguments through Community Studies', *Social Research Methodology*, 3: 173–87.

Crow, G. (2004) 'Social Networks and Social Exclusion: An Overview of the Debate', in C. Phillipson, G. Allan and D. Morgan (eds) *Social Networks and Social Exclusion: Sociological and Policy Perspectives*, London: Ashgate, pp. 7–19.

Crow, G. and Allan, G. (1994) *Community Life: An Introduction to Local Social Relations*, Hemel Hempstead: Harvester Wheatsheaf.

Cruddas, J. (2009) 'Labour is in the Middle of its Gravest Crisis in 30 Years. It Needs to Rediscover the Radicalism than Animated its Founders', *New Statesman*, 7 September: 23–5.

Cruddas, J. (2010) 'Social Engineering by Stealth', *New Statesman*, 1 November: 16.

Cruddas, J. and Nahles, A. (2009) *Building the Good Society: The Project of the Democratic Left*, London: Compass.

Cruddas, J. and Rutherford, J. (2008) 'Out Thought by the Tories', *Guardian*, 10 May: 35.

CSDH (Commission on Social Determinants of Health) (2008) *Closing the Gap in a Generation: Health Equity Through Action*, Geneva: World Health Organization.

Cummins, S., Curtis, S., Diex-Roux, A. V. and Macintyre, S. (2007) 'Understanding and Representing "Place" in Health Research: Relational Approaches', *Social Science and Medicine*, 65 (9): 1825–38.

Curtis, P. (2011) 'Big Society Plans Raise Concerns for Parliamentary Democracy', *Guardian*, 22 January: 6.

Curtis, S. (2004) *Health and Inequality: Geographical Perspectives*, London: Thousand Oaks/New Delhi: Sage.

Davey-Smith, G. (ed.) (2003) *Health Inequalities: Life-Course Approaches*, Bristol: Policy Press.

Davis, R. (2011) 'Close Call', *Guardian 2*, 16 February: 1–2.

Day, G. (2006) *Community and Everyday Life*, Abingdon, Oxon./New York: Routledge.

Day, G. and Murdoch, J. (1993) 'Locality and Community: Coming to Terms with Place', *Sociological Review*, 14 (1): 82–111.

DCLG (2006) *The Community Development Challenge*, London: DCLG.

DCLG (2008) *Communities in Control: Real People, Real Power*, London: DCLG.

De Maio (2010) *Health and Social Theory*, New York: Palgrave Macmillan.

De Silva, M., McKenzie, K., Harpham, T. and Huttly, S. (2005) 'Social Capital and Mental Illness: A Systematic Review', *Journal of Epidemiology and Community Health*, 59: 619–27.

de Souza Briggs, X. (1998) 'Doing Democracy Up Close: Culture, Power and Communities in Community Building', *Journal of Planning Education and Research*, 18: 1–13.

Deacon, A. (2002) 'The Cycle of Deprivation, Thirty Years On', *Social Policy Association News*, Oct/Nov: 32.

Deacon, A. and Mann, K. (1999) 'Agency, Modernity and Social Policy', *Journal of Social Policy*, 28: 413–16.

Dench, G., Gavron, K. and Young, M. (2006) *The New East End: Kinship, Race and Conflict*, London: Profile Books.

Dennis, N., Henriques, F. M. and Slaughter, C. (1956) *Coal is Our Life*, London: Eyre and Spottiswode.

Department of Health (2005) *Tackling Health Inequalities: Second Status Report on the Programme for Action*, London: DH.

Department of Health (2010) *Our Health and Well-being Today*, London: DH.

Department of Work and Pensions (2010) *Households Below Average Income: an Analysis of the Income Distribution 1994/5–2008/09*, London: DWP.

Dines, N. and Cattell, V. with Gesler, W. and Curtis, S. (2006) *Public Spaces, Social Relations and Well-being in East London*, Bristol: Policy Press.

Dominy, N. and Kempson, E. (2006) *Understanding Older People's Experience of Poverty and Material Deprivation*, London: DWP.

Donovan, N. and Halpern, D. (2002) *Life Satisfaction: The State of Knowledge and Implications for Government*, London: Prime Minister's Strategy Unit.

Dorling (2010) *Injustice: Why Social Inequality Persists*, Bristol: Policy Press.

Dorling, D., Rigby, J., Wheeler, B., Ballas, D., Thomas, B., Fahmy, E. D. and Lupton, R. (2007) *Poverty, Wealth and Place in Britain 1968 to 2005*, York: Joseph Rowntree Foundation.

Doyal, L. and Gough, I. (1991) *A Theory of Human Need*, Basingstoke: Macmillan.

Dresang, L. T., Brebrick, L., Murray, D. and Shallue, A. (2005) 'Family Medicine in Cuba: Community Oriented Primary Care and Complementary Alternative Medicine', *Journal of the American Board of Family Practice*, 18: 297–303.

Drever, F. and Whitehead, M. (1995) 'Mortality in Regions and Local Authority Districts in the 1990s: Exploring the Relationship with Deprivation', *Population Trends*, 82: 19–26.

Duncan Smith, I. (2006) *Breakdown Britain: Interim Report on the State of the Nation*, London: Social Justice Policy Group, Centre for Social Justice.

Duncan, S. (2007) 'What's the Problem with Teenage Parents? And What's the Problem With Policy?', *Critical Social Policy*, 27 (3): 307–34.

Dupois, A. and Thorns, D. C. (1998) 'Home, Home Ownership and the Search for Ontological Security', *The Sociological Review*, 46 (1): 24–47.

Durkheim, E. (1952/1897) *Suicide*, London: Routledge.

Durkheim, E. (1933/1893) *The Division of Labour in Society*, New York: Macmillan.

Egolf, B., Lasker, J., Wolf, S. and Potvin, L. (1992) 'The Roseto Effect: A 50 Year Comparison of Mortality Rates', *American Journal of Public Health*, 82 (8): 1089–92.

Ehrenreich, B. (2007) *Dancing in the Streets: A History of Collective Joy*, New York: Metropolitan Books.

Elliott, L. (2010) 'Poverty: An 80s Revival We Can Do Without', *Guardian*, 24 May: 24.

Engels, F. (1987/1845) *The Condition of the Working Class in England*, London: Penguin Books.

Etzioni, A. (1995) *The Spirit of Community: Rights, Responsibilities, and the Communitarian Agenda*, London: Fontana.

Euro Commission (2009) *Solidarity in Health: Reducing Health Inequalities in the EU*, Brussels: Euro Commission.

Evans, M. (1972) 'Karl Marx and the Concept of Political Participation', in G. Parry (ed.) *Participation in Politics*, Manchester: Manchester University Press.

Evans, M. and Cattell, V. (2000) 'Place Images, Social Cohesion and Area Regeneration in East London', *Rising East*, 4 (1): 9–39.

Faith in the City: The Report of the Archbishop of Canterbury's Commission on Urban Priority Areas (1985), London: Church House.

Fielding, N. G. and Fielding, J. L. (1986) *Linking Data*, New York: Sage.

Finch, J. (1984) 'It's Great to Have Someone to Talk To: The Ethics and Politics of Interviewing Women', in C. Bell and H. Roberts, *Social Research: Politics, Problems and Practice*, London: Routledge, pp. 70–87.

Flaherty, J., Veit-Wilson, J. and Dorman, P. (2004) *Poverty the Facts, 5th ed.*, London: Child Poverty Action Group.

Foley, M. W. and Edwards, B. (1998) 'Beyond Tocqueville, Civil Society and Social Capital in Comparative Perspective', *American Behavioural Scientist*, 42 (1): 5–20.

Forbes, A. and Wainwright, S. P. (2001) 'On the Methodological, Theoretical and Philosophical Context of Health Inequalities Research: A Critique, *Social Science and Medicine*, 53 (6): 801–16.

Fordham, G. and Lawless, P. (2003) *The Groundwork Movement: Its Role in Neighbourhood Renewal*, York: Joseph Rowntree Foundation.

Fowler, J. H. and Christakis, N. A. (2008) 'Dynamic Spread of Happiness in a Large Social Network: Longitudinal Analysis Over 20 Years in the Framingham Heart Study', *BMJ*, 4 December, 337: a2338.

Frankenberg, R. (1966) *Communities in Britain: Social Life in Town and Country*, Harmondsworth: Penguin.

Freire, P. (1996) *Pedagogy of the Oppressed*, London: Penguin Books.

Friedli, L. (2009) *Mental Health, Resilience and Inequality*, Copenhagen: World Health Organization.

Frohlich, K. L., Dunn, J. R., McLaren, L., Shiell, A., Potvin, L., Hawe, P., Dassa, C. and Thurston, W. E. (2007) 'Understanding Place and Health: A Heuristic for Using Administrative Data', *Health and Place*, 13 (2): 299–309.

Fuhrer, R., Stansfeld, S. A., Chemali, J. and Shipley, M. J. (1999) 'Gender, Social Relations and Mental Health: Prospective Findings from an Occupational Cohort (Whitehall II Study)', *Social Science and Medicine*, 48 (1): 77–87.

Gaillie, D., Marsh, C. and Vogler, C. (1994) *Social Change and the Experience of Unemployment*, Oxford: Oxford University Press.

Galbraith, J. K. (1958) *The Affluent Society*, London: Hamish Hamilton.

Gans, H. (1961) 'Planning and Social Life: Friendship and Neighbour Relations in Suburban Communities', *Journal of the American Institute of Planners*, 27: 134–40.

Gatrell, A., Thomas, C., Bennett, S., Bostock, L., Popay, J., Williams, G. and Shahtahmasebi, S. (2000) 'Understanding Health Inequalities: Locating People in Geographical and Social Spaces', in H. Graham (ed.) *Understanding Health Inequalities*, Buckingham: Open University Press, pp. 156–69.

Gentleman, A. (2010) 'Life on the Edge', *Guardian 7*, 31 March: 6–12.

Gentleman, A. (2011) 'Shouting to be Heard Above a £92m "Tsunami" of Council Cuts', *Guardian*, 25 February: 20.

Gerth, H. H. and Mills, C. Wright (1970) *From Max Weber*, London: Routledge.

Gesler, W. M. (2003) *Healing Places*, Lanham MD: Rowman and Littlefield.

Giddens, A. (1971) *Capitalism and Modern Social Theory: An Analysis of the Writings of Marx, Durkheim and Max Weber*, Cambridge: Cambridge University Press.

Giddens, A. (1984) *The Constitution of Society: Outline of a Theory*, Cambridge: Polity Press.

Giddens, A. (1990) *The Consequences of Modernity*, Cambridge: Polity.

Giddens, A. (1991) *Modernity and Self-Identity: Self and Society in the Late Modern Age*, Stanford: Stanford University Press.

Gingerbread (2009) *Working but Struggling: Single Parents in the Recession*. www.gingerbread.org.uk

Glaser, B. and Strauss, A. L. (1967) *The Discovery of Grounded Theory: Strategies for Qualitative Research*, Chicago: Aldine.

Glasman, M. (2010) 'Labour as a Radical Tradition', *Soundings*, 46: 31–41.

Glasman, M. (2011) 'My Blue Labour Vision Can Defeat the Coalition', *Observer*, 24 April: 24–5.

Goldthorpe, J., Lockwood, D., Bechhofer, F. and Platt, J. (1968) *The Affluent Worker*, Cambridge: Cambridge University Press.

Gordon, D., Levitas, R., Pantazis, C., Patsios, D., Payne, S., Townsend, P., Adelman, L., Ashworth, K., Middleton, S., Bradshaw, J. and Wiliams, J. (2000) *Poverty and Social Exclusion in Britain*, York: Joseph Rowntree Foundation.

Government Equalities Office (2010) *Equalities Act*, London: HMSO.

Graham, H. (1993) *Hardship and Health in Women's Lives*, Hemel Hempstead: Harvester Wheatsheaf.

Graham, H. (2001) 'From Science to Policy: Options for Reducing Health Inequalities', in D. Leon and G. Walt (eds) *Poverty, Inequality and Health: An International Perspective*, Oxford: Oxford University Press, pp. 294–311.

Graham, H. (2007) *Unequal Lives*, Maidenhead: Open University Press.

Graham, H. (ed.) (2000) *Understanding Health Inequalities*, Buckingham: Open University Press.

Granovetter, M. (1973) 'The Strength of Weak Ties', *American Journal of Sociology*, 78 (6): 1360–80.

Gray, R., Headley, J. and Oakley, L. et al. (2009) *Inequalities in Infant Mortality Project, Briefing Paper 3, Towards an Understanding of Variations in Infant Mortality Rates Between Different Ethnic Groups in England and Wales*, Oxford: National Perinatal Epidemiology Unit, Department of Public Health, University of Oxford.

Grice, A. (2010) 'Prime Minister Unveils Happiness index', *Independent*, 26 November, www.google.com/hostednews/afp

Habermas, J. (1989) *The Theory of Communicative Action*, Cambridge: Polity.

Haidt, J. (2006) *The Happiness Hypothesis: Finding Modern Truth in Ancient Wisdom*, Portsmouth, N.H.: Heinemann.

Hall, P. A. (1999) 'Social Capital in Britain', *British Journal of Political Science*, 29 (3): 417–61.

Hallberg, P. and Lund, J. (2005) 'The Business of Apocalypse; Robert Putnam and Diversity', *Race and Class*, 46 (4): 53–67.

Halpern D. (1995) *Mental Health and the Built Environment*, London: Taylor and Francis.

Hammersley, M. and Atkinson, P. (2005) *Ethnography: Principles in Practice*, 2nd ed, London: Routledge.

Hanley, L. (2007) *Estates: An Intimate History*, London: Granta.

Harrison, J. F. C. (1969) *Robert Owen and the Owenites in Britain and America*, London: Routledge.

Harrison, P. (1983) *Inside the Inner City*, Harmondsworth: Penguin.

Harvey, D. (1989) *The Condition of Post Modernity*, Oxford: Blackwell.

Hasan, M. (2010) 'The Sham of Cameron's Big Society', *New Statesman*, 22 November: 16.

Hattersley, R. (2007) 'The Rich Must Be Penalized', *Guardian*, 25 June: 29.

Hawe, P. and Shiell, A. (2000) 'Social Capital and Health Promotion: A Review', *Social Science and Medicine*, 51 (6): 871–85.

Hayek, F. A. Von (1960) *The Constitution of Liberty*, London: Routledge.

Hennessy, P. (1992) *Never Again: Britain 1945–51*, London: Cape.

Henretta, J., Grundy, E., Okell, L. and Wadsworth, M. (2008) 'Early Motherhood and Mental Health in Midlife: A Study of British and American Cohorts', *Aging and Mental Health*, 12 (5): 605–14.

Hildon, Z., Smith, G., Netuveli, G. and Blane, D. (2008) 'Understanding Adversity and Resilience at Older Ages', *Sociology of Health and Illness*, 30 (5): 726–40.

Hill, K., Sutton, L. and Cox, L. (2009) *Managing Resources in Later Life: Older People's Experience of Change and Continuity*, York: Joseph Rowntree Foundation.

Hills, J. (2007) *Ends and Means: The Future Roles of Social Housing in England, CASE report 34*, London: ESRC Research Centre for the Analysis of Social Exclusion, London School of Economics.

Hills, J., Le Grand, J. and Piachaud, D. (eds) (2002) *Understanding Social Exclusion*, Oxford: Oxford University Press.

Hills, J., Sefton, T. and Stewart, K. (eds) (2009) *Towards a More Equal Society?: Poverty, Inequality and Policy since 1997*, Bristol: Policy Press.

Hirsch, B. J., Engel-Levy, A., Du Bois, D. and Hardesty, P. H. (1990) 'The Role of Social Environments in Social Support', in B. R. Sarason, I. G. Sarason and G. Pierce (eds) *Social Support: An Interactional View*, New York: Wiley, pp. 367–93.

Hirsch, D. (2006) *What Will it Take to End Child Poverty*? York: Joseph Rowntree Foundation.

Hirsch, D. and Spencer, N. (2008) *Unhealthy Lives; Intergenerational Links between Child Poverty and Poor Health in the UK*, London: End Child Poverty.

Hirst, P. (1990) 'From Statism to Pluralism', in B. Pimlott, A. Wright and T. Flower (eds) *The Alternative: Politics for a Change*, London: W. H. Allen, pp. 19–29.

Hobsbawm, E. (1981) 'The Forward March of Labour Halted', in M. Jacques and F. Mulhern (eds) *The Forward March of Labour Halted?* London: New Left Books.

Hoggart, R. (1957) *The Uses of Literacy: Aspects of Working Class Life*, London: Chatto and Windus.

Hollingshead, A. B. and Redlich, F. C. (1953) 'Social Stratification and Psychological Disorders', *American Sociological Review*, 18 (2): 163–9.

Horton, T. and Gregory, J. (2009) *The Solidarity Society: Fighting Poverty and Inequality in an Age of Affluence 1909–2009*, London: Fabian Society and Webb Memorial Trust.

House of Commons Select Committee on Health (2009) *Health Inequalities*. HC 206, cmselect/cmhealth/286/28603.htm

Hutton, W. (2010) *Them and Us: Politics Greed and Inequality. Why We Need a Fairer Society*, London: Little Brown.

Innes, M. and Jones, V. (2006*) Neighbourhood Security and Urban Change*, York: Joseph Rowntree Foundation.

Institute for Fiscal Studies (2010) *Spending Review*, London: IFS.

Institute of Economic Affairs (1988) *Acceptable Inequalities*, London: IEA.

Jackson, P. B. (2004) 'Role Sequencing: Does it Matter for Mental Health?', *Journal of Health and Social Behaviour*, 45: 132–54.

Jacobs, J. (1961/1965) *The Death and Life of Great American Cities*, New York: Vintage.

James, O. (2007) *Affluenza: How to be Successful and Stay Sane*, London: Vermilion Books.

Janowitz, M. and Suttles, G. D. (1978) 'The Social Ecology of Citizenship', in R. C. Sarri and Y. Hasenfeld (eds) *The Management of Human Services*, Columbia: Columbia University Press, pp. 80–104.

Jordan, B. (2006) *Social Policy for the Twenty-First Century: New Perspectives, Big Issues*, Cambridge: Polity Press.

Joseph Rowntree Foundation and New Policy Institute (2010) *Monitoring Poverty and Social Exclusion*. http://www.jrf.org.uk/work/workarea/monitoring-poverty-and-socialexclusion.

Joseph, Sir Keith (1972) *The Cycle of Deprivation*, Speech to Pre-School Playgroups Association, 29 June.

Judt, T. (2010) *Ill Fares the Land: A Treatise on Our Present Discontents*, London: Allen Lane.

Kawachi, I. and Berkman, L. F. (2001) 'Social Ties and Mental Health', *Journal of Urban Health*, 78: 458–67.

Kawachi, I., Kennedy, B. P., Lochner, K. and Prothrow-Smith, D. (1997) 'Social Capital, Income Inequality, and Mortality', *American of Journal of Public Health*, 87 (9): 1491–8.

Kawachi, I., Subramanian, S. V. and Kim, D. (eds) (2008) *Social Capital and Health*, New York: Springer.

Keith, M. (2005) *After the Cosmopolitan: Multicultural Cities and the Future of Racism*, London; New York: Routledge.

Kemp, P. A., Bradshaw, J., Doman, P., Finch, N. and Mayhew, E. (2004) *Ladders Out of Poverty*, York: Social Policy Research Unit, University of York.

Keyes, C. (2002) *Flourishing: Positive Psychology and the Life Well-Lived*, Washington DC: American Psychological Association.

Khattab, N. and Fenton, S. (2009) 'What Makes Young Adults Happy? Employment and Non-work as Determinants of Life Satisfaction', *Sociology*, 43 (1): 11–26.

Kirke, D. M. (2006) *Teenagers and Substance Use: Social Networks and Peer Influence*, Basingstoke: Palgrave Macmillan.

Korpela, K. M., Hartig, T., Kaiser, F. G. and Fuhrer, U. (2001) 'Restorative Experience and Self-Regulation in Favourite Places', *Environment and Behaviour*, 33(4): 572–89.

Kunitz, S. J. (2001) 'Accounts of Social Capital: The Mixed Health Effects of Personal Communities and Voluntary Groups', in D. Leon and G. Walt (eds) *Poverty, Inequality and Health*, Oxford: Oxford University Press, pp. 159–74.

Lane, R. (2000) *The Loss of Happiness in Market Democracies*, New Haven: Yale University Press.

Lawler, S. (2005) 'Introduction: Class, Culture and Identity', *Sociology*, 39 (5): 797–806.

Lawson, N. and Harris, J. (2010) 'The Paradigm Shift', *New Statesman*, 6 December: 33–5.

Layard, R. (2005) *Happiness*, London: Penguin Books.

Le Grand, J. (1987) *An International Comparison of Inequalities in Health*, Welfare State Programme discussion paper no. 16, London: London School of Economics.

Lechner, F. J. (1991) 'Simmel on Social Space', *Theory Culture and Society*, 8 (3): 195–201.

Lee, D. and Newby, H. (1983) *The Problem of Sociology*, London: Hutchinson.

Leonard, M. (2004) 'Bonding and Bridging Social Capital; Reflections from Belfast', *Sociology*, 38 (5): 927–44.

Leonard, M. (2005) 'Children, Childhood and Social Capital: Exploring the Links', *Sociology*, 39 (4): 605–22.

Levitas, R. (2005) *The Inclusive Society? Social Exclusion and New Labour, 2nd edition*, Basingstoke: Palgrave.

Levitas, R. (2009) 'Poverty and Social Exclusion'. Paper presented to *The Peter Townsend Memorial Conference*, London: Conway Hall, 20 November.

Levitas, R., Pantaziz, C., Fahmy, E., Gordon, D., Lloyd, E. and Patsios, D. (2007) *The Multi-Dimensional Analysis of Social Exclusion: A Research Report for the Social Exclusion Task Force*, Bristol: Department of Sociology and School of Social Policy, Townsend Centre for the International Study of Poverty, and Bristol Institute for Public Affairs, University of Bristol.

Lewis, J. and Brookes, B. (1983) 'A Reassessment of the Work of the Peckham Health Centre 1926–51', *Millbank Memorial Fund Quarterly/Health & Society*, 61 (2): 307–50.

Lister, R. (2004) *Poverty*, Cambridge: Polity Press.

Lockwood, D. (1966) 'Sources of Variation in Working Class Images of Society', *Sociological Review*, 14 (2): 249–67.

Lomas, J. (1998) 'Social Capital and Health: Implications for Public Health and Epidemiology', *Social Science and Medicine*, 47 (9): 1181–8.

Low, J. (ed.) (2000) *Regeneration in the 21st Century: Policies into Practice. An Overview of the Joseph Rowntree Foundation Area Regeneration Programme*, Bristol: Policy Press.

LSE (London School of Economics) and Political Science, Centre for Economic Performance and the Young Foundation (2006) *The Local Wellbeing Project: Outline*, www.youngfoundation.org.uk

Lukes, S. and Duncan, G. (1963) 'The New Democracy', *Political Studies*, 11 (2): 156–77.

Lynch, J. (1977) *The Broken Heart: The Medical Consequences of Loneliness*, New York: Basic Books.

Lynch, J. W., Davey-Smith, G., Kaplan, G. A. and House, J. S. (2000) 'Income Inequality and Mortality: Importance to Health of Individual Income, Psychosocial Environment, or Material Conditions', *BMJ*, 320: 1200–4.

MacGregor, S. and Lipow, A. (eds) (1995) *The Other City: People and Politics in New York and London*, New Jersey: Humanities Press.

MacGregor, S. and Pimlott, B. (1991) *Tackling the Inner Cities: The 1980s Reviewed, Prospects for the 1990s*, Oxford: Clarendon: Oxford University Press.

Macinko, J. and Starfield, B. (2001) 'The Utility of Social Capital in Research on Health Determinants', *The Millbank Quarterly*, 79 (3): 387–427.

MacInnes, T. and Kenway, P. (2009) *London's Poverty Profile 2009*, London: City Parochial Foundation and New Policy Institute.

MacInnes, T., Parekh, A. and Kenway, P. (2010) *London's Poverty Profile 2010*, London: Trust for London and New Policy Institute.

MacIntyre, S. and Ellaway, A. (2009) 'Neighbourhood Influences on Health', in H. Graham (ed.) *Understanding Health Inequalities, 2nd ed.*, Maidenhead: Open University Press, pp. 84–102.

MacIntyre, S., McIver, S. and Sooman, A. (1993) 'Area Class and Health: Should We be Focusing on People or Places?', *Journal of Social Policy*, 22 (2): 213–34.

Mackenzie, R., Stuart, M., Forde, C., Greenwood, I. and Perrett, R. (2006) '"All That is Solid?" Class Identity and the Maintenance of a Collective Orientation amongst Redundant Steelworkers', *Sociology*, 40 (5): 833–52.

MacNichol, J. (1987) 'In Pursuit of the Underclass', *Journal of Social Policy*, 16 (03): 293–318.

Manzoor, S. (2011) 'Pop-up Arts Tea Rooms Bring People Together in Birmingham', *Guardian 2*, 11 January: 1.

Marmot, Sir M. (2004) *Status Syndrome*, London: Bloomsbury.

Marmot, Sir M. (2005) 'For Richer, For Poorer', *Guardian 2*, 16 February: 10.

Marsh, A. and MacKay, S. (1994) *Poor Smokers*, London: Policy Studies Institute.

Martin, G. (2010) 'Class Still Matters: A Report from Three Studies', *Sociology*, 44 (6): 1197–203.

Marx, K. (1844/1988) *The Economic and Philosophical Manuscripts*, translated by M. Milligan, New York: Prometheus Books.

Marx, K. (1852) *The Eighteenth Brumaire of Louis Bonaparte*. Reproduced in L. S. Feuer (ed.) *Marx and Engels: Basic Writings on Politics and Philosophy*, London: Fontana, 1969.

Mathews, F. (1977) *Quest for an American Sociology: Robert E. Park and the Chicago School*, Montreal: McGill-Queens University Press.

Maude, F. (2010) 'Bigger the Better', *New Statesman*, 4 October: 48.

May, T. (2010) *Social Research, Issues, Methods and Process*, 3rd ed., Buckingham: Open University Press.

Mayo, M. (2000) *Cultures, Communities and Caring*, Basingstoke: Palgrave.

McVeigh, T. (2011) 'Cameron Measuring "Wrong Type of Happiness"', *Observer*, 10 April: 19.

Mercer, S. W. and Watt, G. (2007) 'How Does the Inverse Care Law Operate: An In-depth Characterization of Clinical Encounters in Primary Care Comparing Deprived and Affluent Areas of Scotland', *Annals of Family Medicine*, 5: 503–10.

Merton, R. (1957) *Social Theory and Social Structure*, New York: Free Press.

Milburn, A. (Chair) (2009) *Unleashing Aspiration: The Final Report of the Panel on Fair Access to the Professions*, London: Cabinet Office.

Miliband, D. (2010) *Keir Hardie Lecture*, www.davidmiliband.net/2010/07/09keir-hardie-lecture-2010

Miliband, D. and Cruddas, J. (2010) 'Our Covenant with Britain', *Guardian*, 4 September: 31.

Miliband, E. (2010) 'Labour Can Still Win the Battle of Ideas', *Observer*, 10 January: 25.

Miliband, R. (1994a) 'The Plausibility of Socialism', *New Left Review*, 206: 5–8.

Miliband, R. (1994b) *Socialism for a Sceptical Age*, Cambridge: Polity Press.

Mills, C. Wright (2000/1970) *The Sociological Imagination*, Harmondsworth: Penguin.

Mohnen, S. M., Groenwegen, P. P. and Beate, V. (2011) 'Neighbourhood Social Capital and Individual Health', *Social Science and Medicine*, 72 (5): 660–7.

MORI (2004) *Life Satisfaction and Trust in Other People*, London: MORI Social Research Institute.

Morris, L. (1995) *Social Divisions: Economic Decline and Social Structural Change*, London: UCL Press.

Morris, W. (1884) 'A Letter from Morris to Arthur Spencer, 25 June 1884', *The Last Word: The William Morris Society Newsletter*, Summer 2007: 32.

Morris, W. (1888) *The Dream of John Ball*, London; New York: Longmans Green.

Morris, W. (1974/1890) *News from Nowhere*, ed. by J. Redmond, London: Routledge.

Morris, W. (1979) *The Political Writings of William Morris*, ed. by A. L. Morton, London: Lawrence and Wishart.

Morrow, V. (1999) 'Conceptualizing Social Capital in Relation to the Well-being of Young People: A Critical Review', *The Sociological Review*, 437 (4): 744–65.

Mowlam, A. and Creegan, C. (2008) *Modern-day Social Evils: The Voices of Unheard of Groups*, York: Joseph Rowntree Foundation.

Muntaner, C. and Lynch, J. (1999) 'Income Inequality, Social Cohesion, and Class Relations: A Critique of Wilkinson's neo-Durkhemian Research Programme', *International Journal of Health Services*, 28 (1): 59–81.

Murray, C. (1984) *Losing Ground: American Social Policy 1950–1980*, New York: Basic Books.

Murray, C. (1994) *Underclass: The Crisis Deepens*, London: IEA.

National Audit Office (2010) *Tackling Inequalities in Life Expectancy in Areas with the Worst Health and Deprivation*, London: HMSO.

NCVO (National Council for Voluntary Organisations) (2010) *Briefing on the Big Society*, http://www.ncvo-vol.org.uk/sites/default/files/Big_Society_Programme_briefing_final.pdf.

Nettleton, S. (2007) *Retaining the Sociology in Medical Sociology*, Editorial, *Social Science and Medicine*, 65 (12): 2409–12.

Newton, K. (1997) 'Social Capital and Democracy', *American Behavioural Scientist*, 40 (5): 575–86.

Norman, J. (2010) *The Big Society: The Anatomy of the New Politics*, Buckingham: University of Buckingham Press.

North, F., Syme, S. L., Feney, A., Head, J., Shipley, M. J. and Marmot, M. G. (1993) 'Explaining Socioeconomic Differences in Sickness Absence: The Whitehall II Study', *BMJ*, 306 (6874): 361–6.

Nuffield Foundation (2009) *Time Trends in Adolescent Well-being; Update*, London; Oxford: Nuffield Foundation.

Oakley, A. (1981) 'Interviewing Women: A Contradiction in Terms', in H. Roberts, *Doing Feminist Research*, London: Routledge.

Oakley, A. (1992) *Social Support and Motherhood: The Natural History of a Research Project*, Oxford: Blackwell.

ODPM (2004) *The English Indices of Deprivation*, Wetherby: ODPM Publications.

ODPM (2005a) *Formative Evaluation of the Take-Up and Implementation of the Well-Being Powers, 2004–2006*, London: ODPM.

ODPM (2005b) *Citizen Engagement and Public Services: Why Neighbourhoods Matter*, London: ODPM.

OECD (2008) *Growing Unequal? Income Distribution and Poverty in OECD Countries*, Paris: OECD.

ONS (2002) *People's Perceptions of Their Neighbourhood and Community Involvement*, London: HMSO.

ONS (2010) *Social Trends 40*, Newport: ONS.

Orwell, G. (1949) *1984*, London: Secker and Warburg.

Pahl, R. (1995) 'Are All Communities, Communities in the Mind?', *Sociological Review Monograph*, 4 (53): 621–40.

Pahl, R. (1996) 'Friendly Society', in S. Kraemer and J. Roberts (eds) *The Politics of Attachment*, London: Free Association Books.

Pahl, R. (2000) *On Friendship*, Cambridge: Polity Press.

Parekh, A., MacInnes, T. and Kenway, P. (2010) *Monitoring Poverty and Social Exclusion in the UK 2010*, York: Joseph Rowntree Foundation; London: New Policy Institute.
Parkes, A. and Kearns, A. (2006) 'The Multidimensional Neighbourhood: A Cross Sectional Analysis of the Scottish Household Survey, 2001', *Health and Place*, 12 (1): 1–18.
Pateman, C. (1970) *Participation and Democratic Theory*, Cambridge: Cambridge University Press.
Pearlin, L. I. (1985), 'Social Structure and Processes of Social Support', in S. Cohen and S. L. Syme (eds) *Social Support and Health*, Orlando, Fla: Academic Press, pp. 43–60.
Pearlin, L. I. (1989) 'The Sociological Study of Stress', *Journal of Health and Social Behaviour*; 30: September, pp. 241–56.
Peren, K., Arber, S. and Davidson, K. (2004) 'Neighbouring in Later Life: The Influence of Socio-Economic Resources, Gender and Household Composition on Neighbourly Relationships', *Sociology*, 38 (5): 965–84.
Phillimore, P. and Morris, D. (1991) 'Discrepant Legacies: Premature Mortality in Two Industrial Towns', *Social Science Medicine*, 33 (2): 139–52.
Phillips, A. and Taylor, B. (2008) *On Kindness*, London: Hamish Hamilton/ Penguin Books.
Piachaud, D. (1997) 'Down but Not Out', Review of When Work Disappears; the World of the New Urban Poor, by W. J. Wilson, New York: Knopf, 1996, in the *Times Literary Supplement*, 24 January: 3–4.
Pickering, J. (2001) 'Eco-psychology and Well-being'. Paper presented to the *ESRC Seminar Series on Well-being: Social and Individual Determinants*, London: 11 September: Queen Mary, University of London.
Pierson, J. and Worley, C. (2005) 'Housing and Urban Regeneration Policy: Citizen and Community under New Labour', in P. Somerville and N. Sprigings (eds) *Housing and Social Policy*, Abingdon: Routledge, pp. 217–41.
Play England (2010) *A Manifesto for Children's Play*, London: Play England.
Plummer, K. (1983) *Documents of Life: An Introduction to the Problems and Literature of a Humanistic Method*, London: Allen and Unwin.
Popay, J. (2000) 'Social Capital; the Role of Narrative and Historical Research', *Journal of Epidemiology and Community Health*, 54 (6): 401.
Popay, J., Williams, G., Thomas, C. and Gatrell, A. (1998) 'Theorizing Inequalities in Health; the Place of Lay Knowledge', in M. Bartley, D. Blane and G. Davey-Smith (eds) *The Sociology of Health Inequalities*, Oxford: Blackwell, pp. 89–94.
Popcorn, F. (1992) *The Popcorn Report*. New York: Harper Collins.
Portes, A. (1998) 'Social Capital: Its Origins and Applications in Modern Sociology', *Annual Review of Sociology*, 24: 1–24.
Power, A. and Mumford, K. (1999) *The Slow Death of Great Cities*? York: Joseph Rowntree Foundation.
Power, A. and Tunstall, R. (1995) *Swimming against the Tide: Polarisation and Progress on 20 Unpopular Council Estates, 1980–95*, York: Joseph Rowntree Foundation.
Putnam, R. D. (1995) 'Tuning In, Tuning Out: The Strange Disappearance of Social Capital in America', *Political Science and Politics*, 28 (4): 664–83.
Putnam, R. D. (2000) *Bowling Alone: The Collapse and Revival of American Community*, New York: Simon and Schuster.
Ramesh, R. (2010) 'The Reluctant Seer', *Guardian 2*, 3 November: 1–2.

Rawls, J. (2001) *Justice as Fairness: A Restatement*, Cambridge, Mass.: Harvard University Press.
Reeves, R. (2007) 'We Love Capitalism', *New Statesman*, 19 February: 28–30.
Room, G. (ed.) (1995) *Beyond the Threshold: The Measurement and Analysis of Social Exclusion*, Bristol: Policy Press.
Runciman, W. G. (1965) 'Social Justice', *The Listener*, 29 July: 152–3, 169.
Runciman, W. G. (1966) *Relative Deprivation and Social Justice*, London: Routledge and Kegan Paul.
Runciman, W. G. (1995) 'Hearing What They Say, Knowing What They Mean', in G. Dench, J. Flower and K. Gavron (eds) *Young at Eighty: The Prolific Public Life of Michael Young*, Carcanet, pp. 85–92.
Rutherford, J. (2010) 'Labour's Good Society', *Soundings*, 46: 6–17.
Sampson, A. (2004) *Who Runs This Place: The Anatomy of Britain in the 21st Century*, London: John Murray.
Sandel, M. (2009) *A New Politics of the Common Good*, Reith Lecture, BBC Radio 4, 10 June.
Sandel, M. (2010) *Justice: What's the Right Thing to Do?* Harmondsworth: Penguin.
Saunders, P. (1990) *Social Class and Stratification*, London: Routledge.
Saunders, P. (2010) *Beware False Prophets: Equality, the Good Society and the Spirit Level*, London: Policy Exchange.
Savage, M. (2000) *Class Analysis and Social Transformation*, Buckingham: Open University Press.
Savage, M. and Burrows, R. (2007) 'The Coming Crisis of Empirical Sociology', *Sociology*, 41 (5): 885–99.
Sayers, S. (1995) 'Commentary: The Value of Community', *Radical Philosophy*, 69: 2–5.
Scharf, T. and Smith, A. (2003) 'Older People in Urban Neighbourhoods: Addressing the Risk of Social Exclusion in Later Life', in C. Phillipson, G. Allan, and D. Morgan (eds) *Social Networks and Social Exclusion: Sociological and Policy Issues*, Aldershot, Hants: Ashgate, pp. 163–79.
Schonfield, A. (1969) *Modern Capitalism: The Changing Balance of Public and Private Power*, Oxford: Oxford University Press.
Schuller, T., Baron, S. and Field, J. (2000) 'Social Capital, a Review and a Critique', in S. Baron, J. Field and T. Schuller (eds) *Social Capital: Critical Perspectives*, Oxford: Oxford University Press, pp. 1–38.
Scott-Samuel, A. (2004) *Health Inequalities Politics and Policy under New Labour*, London: Socialist Health Association, www.sochealth.co.uk/news/ukheg.htm
Scottish Homes (2000) *Reconnecting Excluded Communities: The Neighbourhood Impacts of Owner Occupation*, Glasgow: University of Glasgow.
Seabrook, J. (1985) *Landscapes of Poverty*, Oxford: Blackwell.
Sen, A. (2001) 'Economic Progress and Health', in D. Leon and G. Walt (eds) *Poverty, Inequality and Health: An International Perspective*, Oxford: Oxford University Press, pp. 333–45.
Sennett, R. (2006) *The Culture of the New Capitalism*, New Haven: Yale University Press.
SEU (Social Exclusion Unit) (2000) *National Strategy for Neighbourhood Renewal: A Framework for Consultation*, London: Cabinet Office.
Shaw M., Davey-Smith, G. and Dorling D. (2005) 'Health Inequalities and New Labour: How the Promises Compare with Real Progress', *BMJ*, 330 (7499): 1016–21.

Shaw, M., Thomas, B., Davey-Smith, G. and Dorling, D. (2008) *The Grim Reaper's Road Map*, Bristol: Policy Press.

SIGOMA (Special Interest Group of Local Authorities) (2010) *All in this Together? The Need for a Fair Approach to Local Government Cuts*, Barnsley: Sigoma.

Silverman, D. (2010) *Doing Qualitative Research*, 3rd ed., London: Sage.

Smith and Beazley (2000) 'Progressive Regimes, Partnerships and the Involvement of Local Communities: A Framework for Evaluation', *Public Administration*, 78 (4): 855–78.

Sooman, A. E. and MacInyre, S. (1995) 'Social Variations in the Use of Neighbourhoods'. Paper presented to the *British Sociological Association Annual Conference*, 10–13 April, Leicester: University of Leicester.

Stack, C. (1974) *All Our Kin: Strategies for Survival in a Black Community*, New York: Basic Books.

Stafford, M., Cummins, S., MacIntyre, S., Ellaway, A. and Marmot, M. (2005) 'Gender Differences in the Association between Health and the Neighbourhood Environment', *Social Science and Medicine*, 60 (8): 1681–92.

Stafford, M., De Silva, M. J., Stansfeld, S. A. and Marmot, M. (2008) 'Neighbourhood Social Capital and Mental Health: Testing the Link in a General Population Sample', *Health and Place*, 14: 394–405.

Stansfeld, S. A. (1999) 'Social Support and Social Cohesion', in M. Marmot and R. Wilkinson (eds) *Social Determinants of Health*, Oxford: Oxford University Press, pp. 155–78.

Stansfeld, S. and Candy, B. (2006) 'Psychosocial Work Environment and Mental Health: A Meta-Analytical Review', *Scandinavian Journal of Work, Environment and Health*, 32 (6): 443–62.

Stedman Jones, G. (1976) *Outcast London*, London: Penguin.

Stiglitz, J. E., Sen, A. and Fitoussi, J. P. (2009) *Report by the Commission on the Measurement of Economic Performance and Social Progress*, www.stiglitz-sen-fitoussi.fr

Stronks, K. (2002) 'Generating Evidence on Interventions to Reduce Inequalities in Health: The Dutch Case', *Scandinavian Journal of Public Health*, 30 (1): 20–5.

Subramanian, S., Lochner, K. and Kawachi, I. (2003) 'Neighbourhood Differences in Social Capital, a Compositional Artifact or a Contextual Construct', *Health and Place*, 9 (1): 33–44.

Sutherland, H., Sefton, T. and Piachaud, D. (2003) *Progress on Poverty, 1997 to 2003/4*, York: Joseph Rowntree Foundation.

Swann, W. B. and Brown, J. D. (1990) 'From Self to Health: Self Verification and Identity Disruption', in B. R. Sarason, I. G. Sarason and G. Pierce (eds) (1990) *Social Support, an Interactional View*, New York: Wiley, pp. 150–71.

Szreter, S. and Woolcock, M. (2004) 'Health by Association? Social Capital, Social Theory, and the Political Economy of Public Health', *International Journal of Epidemiology*, 33 (4): 650–7.

Tawney, R. H. (1931/1964) *Equality*, London: Allen and Unwin.

Taylor, M. (2000), *Top Down Meets Bottom Up: Neighbourhood Management*, York: Joseph Rowntree Foundation.

Taylor, M. (2003) *Public Policy in the Community*, Basingstoke: Palgrave Macmillan.

Taylor, M. (2008) 'Why Life is Good', *New Statesman*, 7 January: 26–8.

Taylor, S. and Ashworth, C. (1987) 'Durkheim and Social Realism: An Approach to Health and Illness', in G. Scambler (ed.) (1987) *Sociological Theory and Medical Sociology*, London: Tavistock, pp. 37–58.

Taylor-Gooby, P. and Stoker, G. (2011) 'The Coalition Programme: A New Vision for Britain or Politics as Usual?', *The Political Quarterly*, 82 (1): 4–15.

The Marmot Review (2010) *Fair Society, Healthy Lives: Strategic Review of Health Inequalities in England post-2010*, www.ucl.ac.uk/marmot review.

Thoits, P. A. (1995) 'Stress, Coping, and Social Support Processes: Where Are We? What Next?', *Journal of Health and Social Behaviour*, Extra Issue: 53–79.

Thompson, E. P. (1968) *The Making of the English Working Class*, London: Penguin.

Thompson, E. P. (1977) *William Morris: Romantic to Revolutionary*, London: Merlin Press.

Thompson, P. (1978) *The Voice of the Past*, Oxford: Oxford University Press.

Titmuss, R. (1962) 'Preface', in M. Young and P. Willmott, *Family and Kinship in East London*, London: Routledge.

Titmuss, R. (1987) *The Philosophy of Welfare: Selected Writings of Richard M. Titmuss*, ed. by B. Abel Smith and K. Titmuss, London: Allen and Unwin.

Tocqueville, A. de (1968/1835) *Democracy in America*, London: Fontana.

Tonnies, F. (1955/1887) *Community and Association*, London: Routledge.

Townsend, P. (1979) *Poverty in the UK*, Harmondsworth: Penguin.

Townsend, P. (1991) 'Living Standards and Health in the Inner Cities', in S. MacGregor and B. Pimlott, (eds) *Tackling the Inner Cities*, Oxford: Clarendon/Oxford University Press, pp. 93–126.

Townsend, P. (1993) *The International Analysis of Poverty*, Hemel Hempstead: Harvester Wheatsheaf.

Townsend, P., with Corrigan, P. and Kowarzik, U. (1987) *Poverty and Labour in London*, London: Low Pay Unit.

Toynbee, P. (2006) 'These Nice New Tories Offer the Same Old Cure: Marriage', *Guardian*, April 25: 29.

Toynbee, P. (2011) 'So Simon, What Would it Take for You to Walk Away?', *Guardian*, 11 January: 33.

Toynbee, P. and Walker, D. (2010) *The Verdict: Did Labour Change Britain*, London: Granta.

Turner, S. (1988) 'Extended Review: Classical Sociology and its Legacy', *Sociological Review*, 36 (1): 146–57.

Valente (2010) *Social Networks and Health: Models, Methods and Applications*, Oxford: Oxford University Press.

Veenstra, G., Luginaah, I., Wakefield, S., Birch, S., Eyles, J. and Elliott, S. (2005) 'Who You Know, Where You Live: Social Capital, Neighbourhood and Health', *Social Science and Medicine*, 60 (12): 2799–818.

Wakefield, S. E. and Poland, B. (2005) 'Family, Friend or Foe? Critical Reflections on the Relevance and Role of Social Capital in Health Promotion and Community Development', *Social Science and Medicine*, 60 (12): 2819–32.

Waldfogel, J. (2010) *Britain's War on Poverty*, New York: Russell Sage Foundation.

Walker, A. (2009) 'Older People'. Paper presented to the *Peter Townsend Memorial Conference*, Conway Hall London, 20th November.

Walker, A. and Walker, C. (1997) *Britain Divided: The Growth of Social Exclusion in the 1980s and 1990s*, London: Child Poverty Action Group.

Walker, A. and Walker, C. (2009) *Peter Townsend 1928–2009*, Bristol: Policy Press.

Walker, D. (2002) *In Praise of Centralism: A Critique of the New Localism*, London: Catalyst.

Wanless, D. (2004) *Securing Good Health for the Whole Population*, Norwich: DH.

Watts, B. (2008) *What are Today's Social Evils? The Results of a Web Consultation*, York: Joseph Rowntree Foundation.

Wellman, B. (1979) 'The Community Question: The Intimate Networks of East Yorkers', *American Journal of Sociology*, 84 (5): 1201–31.

Wellman, B. (2001) 'Physical Place and Cyberspace; the Rise of Personalized Networking', *International Journal of Urban and Regional Research*, 25 (2): 227–53.

Wellman, B. and Wortley, S. (1990) 'Different Strokes from Different Folks: Community Ties and Social Support', *American Journal of Sociology*, 96 (3): 558–88.

Westergaard, J. (1975) 'Radical Class Consciousness: A Comment', in M. Bulmer (ed.) *Working Class Images of Society*, London: Routledge, pp. 251–6.

Westergaard, J. and Resler, H. (1976) *Class in a Capitalist Society*, Harmondsworth: Penguin.

Wheaton, B. (1980) 'The Socio Genesis of Psychological Disorder: An Attributional Theory', *Journal of Health and Social Behaviour*, 21: 100–24.

Whelan, C. (1993) 'The Role of Social Support in Mediating the Psychological Consequences of Economic Stress', *Sociology of Health and Illness*, 15 (1): 86–101.

White, S. (2009) 'Thinking the Future', *New Statesman*, 7 September: 20–2.

Whitehead, M. (1993) *The Health Divide*, 2nd ed., London: Health Education Council.

Whitley, R. and Prince, M. (2005) 'Are Inner Cities Bad for Your Health? Comparisons of Residents' and Third Parties' Perceptions of the Urban Neighbourhood of Gospel Oak, London', *Sociology of Health and Illness*, 27 (1): 44–60.

WHO (World Health Organization) (1948) *Constitution*, New York: WHO.

Widgery, D. (1991) *Some Lives! A GP's East End*, London: Simon and Schuster.

Wilby, P. (2008) 'Creativity Generates a Climate of Social Inclusion', *New Statesman*, September 22: 4.

Wilkinson, R. G. (1996) *Unhealthy Societies*, London: Routledge.

Wilkinson, R. G. (1999) 'Health, Hierarchy and Social Anxiety', Paper presented to the *New York Academy of Sciences Conference on Socioeconomic Status and Health in Industrial Nations*, Bethesda, Maryland, May.

Wilkinson, R. G. (2000) 'Inequality and the Social Environment: A Reply to Lynch et al.', *Journal of Epidemiology and Community Health*, 54 (6): 411–13.

Wilkinson, R. G. (2001) *Mind the Gap: Hierarchies, Health and Human Evolution*, London: Weidenfeld and Nicholson.

Wilkinson, R. G., Kawachi, I. and Kennedy, B. P. (1998) 'Socioeconomic Determinants of Health and Social Cohesion: Why Care about Income Inequality?', *BMJ*, 314 (7086): 1037–40.

Wilkinson, R. G. and Pickett, K. E. (2006) 'Income Inequality and Population Health: A Review and Explanation of the Evidence', *Social Science and Medicine*, 62 (7): 1768–84.

Wilkinson, R. G. and Pickett, K. E (2010) *The Spirit Level: Why Equality is Better for Everyone*, London; New York: Penguin Books.

Williams, G. H. (2003) 'The Determinants of Health; Structure, Context and Agency', *Sociology of Health and Illness*, 25 (3): 131–54.

Williams, R. (1976) *Keywords*, Glasgow: Fontana/Croom Helm.

Williams, R. (1988) *Resources of Hope*, London: Verso.

Williams, R. (2011) 'Young Could Lose Chance to Improve Their Lives', *Guardian*, 5 January: 8.

Williams, R. (2008) *Archbishop's Lecture Celebrating the 60th Anniversary of the William Temple Foundation*, http//www.archbishopofcanterbury.org/2039
Willis, P. and Trondman, M. (2000) 'Manifesto for Ethnography', *Ethnography*, 1 (1): 5–16.
Willmott, P. (1986) *Social Networks, Informal Care and Public Policy*, London: Policy Studies Institute.
Willmott, P. (1987) *Friendship Networks and Social Support*, London: Policy Studies Institute.
Willmott, P. (1989) *Community Initiatives: Patterns and Prospects*, London: Policy Studies Institute.
Willmott, P. and Young, M. (1960) *Family and Class in a London Suburb*, London: Routledge and Kegan Paul.
Wilson, D. (1993) 'Everyday Life, Spatiality and Inner City Disinvestment in a US City', *International Journal of Urban and Regional Research*, 17 (4): 578–94.
Wilson, W. J. (1987) *The Truly Disadvantaged*, Chicago: University of Chicago Press.
Wilson, W. J. (1996) *When Work Disappears: The World of the New Urban Poor*, New York: Knopf.
Wirth, L. (1938) 'Urbanism as a Way of Life', *American Journal of Sociology*, 44 (1): 1–24.
Wolf, S. and Bruhn, J. G. (1993) *The Power of Clan*, New Brunswick, N.J.: Transaction.
Woolcock, M. (1998) 'Social Capital and Economic Development: Towards a Theoretical Synthesis and Policy Framework', *Theory and Society*, 27: 151–208.
Woolcock, M. (2001) 'The Place of Social Capital in Understanding Social and Economic Outcomes', *Isuma: Canadian Journal of Policy Research*, 2 (1): 1–17.
Young, I. M. (1990) *Justice and the Politics of Difference*, Princeton, N.J.: Princeton University Press.
Young, M. (1996) 'Love Thy Neighbour', *Guardian 2*, 18 September: 6.
Young, M. and Willmott, P. (1962) *Family and Kinship in East London*, Harmondsworth: Penguin.
Young, M. and Willmott, P. (2007/1986) 'New Introduction', in *Family and Kinship in East London*, London: Penguin, pp. xiii–xxiv.
Ziersch, A. M., Baum, F. E., MacDougall, C. and Putland, C. (2004) 'Neighbourhood Life and Social Capital: The Implications for Health', *Social Science and Medicine*, 60 (1): 71–86.

Index